THE INTERVENTION
OF THE OTHER

THE INTERVENTION
OF THE OTHER

ETHICAL SUBJECTIVITY
IN LEVINAS AND LACAN

DAVID ROSS FRYER

OTHER

Other Press
New York

Production Editor: Robert D. Hack

This book was set in 11pt. Berkeley by Alpha Graphics of Pittsfield, NH.

10 9 8 7 6 5 4 3 2

Library of Congress Cataloging-in-Publication Data

Fryer, David Ross.
  The intervention of the other : ethical subjectivity in Levinas and Lacan / by David Ross Fryer.
    p. cm.
Includes bibliographical references and index.
  ISBN 1-59051-088-7 (pbk. : alk. paper)
    1. Levinas, Emmanuel—Ethics.   2. Lacan, Jacques, 1901—Ethics.
3. Other (Philosophy).   I. Title.
B2430.L484F79 2004
194—dc22

2003022681

To Terry and Elie,
for so much more . . .

Contents

Acknowledgments   ix

Abbreviations and Citations   xi

Introduction: Post-Humanism and Ethical Subjectivity   1
in Levinas and Lacan

1. The Other and the Self: Creating the Subject   31

2. Sexed Subjectivity, Symbolic Subjectivity   71

3. Linguistic Subjectivity and the Speaking Subject   115

4. Ethical Subjectivity: God, An-Archy, the Subject,   155
   and Desire

Conclusion: Post-Humanist Ethical Subjectivity   215

References   239

Index   247

Acknowledgments

In this work, I argue, following Levinas, that the ethical is an an-archic structure of subjectivity and that, as an an-archic structure of subjectivity, the ethical constantly presents itself to us as we live our daily lives. It is, thus, in a very real sense our lived reality, whether we choose to accept it or not. I further argue, following Lacan, that it is up to us to make the choice to accept it and take it upon ourselves, as a desire for the good of the other. As such, I offer this project not as a study of two dense thinkers in an esoteric field, though it may in some sense be that, but rather as a work of chosen responsibility, as the work of life, and it is a work that I can only be engaged in because of the others who surround and guide me and who have helped shape me such that I strive to embrace the ethical structure that lies at the base of my being a subject. It is in this spirit that I offer my thanks to the many friends, family, and colleagues who have played such important parts in my life and in this work's coming to be. Thanks to the scholars—teachers, students, and colleagues—from whom I have learned so much in our conversations over the years, especially Bettina Bergo,

Lenny Clapp, Carolyn Cusick, Wendell Dietrich, Mary Ann Doane, Stephen Dunning, Lewis Gordon, Ben Haines, Carter Heyward, Vincent Hope, Thomas Kniesche, Alan Kors, Michael Michau, Michael Monahan, Marilyn Nissim-Sabat, Stephen Priest, Jock Reeder, Ellen Rooney, Zach Summers, Barney Twiss, and Elizabeth Weed. Special thanks to Wendell Dietrich for years of support, guidance, and the very best kind of teaching, advising, and friendship a student could hope for. Thanks to Jean-Michel Rabaté for a generous and constructive reading of the manuscript and for his enthusiastic support in helping me publish it. Thanks to Judith Feher Gurewich for signing up this book for Other Press and to the staff at Other Press for their hard work in producing the book, especially Blake Radcliffe and Bob Hack. Thanks to Zach Summers for help with proofreading and preparing the index. Thanks to the friends who have supported me in so many way over the years of writing and rewriting, in particular Lexi Adams, Josh Bartok, Michael D'Esopo, Lisa Fabish, Becca Galuska, Lewis and Jane Gordon, Michelle Gorenstein, April Herms, Liz Loeb (theory whore), Marilyn and Charley Nissim-Sabat, Zach Summers, and Alex Wolfson. Special thanks to Zoë Mizuho, just for being Zoë. Thanks to my family, especially my brothers and sisters, Eric and Jennifer Fryer, Beth and Michael Blumberg, and Andrea Fryer, for the love and support they give me. Thanks to Sue and Alan Lubin for welcoming me into their family. Special thanks to my parents, Sandy and Larry Fryer, who taught me from a young age just what it is to desire the good of the other. Finally, immeasurable thanks to my partner, Terry Lubin, for supporting me, encouraging me, and giving me more every day, and to our daughter, Elie, in whom we see the future. It is with the greatest of love that I dedicate this work to them.

Abbreviations and Citations

All citations to major texts by Levinas and Lacan are cited parenthetically in the text following the standard convention of citing page numbers from the original language text first, followed by page numbers from the standard English translation.

Major Works by Levinas:

AE/OTB   *Autrement qu'être ou au-delà del'Essence*. Dordrecht: M. Nijhoff, 1974. Trans. Alphonso Lingis as *Otherwise than Being or Beyond Essence*. Boston: Kluwer, 1991.

CPP   *Collected Philosophical Papers*. Boston: Kluwer, 1993.

DD/OG   *De Dieu qui Vient à l'Idée*. Paris: J. VRIN, 1982. Trans. Bettina Bergo as *Of God Who Comes to Mind*. Stanford: Stanford University Press, 1998.

EDE   *En Decouvrant l'existence avec Husserl et Heidegger*. Paris: J. VRIN, 1967.

EN/EN   *Entre Nous: Essais sur le penser à-l'autre.* Paris: Éditions
Grasset & Fasquelle, 1991. Trans. Michael B. Smith
and Barbara Harshav as *Entre Nous: Thinking-of-the-
Other.* New York: Columbia University Press, 1998.

TI/TI   *Totalité et Infini.* Dordrecht: M. Nijhoff, 1961. Trans.
Alphonso Lingis as *Totality and Infinity.* Pittsburgh,
PA: Duquesne University Press, 1969.

TA/TO   *Le Temps et l'autre.* Paris: Fata Morgana, 1979. Trans.
Richard Cohen as *Time and the Other.* Pittsburgh, PA:
Duquesne University Press, 1987.

Major Works by Lacan:

E/E   *Écrits.* Paris. Éditions de Seuil, 1966. Partial translation, Alan Sheridan as *Écrits: A Selection.* New York:
Norton, 1977.[1]

S VII/S VII   *Le Seminaire de Jacques Lacan VII: L'éthique de la
psychanalyse.* Paris: Éditions de Seuil, 1986. Trans.
Dennis Porter as *The Seminar: Book VII. The Ethics
of Psychoanalysis.* New York: Norton, 1992.

S XI/S XI   *Le Seminaire de Jacques Lacan XI: Les quatre concepts
fondamentaux de la psychanalyse.* Paris: Éditions de
Seuil, 1973. Trans. Alan Sheridan as *The Four Fundamental Concepts of Psychoanalysis.* New York: Norton,
1981.

S XX/S XX   *Le Seminaire de Jacques Lacan XX: Encore.* Paris:
Éditions de Seuil, 1975. Trans. Bruce Fink as *The
Seminar: Book XX: Feminine Sexuality.* New York:
Norton, 1998.

---

1. The new translation by Bruce Fink of *Écrits: A Selection* was published
after this work was completed. As such, this work references the old Sheridan
translation. However, upon reading the Fink translation, I am convinced that it
is a substantial contribution to Lacan scholarship, offering a far more precise and
accurate translation than had the Sheridan volume.

As a matter of practice, where English translations were available, I read the texts first in English, consulting the French with the English translations close at hand. When writing, I worked with both the French and the English versions at my side. In citing quotations, I consulted both the French and English versions. In some cases, where I have found the English translations particularly misleading, I have modified them; for the most part, I have followed them.

Note: On the terms *autre, Autre, autrui, moi,* and *je:*

Both Levinas and Lacan use certain technical terms that bear notice. In the case of Levinas, *autre* and *autrui* are conventionally translated as *other* and *Other,* respectively. However, this convention has caused problems when Levinas intentionally capitalizes *l'Autre,* specifically when contrasting it with *l'Même.* Additionally, Lacan makes a formal distinction between *autre* and *Autre.* Accordingly, I will translate Levinas's *autre* as *other* and his *autrui* as *other person,* capitalizing *l'Autre* in relation to *l'Même,* and will translate Lacan's *autre* as *other* and his *Autre* as *Other.* Additionally, where in Levinas's writings *le moi* is most often translated as *the I,* for Lacan, following a standard psychoanalytic reading, *le moi* is most often translated as *the ego* with *le je* translated as *the I.* Here I will follow those standard conventions.

Introduction: Post-Humanism and Ethical Subjectivity in Levinas and Lacan

Emmanuel Levinas, Lithuanian-born French phenomenologist of the non-phenomenon, and Jacques Lacan, controversial French psychoanalyst and (post)structuralist theorist of the Freudian Unconscious, lived and wrote in the same city, at the same time, among the same colleagues, often using the same language and the same sources, sometimes writing to the same audiences, and yet they never wrote to or about one another. Emmanuel Levinas was suspicious of psychoanalysis, to say the least. He, following Sartre, thought that Freud had fundamentally misunderstood the nature of consciousness by positing the Unconscious as a second but hidden consciousness, although his own work celebrated a certain something that could not be contained by thought. Jacques Lacan was suspicious of philosophical ethics, having subscribed to a Freudian critique of morality as pathogenic, even while he saw his own work as fundamentally about a form of ethics, specifically one concerned with the way people live their lives in already normative society. Among all the sources they shared in common (Kant, Hegel, Heidegger, to mention the most striking) and all the interlocutors they shared (Derrida and Irigaray, to name the most significant), they never engaged with one another's thought—at all.

The time has come to read them together.

Reading Levinas and Lacan together will seem to some a rather odd project. Indeed it is. Until recently, very little has been done in the way of comparative analysis of these two thinkers. For years, they were read in isolation from one another, owing to a rather overdetermined antagonism between their respective methodological approaches—again, a modification of Husserlian phenomenology for Levinas and a (post)structuralist version of Freudian psychoanalysis for Lacan.[1] In the past ten years, a few significant works have been published that have read Levinas and Lacan side by side, resulting in new approaches to old questions, and even some new questions.[2] Additionally, in the past ten years another

---

1. Levinas's relationship to phenomenology is worthy of attention. While his early work is clearly phenomenological in method, proceeding with all the moves of static phenomenology aimed at eidetic reduction, he quickly moves into tricky territory when he discovers the non-phenomenon of the face, that which cannot be contained in consciousness. By the time he moves from *Totality and Infinity* (1961/1969) to *Otherwise than Being* (1974/1991), it is unclear whether he is indeed doing phenomenology at all anymore. Robert Gibbs (1992, Chapter 9) sees this as a shift from phenomenology to "ethical language." I still read Levinas as operating within a broadly construed phenomenological framework. For Levinas's own discussion of phenomenology, see his treatment of Husserl in Levinas (1995). For a good introduction to Levinas's relation to phenomenology, see Davis (1996), Chapter 1. For a thorough assessment of Levinas's relationship to Heidegger, see Manning (1993). For a strong critique of Levinas as more metaphysician than phenomenologist, see Moran (2000), Chapter 10. For a very different take on Levinas, phenomenology, and metaphysics, see Cohen (1994), Chapter 10. Far and away the best discussion of Levinas's relationship to phenomenology, however, is Drabinski (2001).

2. In his recent work, Simon Critchley (1999) puts Levinas in conversation with both Freud and Lacan. Additionally, a small volume on Levinas and Lacan edited by Sarah Harasym (1998) offers several pieces in which the two are put into contact with one another. Included in that volume are insightful and instructive essays by Tina Chanter, Hans-Dieter Gondek, Donna Brody, and Paul-Laurent Assoun, as well as a significant contribution by Alain Jurainville, who has for some time now been attempting to make the Levinas–Lacan connection in his native France. I would also cite the recent work of Bettina Bergo (2004), who has been working on the question of the Levinasian good as an "uncon-

set of books has emerged. These are not books that read Levinas and Lacan together, but rather books that bring together similarly disparate thinkers in order to explore their competing conceptions of ethics and/or subjectivity.[3] *This* book adds to these two slowly growing literatures, in trying to see just what new approaches and new questions open up when we do read two seemingly disparate thinkers—in this case these two particular thinkers—together, attempting to explore what answers might be formulated in response to these lines of inquiry.

In order to better understand what this work is, perhaps we should be clear on what it is not. This is not an introduction to the thought of Emmanuel Levinas or Jacques Lacan. Many excellent

---

scious." Additionally, I would add an article on Levinas and Lacan by Ken Reinhard (1995). Finally, I would note the excellent paper by Suzanne Barnard (2002) entitled "Diachrony, *Tuché*, and the Ethical Subject in Levinas and Lacan."

3. Here three works stand out as particularly noteworthy. Alenka Zupancic's *Ethics of the Real* (2000) explores Kant and Lacan together in the hopes of providing "a conceptual framework for an ethics which refuses to be an ethics based on the discourse of the master, but which equally refuses the unsatisfactory option of a '(post)modern' ethics based on the reduction of the ultimate horizon of the ethical to one's own life" (p. 5). As a study of Lacan, Zupancic's work is worthy of special note. It provides what is undoubtedly the most sophisticated and provocative interpretation of Lacanian ethics to date. Her juxtaposing of Kant and Lacan is in many ways similar to my juxtaposing of Levinas and Lacan. Next, Eric Santer's *On the Psychotheology of Everyday Life: Reflections on Freud and Rosenzweig* (2001) reads Rosenzweig and Freud together as thinkers of human life as containing a "surplus that is no longer referred to a life beyond this one" (p. 110). Next, John Rajchman's classic *Truth and Eros: Foucault, Lacan, and the Question of Ethics* (1991) explores Foucault and Lacan to show how each "tried to raise again the ancient question of truth and eros; each of them in different ways re-eroticized the activity of philosophical or critical thought for our times" (p. 1). As a study of Lacan, Rajchman's work, too, is worthy of special note. It is indispensable to anyone seeking to understand Lacan's (1986/1992) seminar on ethics, in particular by explaining Lacan as interpreter of past ethical system-builders. His work is similar to mine in that its primary emphasis is more exegetical than interpretive; however, his work is not meant to be comparative in nature. Additionally, I offer more in the way of constructive conclusions, a prolegomena, if you will, while he concludes with mostly questions. Each of these books stands as a bold attempt to show how disparate thinkers stand in relation to one another and why both visions are worthy of our serious attention.

introductions to each have already been written.[4] This is not a study of one facet of the thought of either thinker, nor is it a *particular kind of reading* of either thinker or a reading of either as a *particular kind of thinker*. Again, these have been done quite well.[5] Nor is this book intended as a record of the shared philosophical ancestors or mutual philosophical heirs of the two thinkers. Even less is it intended as a reading of a dialogue in which the two were engaged, for, as we have already noted, no such dialogue took place.

Positively, how is this book different from the literature on Levinas and Lacan already circulating? What is unique about what this book does offer?

First and foremost, this book is a comparative analysis of the texts of Levinas and Lacan, engaged in a side-by-side, in-depth reading to see where and how they stand in proximity to each other and where and how they depart. In this, it is the first book of its kind—a sustained, detailed *text-based* comparative analysis of these two thinkers.

---

4. There are many excellent introductions to Lacan. Jane Gallop's *Reading Lacan* (1985) does a wonderful job of introducing the American reader to the difficulty of entering into Lacanian discourse. Malcolm Bowie's *Lacan* (1991) and Jonathan Scott Lee's *Jacques Lacan* (1990) are both clear and cogent discussions of Lacan's thought. Joël Dor's instructive *An Introduction to the Reading of Lacan* (1998) offers its reading from a clinical perspective. My favorite introduction to Lacan, however, is probably Bruce Fink's *The Lacanian Subject: Between Language and Jouissance* (1995). There are equally excellent introductions to Levinas. Edith Wyschogrod's *Emmanuel Levinas* (1974) is a sophisticated introduction to Levinas's early work, culminating in his first magnum opus, *Totality and Infinity* (1961/1969). Davis (1996) is an accessible work covering a significant chunk of Levinas's corpus. Adriaan Peperzak's *To the Other* (1993) is a textbook-style introduction that includes careful readings of some of Levinas's important earlier work, with a brief look at his later work. Additionally, many excellent anthologies cover the work of each thinker, including Rabaté (2000b) and Nobus (1999b) on Lacan, and Bernasconi and Critchley (1991) on Levinas.

5. Particularly worthy of mention in these categories are, on the Levinas side: Simon Critchley's reading of Levinas as deconstructionist in *The Ethics of Deconstruction* (1992) and Robert Gibbs's (1992) reading of Levinas as Judaic thinker; on the Lacan side, see Elizabeth Grosz's feminist engagement with Lacan in *Jacques Lacan: A Feminist Introduction* (1990) and Jean-Michel Rabaté's reading of Lacan as literary theoretician in *Jacques Lacan* (2001).

Next, this book organizes its study of Levinas and Lacan around two important themes: post-humanism and ethical subjectivity, and in this it is a unique and new contribution to the field. By *post-humanism* I mean to designate a theoretical landscape in which contemporary philosophical thought is taking place—a landscape in which liberal modernist assumptions about humanism have been called into question and in which any attempts to explicate the concept of the human now begin from the antihumanist critique before moving any further. By *ethical subjectivity* I mean to designate both an approach to the study of ethics that takes as its goal the explication of the ethical nature of the human person, and an approach to the study of the human person that takes as its starting point the antihumanist critique of the self and positing of the "subject" in its place. It is my contention that Levinas and Lacan offer unique contributions to these two themes, and that they are excellent themes for understanding Levinas and Lacan as thinkers in their own right, thus helping illuminate our understanding of their thought. Moreover, I believe that these two themes are not only those that bring Levinas and Lacan together, but also those that I find particularly worthy of exploring in Continental philosophy today. As such, I hope that this book also stands as a preliminary foundation on which future work can be built. But, in terms of focus, this book is *first* a comparative analysis of the thought of Emmanuel Levinas and Jacques Lacan, and *second* a positive contribution to studies of post-humanism and ethical subjectivity. In this it aims merely to lay the groundwork for what I hope will be my (and others') further work in the study of both post-humanism and ethical subjectivity. My concluding remarks on what Levinas and Lacan offer a post-humanist theory of ethical subjectivity will thus be preliminary and incomplete.[6]

---

6. There have been other studies of Levinas that focus on ethical subjectivity, and studies of Lacan that claim to discuss his take on either subjectivity or ethics, as well as a few books that mention his post-humanism, but none of these has taken either ethical subjectivity or post-humanism as its organizing principle, nor have any of them engaged in *sustained* analyses of these concepts. On ethical subjectivity, Simon Critchley often discusses Levinas as a theorist of "subjectivity

Finally, this book offers unique readings of both Levinas and Lacan, and does so in two ways. In terms of Levinas scholarship, first, while Levinas has all too often been misread as either describing mundane human encounters or presenting abstract metaphysical musings, this book recognizes Levinas's work within a broadly conceived phenomenology. As such, it reads Levinas's descriptions

---

as ethical," and once even used the term "ethical subjectivity" to refer to both Levinas and Lacan. However, Critchley has not offered a sustained analysis using this phrase, nor has he fully explicated it as a philosophical theme/position. For his use of "ethical subjectivity" see his excellent article "*Das Ding*: Lacan and Levinas" in Critchley (1999). Suzanne Barnard (2000) discusses the "ethical subject" in Levinas and Lacan in her excellent piece, in which she is interested in the status of the subject as ethical, but does not elucidate the concept of subjectivity itself in the work. Additionally, Lisa Walsh (2001) uses the phrase "ethical subjectivity" in the title of her important article on Levinas and Kristeva, "Between Maternity and Paternity: Figuring Ethical Subjectivity," although this term does not take center stage in the essay itself. Bruce Fink (1995) wrote the definitive work on Lacan's conception of the subject, but he did not focus on Lacan's reading of subjectivity as ethical, while John Rajchman (1991) wrote the definitive work on *Lacan's Seminar VII: The Ethics of Psychoanalysis* without focusing on the ethics of subjectivity. As well, of course, I am not the first to use the term "post-humanist," nor am I the first to pose the question of thinking the human in the post-humanist landscape. See, for instance, Donna Haraway's (1992) "Ecce Homo, Ain't (Ar'n't) I a Woman, and Inappropriate/d Others: The Human in a Post-Humanist Landscape." Haraway focuses more on the question of who counts for human after antihumanism than it does on the question of how to theorize the human after antihumanism, which is my question here. Also see the collection of essays edited by Diana Fuss (1996), in which the question is posed, "In the wake of humanism's recession, what has become of the human?" (p. 1). The essays in that volume tend to focus either on the historical decline of humanism, on particular theses of humanism that must be rejected, or on particular facets of the human that can now be thought of through post-humanism. The essays do not focus on the larger questions of what it is to think of the human post-humanism or what larger, deeper structures of the human might be uncovered after humanism's demise. On post-humanism, the most promising use of the term comes on the jacket blurb for Tamise Van Pelt's *The Other Side of Desire: Lacan's Theory of the Registers* (2000), which tells us that "Van Pelt demonstrates Lacanian theory's pivotal role in the intellectual transition from the poststructuralism of the mid-twentieth century to the post-humanism of the twenty-first" (back cover). However, post-humanism does not emerge in any explicit, systematic, or sustained way in the text, even if it operates implicitly throughout.

as descriptions of the very structures that underlie our experiences of the world, in particular as descriptions of the structure of subjectivity and intersubjectivity. Second, while most works on Levinas still stress the centrality of his earlier work over his later work, this book, while offering attention to both, is attuned to the significance of the later work, and thus offers a more thorough treatment than is usually given, for instance in the careful reading of what I would argue is the most succinct and well-argued explication of Levinas's mature thought, his important essay, "Diachrony and Representation" (1991).[7] In terms of Lacan scholarship, first, while most older work on Lacan failed to situate him within a clinical framework, this book adds to the growing literature that sees Lacan as analyst first, theorist second. However, my interest here is not in Lacan as analyst per se. Rather, it is in Lacan as theorist. To achieve this dual goal, I read Lacan's theory as arising from his analytic practice, and in keeping true to this I offer in places what turns out to be quite a novel reading of Lacan's theory, one that at times is at odds with more traditional, accepted views of Lacan in the English-speaking world.[8] Second, even though certain works have emerged that focus more on the Real as the key to Lacan, such a focus is not yet widely recognized as essential for a proper understanding of his work.[9] This book takes the Real to be central to an understanding of Lacan's theories of ethics and subjectivity, and thus focuses a great deal on his discussions of this most elusive concept.

Overall, then, this book is an engagement with the thought of both thinkers, side by side, ultimately aimed at a co-reading of their thought that seeks to connect the insufficiently connected, to

---

7. Take for instance Peperzak (1993), which devotes only one chapter to Levinas's later works.

8. Several excellent works mark the recent focus on Lacan as analyst and analytic theorist. Every book in Other Press's The Lacanian Clinical Field series, edited by Judith Feher Gurewich, is worthy of attention on this matter.

9. Consider two recent books: Zupancic's *Ethics of the Real* (2000) offers one of the best readings of the Real in Lacan to date, whereas Van Pelt's *The Other Side of Desire: Lacan's Theory of the Registers* (2000) has very little to say about the Real, focusing almost exclusively on the other two registers.

underscore the insufficiently underscored, and to put forth the beginnings of philosophical claims of its own. On the whole, it is my contention that in a philosophical landscape that I label "post-humanism," Levinas and Lacan stand as two contemporary options in our thinking about both the question of ethics and the question of the human person, and that in bringing together these two seemingly disparate thinkers, new doors may be opened up for our thinking about the human person as an ethical subject. As a reading of two disparate thinkers, this work attempts to find points of contact as well as points of divergence in order to (1) deepen our understanding of these two important thinkers, (2) shed light on each thinker as a representative of what I am calling the post-humanist landscape of contemporary Continental philosophy, and (3) show what each thinker has added to our understanding of an important subject in philosophical theory today—that of ethical subjectivity.

In order to better frame this project, then, we begin by exploring our first theme: post-humanism. To explore this theme, we ask the following question: What does the contemporary philosophical landscape, that place in which we are seeking to stake our claim that Levinas and Lacan ought to be brought together, look like?

HUMANISM, ANTIHUMANISM, AND THE CONTEMPORARY PHILOSOPHICAL LANDSCAPE

In her 1993 biography of Jacques Lacan, Elisabeth Roudinesco writes of an unpublished interview between Didier Eribon and Michel Foucault in which Foucault labeled Jean-Paul Sartre and Lacan "alternate contemporaries": two thinkers trained in the reading of the same thinkers, occupied with the same issues, and taking two alternate approaches (Roudinesco 1997, pp. 332–333). The basic topic that interested them both was the nature of human subjectivity, and the basic approach that each of them took can roughly be labeled "humanist" (Sartre) and "antihumanist" (Lacan). Sartre's existentialism was humanist in that it hailed the autonomy and self-sufficiency of the human person, while Lacan's psycho-analytic theories were antihumanist in that they adhered to a theory of the human subject as split, fragmented, and, to some degree, determined.[10]

Humanism is a belief in the autonomy and self-sufficiency of the human self, whereas antihumanism is a belief in the human being as constitutively subject to external forces. Or at least this is the essence of Foucault's charge. Of course, this is not what every-one means by these terms. "Humanism" in particular is a diffi-cult term, one not easily reduced to a single definition. For even when Sartre hailed existentialism to be humanist, he did specify it as one *kind* of humanism, distinguishing it from other kinds. Sartre's humanism is a humanism of choice and freedom, of power and possibility, and of transparency and knowledge. It is not a humanism of essence, rights, or community. In these ways it dif-fers from the humanism of such thinkers as Descartes, Kant, Rawls, Habermas, or even Husserl. It does not claim the essence of the human person to be reason, or rationality, or even some-thing as simple as "thinking." It does not argue for the human person as a participant in a liberal community ultimately aimed at the positing of basic human rights to be respected by all its members. It does not posit the human person as formed in discourse with the other, nor does it point to the possibility of communities in dialogue, or, arising out of and following that dialogue, a coex-istence in harmony. And it certainly is not a humanism of the tran-scendental ego. These are all equally valid definitions of humanism, none of which apply to Sartre's views. In short, humanism means many things to many people.

Whatever humanism is, it is a thoroughly liberal and modern ideal. It emerged as the dominant way of thinking about the human person in the Enlightenment and continued its reign in Western thought well into the twentieth century. It forms the basis of the

---

10. Foucault's characterization of Sartre's humanism should not be too easily adopted, for it is possible to see in Sartre the beginnings of a post-humanism. On this point, see the presentation of Sartre found in Gordon (1995a).

broad landscape upon which modern thought has emerged. It has been the dominant set of beliefs through which philosophers have thought about the human person for the last two to three hundred years. In other words, modern philosophy emerged in a thoroughly humanist landscape.[11] At least until things changed.

How can we better define what I am calling this "humanist landscape"? Let us take the following, and other varied definitions and aspects of humanism, as a way of summarizing the tenets of the humanist landscape of modern thought:[12] (1) the human person is a self-sufficient and autonomous subject, free in his decisions and in his actions;[13] (2) the human person is fully cognizant of the motives behind his actions;[14] (3) knowledgeable of the motives behind his actions, the human person is a moral agent capable of making decisions about the ethical status of his actions;[15] (4) morality is located within the human person as the product of either an internal sense of the right or the good, or through an inner capacity for moral empathy as enacted through "sentiment";[16] (5) the

---

11. For the sake of clarity, I will sometimes refer to this as "modernist" or "liberal" humanism, distinguishing it from the post-humanisms that have emerged in the wake of the antihumanist critique.

12. This attempt at a complete definition is meant solely as a heuristic device used to distinguish humanism from antihumanism, and what I will call the humanist landscape from the post-humanist landscape. We could cite many texts on each of these points. I will mention just a few authors who might be considered classic examples for each point, citing what I find to be either their more accessible texts or the best representative statements of their positions, and will try to offer a range of positions within humanism as I do so. While I don't cite Marx individually below as a representative of any one particular aspect of humanism or antihumanism, it is worth noting that he can be read as a representative of both humanism and antihumanism. This is a move most often made with reference to Marx's early humanism and his late antihumanism, but a careful reading exposes both trends in both his early and late writings. On the humanism and antihumanism in his early work, see his "On the Jewish Question," and on humanism and anti-humanism in his late work, see his "The Eighteenth Brumaire of Louis Bonaparte," both collected in Tucker (1978).

13. See Rawls (1971 and 2001), and Sartre (1991).

14. See Husserl (1962) and Sartre (1960).

15. See Kant (1997).

16. See ibid. and Hume (1978).

human person is a bearer of certain inalienable rights;[17] (6) as a member of a community, the human person is bound to certain laws and codes of action to which he has freely assented (that is, he is individual first, member of a community second);[18] (7) these are universal traits of the human person, cross-cultural and essential;[19] and (8) the moral person makes his decisions in light of his personal freedom to choose his own path.[20]

While humanism still thrives in many academic circles, in others it has come under considerable attack over the last fifty years or so. Critics from varied disciplines and ideological commitments have found humanism to be a remnant of a universalist project that they no longer consider valid in a fragmented world that has come increasingly to be labeled "postmodern."[21] Ideas such as "self-sufficiency," "autonomy," "universality," and "existential freedom," not to mention discussion of "rights" in general, are read as remnants of a dying liberal project. Since (at least) the 1950s, the humanist landscape of modern thought has come under a stringent attack from thinkers who called themselves "antihumanist." Like "humanist," the term "antihumanist" means many things. For one thing, it explicitly challenges the claims of the humanism it seeks

---

17. See Rawls (2001).

18. See ibid. For the application of definition to the question of religion, see Kant (1960). For a still humanist critique of subject-centered individualism, see Habermas (1995), especially lecture eleven, "An Alternative Way Out of the Philosophy of the Subject: Communicative versus Subject-Centered Reason."

19. See the essays by Gewirth, Donagan, and Little in Outka and Reeder (1993).

20. See Sartre (1992).

21. Postmodern is a highly contested term, and one that we will use here only as a heuristic device meant to designate a particular intellectual landscape in which I will locate Levinas and Lacan. Here, I borrow the definition of postmodern offered by Robert Gibbs. For Gibbs (1992), the term "modern" signifies a certain adherence to principles of universality and comprehensiveness of theory. The term "postmodern," on the other hand, signifies a rejection of theories of totality and comprehensive universalization, and an adherence to principles of partiality and tentative construction. Hence, Gibbs refers to postmodern philosophy's "acceptance of heterogeneous elements into its thought without assimilating them into a single model" (p. 21).

to displace. As I suggested above, for instance, it posits a human person who is fragmented, split, and subject to forces outside of herself. But, again, it does more than this, for it posits its own ideas about the nature of the human person.

We might summarize the antihumanist critique of humanism as follows: (1) the human subject is the product of forces beyond his immediate control, and is therefore free only within the realm of those choices given to him as viable;[22] (2) the forces that drive the human subject are not only not transparent to him, but also are often in conflict with one another;[23] (3) the human subject is a moral agent only insofar as he subscribes to a particular code of morality, and moral judgments are made via this code;[24] (4) this code to which the human subject accedes is by definition a historical and social construct (it does not arise out of an inner sense of reason or moral sentiment);[25] (5) the human subject is the bearer of rights only insofar as society confers those rights upon him;[26] (6) as a member of a community, the human subject is first and foremost "subjected" (that is, the communal defines the individual);[27] (7) any traits commonly associated with a universal "humanitas" are the false projections of a particular model onto a universal construct;[28] and (8) freedom, as the act by which one

---

22. The first thing one might notice is that, from an antihumanist perspective, we are no longer talking about the human self, but rather the human subject. This distinction is crucial, and we will return to it in the next section, "Contemporary Continental Philosophy and Ethical Subjectivity." On the question of freedom and constriction, see Heidegger's discussion of thrownness in *Being and Time* (1992).

23. See Althusser (1971).

24. See MacIntyre (1981).

25. Though he would most certainly contest the term "antihumanist," on this point see the pragmatist position of Stout (1988). For a more strictly social constructionist position, see, for instance, Berger and Luckmann (1967).

26. See Foucault (1970 and 1977).

27. See ibid.

28. See Derrida (1972 and 1987), and Lacoue-Labarthe (1990). Writing specifically on the ways in which Nazism can be considered a humanism, Lacoue-Labarthe offers a fine summary of the antihumanist critique of humanist thought:

chooses to be her or his moral self free from external constriction, is in fact a false category constructed to mask the reality of subjectivity (subjection and subjugation).[29] A theory that adheres to some or all of these tenets may, then, properly be called an "antihumanism."

Since the 1950s, antihumanism has grown to prominence in some fields of intellectual inquiry. Continental philosophy has endorsed much of the antihumanist critique, as has Anglo-American literary theory.[30] In many departments in the humanities in the United States, Great Britain, and Australia, not to mention the European continent, antihumanism is dogma. This is not to say that even in what can be roughly called postmodern circles humanism can be considered completely dead. Putting aside the old humanism that still remains in some areas of the social sciences and analytic philosophy departments, there are now thinkers who, following certain antihumanist critiques, agree that past humanisms have been problematically universal, totalizing, and insufficiently sensitive to the question of human otherness. At the same time, they believe that certain humanist claims are worth retaining: claims to self-knowledge, the possession of rights, the universality of the ethical, and even some attenuated unity of the human subject. However, they only retain these ideas within a system of thought that has absorbed the critique of antihumanism and taken seriously its place in the postmodern landscape. In place of a modernist

---

[an ideology] is a humanism in so far as it rests on a determination of a humanitas which is, in its view, more powerful—i.e., more effective—than any other. The subject of absolute self-creation, even if, occupying an immediately natural position . . . transcends all the determinations of the modern subject, brings together and concretizes these same determinations . . . and constitutes itself as the subject, in absolute terms. [pp. 95–96]

29. See Foucault (2000).
30. This, of course, is not true of analytic philosophy departments, which, when speaking of the human person at all, tend to remain humanist. Nor is it true of the social sciences in general, though it has made headway in political science, and emerges occasionally in history and sociology departments.

liberal humanism, these thinkers offer what they see as a humanism better suited to the commitments of a postmodern outlook.
These new humanisms are, in my opinion, not modernist humanisms at all. In their acceptance of certain tenets of antihumanism
and in their firm commitment to a postmodern outlook, they have
moved beyond modernist humanism and offered a new set of ideals
in its place. As they lie in a landscape that has moved beyond
modernist humanism into new terrain, and as they have accepted
much of the antihumanist critique, these new humanisms are in a
very definite sense post-humanist humanisms, or *post-humanisms*.
By post-humanism, then, we mean to designate these new attempts
to think the human in the wake of the antihumanist critique. By
post-humanist we mean to designate an intellectual landscape that
takes as its starting point the antihumanist critique, and that thereby
includes both what we have called antihumanisms and these new
post-humanisms. This post-humanist landscape is the terrain on
which nearly all Continental philosophy and critical theory, and
much contemporary religious thought now does its work, and is
the place from which this work is written.

　　　This leads to our next question: From this post-humanist landscape, what, in particular, is that issue through which we will make
progress if we now do bring together Levinas and Lacan?

CONTEMPORARY CONTINENTAL PHILOSOPHY AND ETHICAL SUBJECTIVITY

The question of ethics is one that plagues contemporary Continental philosophy. Major figures in its history have been chided
for insufficient attention to ethical concerns, ethical questions,
and ethical issues. High-profile events, such as those referred to
as the Heidegger affair, have drawn attention to the ethical short-
comings of some of its most powerful voices.[31] Yet some of the
most prominent voices in Continental philosophy have been

---

31. See Fryer (1996).

deeply concerned with the question of ethics. The most obvious are Emmanuel Levinas, Karl Marx, and Herbert Marcuse. Ethics are, however, equally concerns of Jacques Derrida, Michel Foucault, and Jacques Lacan.

Continental ethics differs from analytic ethics in important ways. Continental ethics tends not to be as concretely case-centered, and instead often focuses on what one might term "broader pictures." It tends not to abstract ethical situations from social and political contexts, instead seeing historical situatedness as central to ethical issues. It tends not to adhere to strict classical moral traditions (utilitarianism, deontology, virtue ethics), instead operating under different categories unfamiliar to most analytic philosophers (Foucauldian ethics, ethics of the other, feminist ethics, psychoanalytic ethics). But perhaps the most significant way in which Continental ethics differs from analytic ethics is that for many (not all) Continental ethicists, the question of human subjectivity is of central concern. Indeed, for some, the question of the human subject is inseparable from the question of ethics. Making this clear and explaining how ethics and subjectivity connect need to be of central concern to any Continental philosopher wishing to further the debates in these areas, especially if she or he hopes to cross the all too destructive fence between Continental and analytic traditions.[32]

But what do we mean by "human subjectivity?" Since its inception, Continental philosophy has been deeply concerned with the question of the human. From Husserl's deduction of the transcendental ego to Derrida's antihumanist critique of the transcendental ego, Continental philosophy has always taken the question

---

32. Several important works have been published in Continental ethics in the past twenty years. I have already mentioned important works by Simon Critchley, John Rajchman, Eric Santer, and Alenka Zupancic. I would further highlight Caputo (1993), Gibbs (2000), and Gordon (1995b), as well as recent works by Derrida and Irigaray. Additionally, two recent edited volumes are worthy of note: Kearney and Dooley (1999) and Madison and Fairbairn (1999). Of course, one ought also go back to Beauvoir's classic *Ethics of Ambiguity* (1948).

of the human person as a, if not the, central concern. So, by human subjectivity, first, we mean to signify a phenomenologically based understanding that the human subject is, in a very real sense, the center of the human universe. Following Husserl, we recognize that all knowledge of the world is fundamentally knowledge achieved by human subjectivity, and thus the world only exists for us as a world of, through, and by the subject. Second, we mean to signify the belief that the active subject who constitutes the world around her is at one and the same time subjectified, that is, subjected and subjugated, and only thereby subjectivated.[33]

By calling the human person a subject, then, we are doing several things. First, we are calling attention to the Husserlian underpinnings of our investigations, recognizing subjectivity as our necessary starting point. Second, we are calling attention to the fact that the identities of our subjectivities are subject to social and

---

33. To read it from the antihumanist perspective alone, some postmodern thinkers have removed and attacked the self-conscious, self-sufficient human *person*—that which they designate "the self"—as the center of philosophical knowledge, removed "him" from his privileged place, torn him into contradictory pieces, and left him for dead. Some responded by replacing the term "self" with the term "subject," a move that Étienne Balibar (1994) suggests has its origins in Kant's *Critiques*. Still, in poststructuralism the very term "subject" has further been called into question. Critiques emerged in the works of thinkers such as Louis Althusser, Michel Foucault, and Luce Irigaray. Ultimately, this has led to cries of the death of the Man, the death of the self, *and* the death of the subject. The death of Man, due to the decentering of the human person as a self, is *not*, however, equivalent to the death of the subject. As Balibar has shown, the concept of subjectivity is not reducible to the Cartesian cogito, the standard whipping boy of much contemporary Continental philosophy. Rather, the concept of subjectivity stands as a challenge to precisely that idea of self-knowledge implicitly in the cogito, in all its post-Cartesian forms. For Balibar, then, the "subject" is a subject that can be utilized to explain old concepts in new and different ways, furthering Kant's critical project beyond the confines of an all-too-simple positivism or narrowly defined Enlightenment search for essence. The subject, argues Balibar, is an inherently *political* concept, but this does not mean that the Kantian (and Husserlian) starting points are completely destroyed. Balibar is right—the subject is a political concept—and this is reconcilable with a conception of the subject as active in the constitution of her world. See Balibar (1994).

historical contingencies. Our conceptions are all shaped by the shared conceptions of our culture, our history, our society, our family, and more. Third, we are calling attention to the fact that our identities are shaped by other hidden forces and agencies not as readily identifiable as "society" or "culture," forces such as the Unconscious (Lacan) or Ideology (Althusser) or an-archy (Levinas). These forces and agencies are buried within our psyches in ways not readily transparent to us. Fourth, we are calling attention to the fact that our subjectivities, at least on the level of the mundane ego, are shaped by our identities and our adherence to them. When I call myself an academic, I am attaching myself to a particular system of practice and belief that shapes much of how I see the world and act in it. When I identify as a man, I am attaching myself to certain cultural and social assumptions about not only the gender identity "man," but also the sex "male." Even when I resist stereotypical gendered "masculine" behavior, I do so within the context of being a different kind of "man." Taking these four points together, I am calling attention to the fact that, even as subjects who constitute our world in the strict sense of being intentional consciousnesses, in being shaped by social and historical contingencies, hidden agencies of power, and our own identificatory practices, we subjects are constructed into being the selves we think we naturally are. Subjectivity, then, is the state of being of what are not purely self-determining selves, but rather highly constructed and overdetermined agents of external as well as internal identificatory practices that nevertheless constitute our world. As Étienne Balibar describes it, in our subjugation, we are subjectivated.

In accepting this basic theory of subjectivity, we are not committing ourselves to a thorough antihumanism. It is possible to adhere to a theory of subjectivity that still seeks to retain some notions of unity and coherence, as well as to claim certain rights and dues. We are, however, firmly placing ourselves in the posthumanist landscape, for our subjects are not freely self-determining and fully self-transparent. So, while antihumanism necessitates a model of subjectivity, subjectivity does not necessarily entail a thoroughgoing antihumanism.

But recall that our theme here is not simply subjectivity, but rather ethical subjectivity.[34] By ethical subjectivity we mean to specify a particular field of inquiry within studies of subjectivity, as well as particular philosophical and ideological commitments. A theory of ethical subjectivity posits two things: (1) that there is an intimate connection between a person's subjectivity and her being ethical, that is, the structure of the human subject is an ethical structure, and (2) that an ethics is best conceived when one first understands that the structure of the human subject is ethical. But what does that mean? It means that in studying both ethics and subjectivity, our focus is on the ways in which we, as subjects, are ethical. That is, our focus is on the ways in which those things that structure us (social law, language, the Unconscious, ideology) make us, or fail to make us, ethical—ethical in the sense of responsible for others and responsible to ourselves, ethical in the sense of being originally bound to each other in ways that cannot, or at least should not, be denied or ignored, ethical in the sense that, at our very core, we, as subjects, have commitments that we need to be aware of, that we need to nurture and cultivate, and that is it these commitments that make us who and what we are.

Of course, what this means varies from thinker to thinker. For some, ethical subjectivity equates the relational nature of the human person with her ethicalness (Buber). For others, ethical subjectivity posits a subordination to the introjection of an external ethical law, an introjection that is constitutive of a human person's sense of self (and in fact may be pathogenic) (Freud). Regardless of the specifics of a theory of ethical subjectivity, the positing of the human subject as ethical and the positing of the study of ethics as a study of human subjectivity are two of the hallmarks of Continental ethics, particularly given its post-humanist framework.[35]

---

34. Again, Critchley has been the leader in examining the question of the ethics of subjectivity from a Continental perspective. For a helpful and instructive overview of his position, see his "Prolegomena to Any Post-Deconstructive Subjectivity" in Critchley and Dews (1996).

35. This is but a tentative explanation of a difficult concept, but for now it must suffice, for a full understanding of what I mean by ethical subjectivity can

READING LEVINAS AND LACAN

In this post-humanist landscape, we now need to rethink Foucault's statement to see if we can come up with another illustrative pairing. It is my contention that similar to the contrastive pairing of Sartre and Lacan, the contrastive pairing of Levinas and Lacan is precisely the set of post-humanist alternate contemporaries we are seeking. Both Levinas and Lacan share some basic interests, and both view their projects as attempts to intervene in the liberal humanist constructions of ethical systems, examining and questioning the nature and the role of the subject in moral action. As such, they stand as two powerful alternatives when discussing in a post-humanist context the question of human subjectivity in general and ethical subjectivity in particular.

Let us make this point more strongly. First, consider that Levinas and Lacan certainly both stand tall in the field of twentieth-century French intellectual thought. Both were occupied with the same philosophical thinkers and questions, both being avid readers of Descartes, Kant, Hegel, Husserl, and Heidegger. This led both of them to their interest in similar questions concerning the

---

only be made through a detailed reading of Levinas and Lacan as theorists of precisely that. I will return to this theme again and again throughout the text, and I will put forth some preliminary comments on the possibilities of constructing a full-blown theory of ethical subjectivity out of Levinas and Lacan in the conclusion. This will be a prolegomena to one of my future projects, which will be a constructive proposal for a conception of ethical subjectivity. Constructively, I will attempt to see how contemporary Continental philosophical and religious thinkers have explained the ethical nature of our subjectivity in order to open us up to different ways of thinking, both about ethics and the human, than we have previously had. Moreover, I will try to construct, out of these thinkers, by combining them in new and interesting ways, my own theory of the ethics of subjectivity, one that is more explicitly about *ethical subjectivity*. What I hope to offer will be a theory that covers more than any of the thinkers I will study have done on their own and that will truly move the discussion centered on the question of ethics and the question of the human forward. It will, I hope, be a theory that will show people working outside of the tradition the kind of thinking that goes on in contemporary Continental philosophical and religious thought. Thus, this books lays the groundwork for more constructively directed work to follow.

proper reading of major philosophical figures (e.g., to what extent
was Kant's view of the human subject simply an extension of Cartesian thought and to what extent was it offering a new, cosmo-
politan view? Was Hegel the last great metaphysician or the first
great philosopher of history?) and the proper approaches and answers to philosophical questions, specifically those involving the
nature of human subjectivity and the role of the human subject in
philosophical discourse (e.g., What is the importance of death in
studying the human person? What is the meaning of Being in relation to beings? What are the relationships between metaphysics,
ontology, ethics, and philosophical anthropology?). That is, they
were two alternate *contemporaries*.

Second, consider that Levinas and Lacan also represent two
competing methodologies in contemporary theoretical analysis: the
phenomenological-philosophical and the psychoanalytic. In his
commitment to the phenomenological method, Levinas remains
committed to a particular way of thinking that takes seriously the
transcendental essence of events (and, as we shall see, nonevents
that have no essence as such) as transparent and knowable through
strict observation and questioning. As well, Levinas takes human
consciousness as an essential starting point in all questioning, even
if he posits a transcendence beyond my (mundane) consciousness
that ultimately becomes the ground of ethics.[36] Lacan, in his commitment to the psychoanalytic method, remains committed to a
very different way of thinking that not only rejects the search for
"essence," but sees motivations and meanings of events as conflicting, hidden, and counterintuitive. Lacan thus may start with the

---

36. Of course, unlike Husserl, Levinas will insist on a radical transcendence,
a transcendence of something beyond human consciousness; this is the fundamental break between Husserlian phenomenology and Levinasian ethical theory.
Simply put, if for Husserl everything that is known, including the other (for
Husserl, as an other consciousness), is known only by virtue of the activity of a
constituting consciousness, for Levinas it is precisely the other that interrupts
consciousness itself that signals a transcendence beyond the mundane, and even
the transcendental ego and its essential constitutive and constituting active structures, thrusting the self into passivity and founding the subject as "for-the-other."

subject, but with what remains hidden to it as the key to subjectivity, and thus as the key to ethics. Levinas sees meaning as readily available, that is, made obvious through strict philosophical analysis; Lacan sees meaning as occluded, covered over, and available only in part and only through an examination of the extraneous. In short, where Levinas is committed to the surface transparency of the event—what Lacan would locate in the realm of the conscious, though as we shall see for Levinas the meaning of the event is not therefore located in "consciousness"—Lacan is committed to the reality of the Unconscious. In this, therefore, they have remained *alternate* contemporaries.

So, within the basic philosophical framework we are calling post-humanist, then, this work operates under the assessment that it is now Levinas and Lacan who stand as alternate contemporaries, with Lacan representing an antihumanism and Levinas representing a post-humanism, specifically what, according to the title of a 1982 book, he calls a "humanism of the other person."

In reading these two thinkers side by side, what jumped out at me, among all of the various themes that occupied each thinker, was the question that stood out as centrally important to both—that of ethical subjectivity.

To begin, we note that both Levinas and Lacan can be read as theorists of subjectivity precisely because they, for the most part, agree with the claims made by Foucault about the nature of the human person. Moreover, both Levinas and Lacan see their projects as studies of the human subject—as attempts to uncover the structures that make us subjects in the world and as attempts to explicate the nature of that subjection. Levinas wants to know, "Who are we subject to?" Lacan asks, "When and where does subjection first arise?" And the question central to both thinkers is "How are we to live in the fact of our subjection?" Both Levinas's ethical philosophy and Lacan's psychoanalysis are studies of the human subject and human subjectivity. And, again, Lacan's subject is clearly antihumanist, where Levinas's subject is decidedly post-humanist.

Continuing, we note that for Levinas the subject is first and foremost an ethical subject, for the very structure of subjectivity in Levinas's thought is the subject as "for-the-other." In this, any study of the ethical is, for Levinas, a study of subjectivity, and any study of subjectivity is a study of the ethical. Moreover, the focus for Levinas is on the ethical, not on morality, or even ethics, because the latter terms designate a field of study in which rules or foundations are put forth to which the subject is expected to subscribe. For Levinas, to call the structure of subjectivity ethical is, by contrast, to identify an an-archic foundation—a non-event from the immemorial past that structures us as subjects for-the-other, but does so without specific prescriptions of content, code, or law. The moral, for Levinas, relies too much on a theory of the categorical imperative as a reflective a priori, while ethics too closely aligns itself with a Hegelian code of the subject as an historical enactment of an overarching spirit.

For Lacan, the situation is a little less clear. According to Lacan, the psychoanalytic study of subjectivity is an *ethical* intervention precisely because, in the uncovering of desire, we are led to a knowledge of the Unconscious, and in turn are put in touch with the conflicts between consciousness and the Unconscious as well as the conflicts within the Unconscious. It is only in understanding unconscious desire that one can lift the symptoms caused by psychic conflict. At first it may seem odd to call this ethical, but Lacan does not hesitate to refer to this as the ethics of psychoanalysis. By doing this he is *in part* co-opting the term for his own uses, thereby ironizing the category of the ethical as used by traditional philosophers such as Aristotle, Kant, and Bentham. However, he is also positively viewing ethics as a historical and situational claim in which the desire of the individual patient is uncovered and the structure of subjectivity as rooted in desire is exposed. As the psychoanalytic study of subjectivity is, for Lacan, an historical enterprise, he goes to great length to focus his study of the subject as a study of a particular historical subject. As such, the ethics of psychoanalysis is not a universalizable study, but rather one limited to a particular time and place—the contemporary West.[37] Lacan's study is not a search for the a priori of the moral; nor is it a study of ethics as the unfolding of a Hegelian spirit; it is, however, the study of a particular kind of "ethics" as an historical enterprise rooted in a specific moment. Lacan's psychoanalytic study of the human subject is a search for a new kind of "ethics." So, when Lacan examines the ethical nature of the human subject, he is clearly doing something different than we may have previously encountered. Still, there is no question that ethical subjectivity, in both its positive and negative forms, is of central concern to Lacan.

So, in order to make the connection between Levinas and Lacan, this book will focus on a problematic central to both of their projects: ethical subjectivity.

Reading these two thinkers together is not, however, an easy task. There is no evidence that either Levinas or Lacan had ever read the other's work. Though they shared much in common, including a certain philosophical heritage, a shared intellectual stage, and a few important personal friends and interlocutors (including Jean Wahl and Jacques Derrida), I have not been able to find a single reference that either made to the other in either of their works; nor has any interpreter I have read. In the few places where Levinas has anything to say about psychoanalysis or Freud, his remarks are markedly critical, often derisive. In the places where Lacan has anything to say about phenomenology, the names adduced are always Husserl and Heidegger, as if Levinas simply does not exist. Their readers, too, have for the most part remained separate, with different schools of thought forming in response to each, schools of thought that do not engage with one another on any meaningful level.[38]

---

37. Lacan makes this point in several places in his work. For instance, in *The Four Fundamental Concepts of Psychoanalysis* (1973/1981) he writes: "Psychoanalysis is neither a *Weltanschauung*, nor a philosophy that claims to provide the key to the universe. It is governed by a particular aim, which is historically defined by the elaboration of the notion of the subject" (Lacan S XI 90/S XI 77).

38. There are notable exceptions to this. Two of the most important philosophers on the contemporary scene, Jacques Derrida and Luce Irigaray, draw

This book stands as an attempt to begin to undo this separation. It is offered as an addition to the small but growing body of literature that does take both Levinas and Lacan seriously, as well as the small but growing body of literature that dares to put the two thinkers into dialogue. It will do so by taking key texts of each thinker and engaging in close readings of them in order to expose points of connection and divergence. It will isolate shared themes, and will explore how each thinker dealt with these themes in very different ways. It will look at some texts in isolation, and others in dialogue, in order to highlight all the more clearly these commonalities and differences. And in the end, it will attempt to bring the two into a more direct dialogue, resulting in something of a co-reading that, regardless of their obvious disagreements, attempts to draw from the best of each thinker.

A NOTE ON THE METHOD AND GOAL OF THIS PROJECT

This book is executed primarily through a series of close readings of primary texts. I do not apologize for this. As this is not a book about interpretations of Levinas and Lacan, it is not my intention here primarily to assess secondary source literature. When I felt that secondary sources helped to enrich my reading, or when they had been particularly instructive in guiding it, I used them. Mostly, I tried not to. I have been more successful in this department in my reading of Levinas than in my reading of Lacan, perhaps given my greater comfort level with things philosophical. However, as contact with secondary literature is a useful way to frame the uniqueness of this project, I have attempted in the footnotes to offer some connections and point out some differences between my project and others. Still, it is my contention that the unique-

---

heavily on the work of both Levinas and Lacan. They each credit both Levinas and Lacan as being major influences on their work in addition to being significant objects of their studies. For an excellent study of Irigaray in her relation to both Levinas and, to a much lesser extent, Lacan, see Chanter (1995).

ness of this project speaks for itself and is sufficiently explained in this introduction.

In reading these two disparate giants, I have continually been confronted with the difficulty of switching out of one theoretical world and into another. Levinas and Lacan are very different writers, thinkers, and theorists. I find myself at different times and in different ways closer to one, and at other times and in other ways closer to the other. My training in religious studies has grounded me in Continental philosophical approaches, but my interest in psychoanalysis has a long history that has been equally supported and nurtured in my studies. At times my readings of one improperly affected my readings of the other. Early on in this project, one reader accused me, in one chapter, of "philosophizing Lacan." Later in this project's gestation, that same reader was bothered by the use of biographical and historical material in my discussions of Lacan and the lack thereof in my readings of Levinas and accused me of furthering the idea that "philosophy is ahistorical." I have attempted to use these two comments as railings on either end, representing extremes that I have tried to steer between, while occasionally bumping into them. As the two thinkers are so different, my own writing style changes when dealing with each. I have attempted to tailor my style to theirs in order to allow each to speak on his own terms. By following closely the styles of the writers in my readings of them, I hope that each voice comes out distinctly alongside my own.[39]

---

39. I find it particularly amusing that when this manuscript first went out for review, I received reviews that were strongly at odds with one another. The manuscript was sent to one Levinas scholar, one Lacan scholar, and one scholar who works with both Levinas and Lacan. Not surprisingly, the Levinas scholar read me as a Lacan person, whereas the Lacan scholar read me as a Levinas person. For instance, the Lacan scholar mentioned my "proximity to Levinas" while the Levinas scholar mentioned that my take on Lacan is "surer of itself." This in and of itself demonstrates the difficulty of writing a text that tries to deal with both on an equal level, with a readiness to praise and criticize both thinkers and to bring them together in a most unorthodox manner. Needless to say, I found the disagreements between these reviews to be both frustrating and amusing and, ultimately, indicative of my being on the right track.

Thus, it is true that I have historicized Lacan more than Levinas. Levinas's philosophy, while not properly ahistorical, is not simply a reading of the day-to-day life of individuals in the contemporary West.[40] It is aimed at things more universal, more timeless—what Husserl called the transcendental. It is, I contend, an attempt to elucidate, through phenomenological analysis, the very nature of our subjectivity. While Levinas believed that his obsession with the Holocaust shaped the trajectory of his thought, he did not believe, so far as I can tell, that it determined the answers he found to the questions he posed. So, following Levinas's lead, I have treated his thought on a more abstract level, and in a decidedly less historical way.

Lacan is a different story. Too often people dismiss Freud and Lacan for their insufficient attention to their own historical situation, to the historical nature of their own thought. This is solidly an unfair critique. Both Freud and Lacan were keenly aware of their own historical situations, and of the situatedness of their thought.[41] Additionally, we must remember that psychoanalysis is at its core a reading of how we live in the world, of our struggles with our past as it shapes our present and future. It takes as its subject matter our everyday occurrences, our daily life. It is inherently historical, contextual, situated, and is best treated as such. Following Lacan's lead, then, I have attempted to read Lacan as he read Freud—as a product of his times, as engaged in the world, and as an historical event of great import.

However, it is also true that at times I have turned Lacan too much into the philosopher he always hoped he would be. There are several works that treat Lacan as a philosopher, or at least translate him into philosophical language. The most notable in this category is Elizabeth Grosz's *Jacques Lacan: A Feminist Introduction*

---

40. This is not to say that Levinas is unconcerned with lived life. Quite to the contrary: as a phenomenologist Levinas is profoundly interested in our lived lives—but with an eye toward the transcendental structures that underlie our experiences.

41. For instance, take Lacan's claim, cited in footnote 37, on the status of psychoanalysis.

(1990). Grosz has a keen eye and is one of the best at making Lacan accessible to the philosophical mind. However, sometimes the result is that Lacan is oversimplified. Other thinkers have attempted to systematize Lacan in ways that fail to do justice to the experimental nature of his work. The most notable in this category is Dylan Evans's *An Introductory Dictionary to Lacanian Psychoanalysis* (1996), one of the more helpful secondary sources on Lacan that I have come across. However, the very nature of the project suggests that Lacan can be categorized and classified in a straightforward manner. In all fairness to his work, Evans tries very hard not to do this. He recognizes that Lacan's thought was always under revision, that Lacan was always thinking up new ways to get his points across, that his language shifted over time, and that he cannot be pinned down in a systematic manner. Still, the very idea of a dictionary is not necessarily the best structure for a reading of Lacan, and when using it one must always remember that Lacan is not a philosopher, not a system builder, and not a theorist who can easily be systematized. Thus, my reading of Lacan has not attempted to take into account the entire Lacanian corpus in a systematic way. To do so, I contend, would not only be a task too large for this project, but also a misguided one. Rather, my reading of Lacan remains closely situated in the text, fragmented and tentative, and not masked by an attempt at mastering he who cannot be mastered.[42]

Others still have accused me of taking Levinas into territory where he should not go. At a Levinas conference at Walsh University a few years ago, I gave a paper on Levinas and Lacan in one of my earliest attempts to read the two together. This paper, a

---

42. Gallop speaks to this the best of anyone. In her "Prefatory Material" she tells of a reader's report to a partial version of the manuscript in which the reader complained that Gallop not only was not in "command" of the material, but also admitted as much. Gallop takes this as an opportunity to reject the very idea that Lacan either can or should be "mastered." If, after all, Lacan is a theorist of the Unconscious, and moreover claims that the Unconscious cannot be mastered, controlled, conquered, then Lacan, more than anyone, offers a theory of impotence for the impotent, moving us to dissolve the "subject supposed to know." See Gallop (1985, pp. 18–21).

critique of William Richardson's (1995) highly problematic essay "The Irresponsible Subject," suggested that the work of both Levinas and Lacan would benefit from their comparison—that Levinas gave Lacan's ideas a stronger ethical structure and that Lacan gave Levinas's theory an Unconscious.[43] One audience member was "appalled at the violence" I was doing to Levinas by suggesting that his theory was strengthened by bringing in something that he himself so vehemently denied the very existence of! This was a sign to me that I was on the right track, for I was indeed pushing Levinas into territory that was not his own. I have continued to do that in this work, and make no excuses for doing so.

Still, the reader should not walk away thinking that in this project I ultimately take a side, either Lacan over Levinas or Levinas over Lacan. Although on certain areas of conflict I may think that one thinker adds something that the other does not, when it comes to an overall endorsement of one over the other, I am careful not to offer one.[44] It is my strong contention that each thinker has something unique and essential to offer a theory of ethical subjectivity and that to fill in the gaps each needs the other.

The book will unfold in four chapters, framed by an introduction and a conclusion. The four chapters will be close readings of key texts by Levinas and Lacan on a particular topic. Chapter 1 will focus on the founding moment of subjectivity in the confrontation with the other for both Levinas and Lacan, looking at key sections of Levinas's *Time and the Other*, *Totality and Infinity*, and *Otherwise than Being*, and Lacan's "Mirror Stage" and "Aggressivity in Psychoanalysis" papers. Chapter 2 will focus on subjectivity as sexed subjectivity in the works of both thinkers, again looking at key sec-

---

43. Richardson's essay can be found in Peperzak (1995).

44. This may, of course, frustrate some readers. I would venture to guess that those more familiar with Lacan will find my reading of Levinas more sure and that those more familiar with Levinas will find my reading of Lacan more sure, and that each will find me siding with the other side. I assure readers that I am neither Levinasian nor Lacanian, and leave it to them to evaluate my position as a *both/and*, though in a very peculiar way, as I will discuss in the conclusion.

tions in Levinas's *Totality and Infinity* and *Otherwise than Being*, and Lacan's "The Signification of the Phallus" and *Seminar XX: Encore*. Chapter 3 will focus on subjectivity as it connects to language and discourse, looking at Levinas's "Language and Proximity" and key sections of his *Otherwise than Being*, and Lacan's "The Function and Field of Speech and Language in Psychoanalysis" and "Agency of the Letter in the Unconscious." Chapter 4 will focus on subjectivity as ethical through an examination of the an-archic as the central ethical category in Levinas and the Unconscious as the central ethical category in Lacan, looking at Levinas's "God and Philosophy" and "Diachrony and Representation," and Lacan's *Seminar VII: The Ethics of Psychoanalysis* and *Seminar IX: The Four Fundamental Concepts of Psychoanalysis*.[45] These chapters will show the progression in each thinker from the undifferentiation of pre-subjectivity into the differentiation of subjectivity, through sex and language as further categories of differentiation and definition, and finally into the fullness of subjectivity as ethical. Through these four chapters, we will have prepared the way for the book's conclusion, in which I will offer suggestions for a constructive theory of post-humanist ethical subjectivity that takes seriously the insights of both Levinasian and Lacanian thought, using the work of both thinkers to put forth my own proposal. The goal here will *not* be a synthesis of the two thinkers, nor a unified and coherent theory of

---

45. The reader may notice that my choice of texts by Levinas covers only the "Greek" and not the "Hebrew" writings. That is, it focuses on only the explicitly philosophical works. This is not an accident. Nor is it a statement about the importance of one over the other. Robert Gibbs (1992) makes an excellent argument that Levinas's philosophy is inherently Judaic. However, I find the style and subject matter of Levinas's philosophical and Judaic writings sufficiently different to merit separate treatment. While there are many points of overlap and connection, I felt that it would obscure my reading of Levinas to bring in the Judaic sources, as it is in his philosophical works where he offers the phenomenological analysis of the ethical structure of human subjectivity. Therefore, some works that may seem appropriate to the reader at certain points were not consulted, such as Levinas's (1982b) discussion of language in *Beyond the Verse*. For an excellent discussion of the "Greek" and the "Hebrew" in Levinas, see Gibbs (1992), Chapter 7.

the ethical subject, but rather a theory of ethical subjectivity that draws on each thinker, without reducing one to the other, and without sacrificing their differences; the two will be brought together in a fractured and fragmented vision that appeals alternatingly to their points of view, not only *even*, but also *especially* in their points of divergence and disagreement. In the end, I argue toward a theory of ethical subjectivity as a theory of the subject desiring-the-good-of-the-other.[46]

---

46. I say "argue toward" not "argue for" because the conclusion will not offer a full-blown theory of ethical subjectivity. That is not the point of this book. Rather, the conclusion will point *toward* what I believe are the essential components of a theory of ethical subjectivity—components that come from the co-readings of Levinas and Lacan that I offer here. As I mentioned above, I hope to fully develop this theory of ethical subjectivity as the subject desiring-the-good-of-the-other in a future work.

1

The Other and the Self:
Creating the Subject

The relationship with the other person, the face-to-face with the other person, the encounter with a face that at once gives and conceals the other person, is the situation in which an event happens to a subject who does not assume it, who is utterly unable in its regard, but where nonetheless in a certain way it is in front of the subject. The other "assumed" is the other person.
—Levinas, TA 67/TO 78–99

I is an other . . . Don't let this impress you! Don't start spreading it around that I is an other—it won't impress anyone, believe me! And what is more, it doesn't mean anything. Because, to begin with, you have to know what an other means. The other—don't use this term as mouthwash.
—Lacan, *Seminar Book II*, p. 7

The point of departure for both Levinas and Lacan is the intervention of the other, be it in the fact of otherness as seen in the reality of death, in the face-to-face encounter with the other person, in the image of the self as self/other in the mirror, or in the image of the other as unity as seen through the eyes of the infant.[1] Prior to the intervention of the other, the self is incomplete. There

---

1. Before going any further, we need to clarify the use of our terms. "Self" is a term that Lacan avoids at every turn. The very term is so wrapped in humanist meaning that he could not in good conscience continue to use it. Instead, Lacan speaks of the creation of "the subject"—a term emphasizing the subjected nature of the person and its radical linguistic and cultural construction. However, in his later work (post 1950), Lacan reserves the term "subject" for the subject in language, that is, he reserves the term for one who has moved from the Imaginary to the Symbolic. The Imaginary ego and the Imaginary I are not yet "subjects" because they are still defined primarily by the intersubjective exchange between child and (m)other. To avoid confusion, I will use the term "self" in referring to what is constructed in the Lacanian Imaginary, but only with reservation, and only when no other term will suffice. More often, I will refer to the Imaginary "ego" (the sense of self) or the "I" (the locus for this construction).

is neither unity nor self-sufficiency; neither a subject resting in reason, nor one secure in its capacity to know. Prior to the other the self is not yet actualized, and not yet a subject. Unity, self-sufficient freedom, contentment in capacity, these are things that are not yet known. It is the intervention of the other that marks the creation of the self as self, gives it its mission and purpose, even its very being, and thus it is the intervention of the other that marks the shift out of the humanist paradigm into the post-humanist paradigm. Here, now, the self finds itself as subject always and only in/through the eyes of the other. This is the post-humanist vision of which Levinas and Lacan are two *competing* representatives. By examining the creation of the subject in Levinas and the creation of the imaginary ego-self in Lacan as marked by the intervention of the other we can shed light on the originary nature of the subject and its primary relationship with the other, and in so doing can begin to see Levinas and Lacan as the visionaries they are.[2]

Levinas began his philosophical career with two relatively short works in which the themes he would later develop were outlined. The first was *De L'existence à l'existant* (*Existence to Existents*) and the second, *Le Temps et l'Autre* (*Time and the Other*). *Time and the Other* was originally a series of four lectures Levinas delivered in 1946–47 at Jean Wahl's Philosophical College in Paris. It was published in 1948, again in 1979, and translated by Richard Cohen in 1987. Although Levinas later gives up the metaphysical language of this early work, *Time and the Other* remains the best succinct introduction to his most basic premise that the subject is constituted in the intervention of the other.[3]

---

2. The term "other" was widely used in France by the 1950s. In fact, the influence of Hegel had made the term something of a cliché. Hence, Lacan's warning not to use the term as "mouthwash." Still, it is Levinas and Lacan who bring this otherwise overused term into sharp focus, where it is not only a term of extreme philosophical importance but also the linchpin of their respective revolutionary projects.

3. *Time and the Other* is a dense and difficult work; however, as it presupposes a deep understanding of Levinas's phenomenological roots, to attempt to

Best read as a response to Heidegger's *Being and Time*, *Time and the Other* seeks to show that time is neither the horizon of being nor the existential structure of Dasein in its solitude.[4] Rather, in *Time and the Other*, time is shown to be that which constitutes the subject in its intersubjectivity: "time is not the achievement of an isolated and lone subject, but . . . is the very relationship of the subject with the other person" (TA 17/TO 39). The work is an adept demonstration of Levinas's phenomenological method, in which he takes single moments of time and expands upon their existential and ontological attributes. The moments of time herein treated are: (1) the solitude of being prior to the intervention of the other, and (2) the confrontation with death as the first intervention of the other itself.

Time and the Other begins with the solitude of existing, in which the existing being is all alone without any determinate mode of existing. The central ontological question that dominates the opening pages of the text is the question of monadism versus monism. Existing, Levinas finds, is a state brought about in solitude; that is, existing belongs to an isolated individual. Solitude is the "indissoluble unity between the existent and its work of existing" (TA 22/TO 43). Existing, then, is an attribute of a lone existent, prior to intersubjectivity and inside of itself, a single consciousness.[5]

Instead of viewing existing as an attribute of a being, Levinas asks if one can return to a time before existents in order to understand existing in itself. This is clearly a modification of Heidegger's question. Translating Heidegger for his own purposes, Levinas

---

"translate it out of" phenemenological language would be to do an injustice to its sophistication and direction. Thus, I will remain true to the text by keeping the language close to Levinas's, while still trying to make it accessible to the nonspecialist.

4. John Drabinski (2001) makes the argument that Levinas's work is best read in relation to Husserl and that *Time and the Other* is best read as a drawing out of the "forgotten possibilities in Husserl's phenomenology" (p. 60). Drabinski's work is both sophisticated and illuminating and offers a much-needed explication of Levinas's indebtedness and proximity to Husserlian phenomenology.

5. In this, we can see that for Levinas the structure of being is monadic, not monistic.

shows how the solitude of Heidegger's *es gibt* (*il y a*) is one of in-somnia, in which impersonal existence is "a vigilance without possible recourse to sleep" (TA 27/TO 48–49). This inability to withdraw signifies an existing that is "not an *in-itself* . . . [but] is precisely the absence of all self, a *without-self*" (TA 27/TO 49). This existing is without self in that it is without boundary, without lo-cation and place. It cannot withdraw because it has nothing into which it can withdraw; all existence is its existing. That this stage of existing is prior to the sense of self marks it as prior to any kind of time. The inability to withdraw thereby marks the "not-yet" of temporality.

When consciousness ruptures the *il y a*, existing, in the event of hypostasis—the taking up of existence by the existent—becomes an attribute. With existence as an attribute, the existent begins to form a certain sense of self, a sense of itself as a thing that pos-sesses. However, to posit hypostasis is "not to introduce time into being" because the attribute of existence is still not yet an attribute of a completed self (TA 32/TO 52). For an existent is not only not a self when it is not yet distinguished from an other, when it does not yet have boundaries and a sense of place, but an existent is also not yet a self so long as it is bound up in only the present. Hypostasis is an event of an ever-present now, in which everything is imme-diately present to the existent. So long as all is present, in the to-tality of its existence, the existent is without time, and thus without self. In hypostasis, "[s]omething that is bears existing as an at-tribute. Existing is its own, and it is precisely through this master . . . that the existent is alone" (TA 31/TO 52). So, the existent is still only that which houses existing, only the place of an ever-present existence. In hypostasis, the self as existent may begin to be, but the self completed is not yet. Existing may be an attribute, but of what?

Here Levinas offers a fascinating description of the phenome-non of the "I." Whereas philosophers, he claims, have always rec-ognized the *I* as substance, here hypostasis creates the form *I* upon which existing rests, and yet the *I* is something different than what we are used to. Here *I* is only a means of locating the ever-present now of hypostasis. The *I* still has no time, and thus no subjectivity. Simply calling the existent "I" is not to give it substance; the *I* that is speaking its word, rather, does not, in actuality, exist. If *I* is an attribute, then we are again confronted with the question, an attribute of what (or whom)? The hypostasized *I* is only a form of existing itself, not initially an existing being, as "properly speaking it does not [yet] exist" (TA 33/TO 53). The *I*, then, is simply the "indissoluble unity between the existent and its existing" (TA 35/TO 54). And as the *I* is the form of existing in which existing belongs to itself, it is alone: "Solitude is the very unity of the existent, the fact that there is something in existing starting from which existence occurs" (TA 35/TO 54).

The existent's mastery over its existing is paradoxical, for the existent is not free in its entirety. Instead, its existing is master, as in its solitude the existent is inescapably "occupied with itself" (TA 36/TO 55). Because the existent is its existing and nothing more, and because all existing is of the existent, the existent is made heavy with itself. In this Levinas argues that "a free being is already no longer free, because it is responsible for itself" (TA 36/TO 55). This is the tragedy of a paradoxical freedom—the solitude of the self leaves us no place to turn but inward.

Levinas now tries to show various attempts of the existent to overcome the tragedy of solitude through material life. In classic phenomenological form, Levinas takes us through various events of existence. In these forms we are confronted with existents in solitude, in which all is for the existence it fills. The attribute of existence thrust upon the anonymous existent leaves the existent alone and unformed. All things are but extensions of the self, as the self absorbs them into itself. All material life, even the *jouissance* of the everyday, is nothing but "absorption of the object" (TA 46/TO 63) It is not until the encounter with the object *in light* that things *begin* to progress. Here, an interval of space is given by light. The existent is confronted with the object and begins to recognize space and boundary. In seeing the other as other, the self "separates from itself . . . every day life is already a way of being free from the initial materiality through which a [self] accomplishes itself"

(TA 46/TO 63). Unfortunately, even though light is "that through which [we can come to recognize] something is other than my-self," the existent recognizes light "already as if it came from me" (TA 47/TO 64). That is, the object in light does not have a funda-mental strangeness because it can still be explained in the reason of the existent. The existent can control and power the object; it is for the existent, and thus by the existent. That is, it is still object. While in some sense "outside" of the existent, the object's "tran-scendence is wrapped in immanence" (TA 47 /TO 65).[6] Unfortu-nately, then,

> The objectivity of rational knowledge removes nothing of the solitary character of reason. The possible reversal of objectiv-ity into subjectivity is the very theme of idealism, which is a philosophy of reason. Subjectivity is itself the objectivity of light. Every object can be spoken of in terms of consciousness— that is, can be brought to light. [TA 48/TO 65–66]

All remains caught up in the circle of the known, or the knowable, or the conscious. It is not until confronted with that which is wholly outside of the existent that the subject actualizes. It is not until the intervention of the other that the subject qua subject, that is, as actor and agent, and not simply vehicle for existing, comes to exist.

The "other" first comes to us in Levinas's work here in his potent analysis of death. The discussion of death is, of course, not an historical accident. Rather, Levinas places himself in direct con-versation with Heidegger. Whereas for Heidegger death signifies that which is Dasein's most "mine," for Levinas death signifies the

---

6. It is striking here to notice the parallels we find between Levinas's work and that of Jewish philosopher Franz Rosenzweig (1886–1929). For instance, in *The Star of Redemption* Rosenzweig (1985) shows us how reason, as a compo-nent of the world, collapses on itself when left in the light of immanence with-out the transcendence of God to point beyond. We also find, for instance, at the end of Book One of the *Star*, that Rosenzweig leaves us with solitary man, the self-willed self who has no relations, and it is only in Book Three that, in his relations with others, man becomes a soul.

advent of that which is not the existent—the other.[7] Death is the future that for the existent is always looming but is never present. As soon as death becomes present, the existent is no more, and as long as the existent is, death is not-yet. Death, then, is the event that will happen to us that we can never control—it is the certain moment at which we will "no longer [be] *able to be able*" (TA 62/ TO 74). As such, death is "the impossibility of having a project" (TA 62–63/TO 74). In this impossibility, death is that which breaks my solitude, for death is that which I cannot control, and thus is that which is the utmost *not*-mine. Death, then, is the absolute insistence of existence's plurality. In this insistence, we are first confronted with the fact of the other.

The confrontation with death serves as a foundationally descriptive event in *Time and the Other*. It is foundationally descriptive both in the sense that it serves as a point of reference for the descriptions Levinas gives of "concrete encounter" with the other later in the work, and in the sense that it serves as a foundational reference for understanding the intervention of the other as it is re-presented in Levinas's later works—specifically, as the face of the other person who calls on me from high in *Totalité et Infini* (*Totality and Infinity*) and as the other person who draws me near in *Autrement qu'être ou au-delà de l'essence* (*Otherwise than Being* or *Beyond Essence*). Thus, it is here present to help us understand the intervention of the other, not to serve as the actual and only event in time in which we come to see otherness as such. The concrete event that becomes significant in Levinas is the erotic encounter with the other person, to which he next moves in *Time and the Other*.

That the event of death cannot be grasped leaves us with a conundrum: "How can the event that cannot be grasped still happen to me?" (TA 65/TO 77). In the face of death, the existent confronts its inability to be able. Husserl's intentional consciousness finds its limit. How, then, can it continue existing in the face of

---

7. For Heidegger's discussion of death, see Part One, Division Two, Section I, Chapters 46 to 53 of Heidegger (1962).

not only its eventual non-being, but in the face of its very impotence? In death, this first confrontation with the other, the existent is thrust into the most passive of its modes of being. In this first encounter with the other, the existent is caught in pure passivity. Yet the existent continues "to be"; it still is, even in the face of this other. Moreover, it now "is" with a sense of boundary, a sense of that which it is not, and which it cannot overcome or control—death, the other. Only now does the existent as subject truly begin to be. Only now does the subject understand itself as such—as not simply alone, but as differentiated in a world among others. And only now does the future hold any meaning, for only now does the self understand the possibility of its impossibility.[8] As such, in the confrontation with death, both time and subjectivity begin.[9] For this self, "time is essentially a new birth" (TA 72/TO 81).[10]

Having shown how death presents itself as the announcing of the multiplicity of existence, Levinas goes on to describe the positivity of alterity in the figure of the feminine. The description here is rich and powerful, and this early description is enriched by more complete descriptions of sexual difference, the topic of Chapter 2 of this book, in *Totalité et Infini* (*Totality and Infinity*). Before turning to that topic, we need to understand Levinas's description of the intervention of the other better, and so move to another description of the birth of the subject, in which we may better understand the existent before and after the intervention of the other.

---

8. The interlocutor here is Jean Wahl, who argued that for Heidegger death is the impossibility of possibility. Levinas disagrees. See Heidegger, *Being and Time* (1992), paragraphs 50–53, pp. 290–311.

9. Thus, John Drabinski aptly titles the chapter in which he deals with *Time and the Other* "The Subject Outside the Self." See Drabinski (2001), Chapter 2.

10. Here the contrast with Husserl is remarkable. Levinas is precisely making the claim that Husserl's account of intersubjectivity is not truly intersubjective, that it is in coming to see others as other consciousnesses like myself that I come to know the other. Rather, it is in the confrontation of an otherness that is alien to consciousness that I come to differentiate myself from others. This differentiation is neither mimetic nor empathetic. For Husserl's (1999) discussion of intersubjectivity, see the fifth meditation in his *Cartesian Meditations*.

Levinas is better able to extend his phenomenology of the subject as his thought moves into deeper realms. Over the next decade, Levinas develops his thought, and the publication of *Totality and Infinity* marks the emergence of Levinas as a major original philosophical thinker whose ideas have begun to form a large and coherent vision. The first two sections of *Totality and Infinity* can be read as a spelling out of the phenomenology of solitude expressed in *Time and the Other*.[11] Where Levinas breaks new ground is in section three of the book, "Exteriority and the Face," in which he introduces what is one of the best-known of all Levinasian concepts—the face. The discussion of the face is, following the description of the confrontation with the idea of death in *Time and the Other*, Levinas's second description of the intervention of the other and marks a fuller vision of the advent of the subject. Where we might call the discussion in *Time and the Other* Levinas's early attempt at a phenomenology of subjectivity, the presentation in *Totality and Infinity* could be called the mature version of that early vision.[12]

The face is that which marks in Levinasian terms the failure of traditional philosophy:

> Inasmuch as the access to beings concerns vision, it dominates those beings, exercises a power over them. A thing is given, offers itself to me. In gaining access to it I maintain myself within the same.

> The face is present in its refusal to be contained. In this sense it cannot be comprehended, that is, encompassed. It is neither

---

11. I don't mean to reduce these sections to simply an expansion of *Time and the Other*. They are serious developments of the work that Levinas began in *Existence and Existents* and *Time and the Other*. For a detailed account of this, see Drabinski (2001), Chapter 3.

12. As is *Time and the Other*, *Totality and Infinity* is a sophisticated work deeply rooted in Husserlian and Heideggerian phenomenology; consequently, I will again stay close to the phenomenological language that Levinas himself uses. To do otherwise would be no longer to talk about Levinas's texts, but to take them into the world of the natural attitude.

seen nor touched—for in visual or tactile sensation the identity of the I envelops the alterity of the object, which becomes
precisely a content. [TI 211/TI 194]

The face is that which refuses to be contained, that which cannot
be comprehended, mastered, encompassed. The face is that fact of
being that exceeds the self's power, indeed overpowers the self, for
it marks the first limit of the self from outside. Whereas in *Time
and the Other* death was an abstract fact of otherness, the fact of
being exceeding the existent, now the face emerges as the concrete
event that places limits on the existent, and in so doing calls attention not only to otherness beyond (my) being, but to the otherness of *a* being, of an existent, as well. The face is concretely the
intervention of the other.

The face is not a phenomenon in any traditional sense, for
phenomena are by definition constituted objects of consciousness,
those things that can be explained, grasped, or, as Levinas would
claim, *reduced.* The encounter with the face is not, then, an experience in the traditional sense. Rather, the encounter with the face
is that which speaks to the inexplicability of the beyond, the infinity beyond any totality, the transcendence of alterity.[13] As such,
it is not a visual encounter, as vision is an experience of dominion, or capturing a moment in time. Instead, the encounter with
the face is a linguistic experience. The other person establishes
her being in speech, "speech [which] proceeds from absolute difference . . . [and] [a]bsolute difference, inconceivable in terms

---

13. Here we begin to see the difficulty in labeling Levinas's work "phenomenology," for he himself states vigorously that what he is describing is not a phenomenon. In this we can see Levinas's work as an attempt at a phenomenology
of the intervention of a non-phenomenon. Is this still philosophy in a traditional
sense? This is a question raised by Jacques Derrida (1978) in his essay "Violence
and Metaphysics." How can Levinas describe a non-experience, a nonevent? What
is it to talk about a non-phenomenon? While these questions are not central to
the thesis of this book, we will return to them periodically to help us better understand the radicality of Levinas's work, and the difficulty we inevitably encounter
when attempting to do something radically new. For more on this topic, see
Derrida's "Violence and Metaphysics" in *Writing and Difference* (1978).

of formal logic, is established only by language" (TI 212/TI 194–195). The face of the other person is the other person calling to the existent, calling it forth into a realization that she, the other person, exists and cannot be contained (by the existent). The face is that of an other and is not part of the existence of the existent, not part of the same. Language, then, "accomplishes a relation between the terms [of logic] which breaks up the unity of a genus" (TI 212/TI 195).

The existent acknowledges the face in its own linguistic response: "Speaking, rather than 'letting be,' solicits the other person" (TI 212/TI 195). The act of speaking acknowledges the fact of the other person, as speech assumes an interlocutor with whom one is in fact speaking. In this relation of language, the *I* validates the other person as other, and thus acknowledges that which exceeds its self. In acknowledging that which exceeds its self, the *I*, now more than an attribute of existence but a marker of finitude in the face of something more, acknowledges the infinite: "The presence of a being not entering into, but overflowing the sphere of the same establishes its 'status' as infinite" (TI 213/TI 195). That the existent cannot contain the other person determines the existent's finite nature, and so establishes within the existent "the idea of the infinite." According to Levinas, the "idea of the infinite, the infinitely more contained in the less, is concretely produced in the form of a relation with the face" (TI 213/TI 196). The existent thus comes to understand the fact of something beyond itself as the impossibility of containing all in the same, in the self, in being, and thus the idea of the infinite is posited.

In acknowledging that which exceeds itself, the infinite, the existent has put its existence, or at least its self-referential understanding of its own existence, into question. Until now, all was by and for the self; with the entry of the other person, the world takes on new meaning:

> The fact that the face maintains a relation with me in discourse
> does not range him in the same. He remains absolute in the
> relation. The solipsistic dialectic of consciousness, always

> suspicious of its captivity in the same, is broken off. The ethical relation that subtends discourse is not, in effect, a species of consciousness whose ray emanates from the I; it puts the I in question. This putting into question emanates from the other.
> [TI 213/TI 195]

The existent is now called to a new existence. In the intervention of the other, the existent comes to recognize itself as a finite being. In this, the existent comes to see itself as one among other selves, not as the transcendental self in dominion over all objects. The existent comes to see itself as self, as subject: subject in that it is subjected to a world of both objects and other beings made known by the face of the other. With this knowledge also comes responsibility. The existent becomes a "subject" not only in seeing itself as a finite being exceeded by the other person, but it also becomes a subject as the existent is subjected to that other. The face of the other person "calls [the subject] to responsibility, it founds it and justifies it" (TI 214–215/TI 197). And this intervention of the other by the face of the other person has a structure that Levinas calls ethical.

The face, Levinas tells us, resists me. When I encounter it, and realize that I cannot contain or possess it, my power is called into question. It also presents itself as a power I am (can) not (have). In escaping my power, the face presents itself as "an existent absolutely independent" (TI 216/TI 198). The other person, therefore, can say "no" to me, and in doing so, in saying "no" to my power over it, the other person, in the form of the face, utters to me the first command, what Levinas calls "the primordial expression": Thou shalt not kill (me) (TI 217/TI 199). It is as such that the presence of the face is ethical, and it is as such that the intervention of the other is the founding not only of a subject, but also an ethical subject. In invading my world of existence, the other person limits me, but does so in a way that demands my attention to its call. It shows itself to me, and I cannot but respond, because I cannot turn away. I cannot return to the pre-differentiated space of hypostasized existence, because I know there is something beyond that finitude.

In this, the other person "imposes itself [on me], but does so precisely by appealing to me with its destitution and nudity—its hunger—without my being able to be deaf to that appeal" (TI 219/TI 200). The face, then, calls me to responsibility, and in so doing "promotes my freedom, in arousing my goodness" (TI 219/TI 200). The existent, now first fully within that sense of space and boundary the hypostasized I lacked, becomes subject, and in so doing, understands itself not as *in-itself* or as *for-itself*, but as first, and always, *for-the-other*.

Inasmuch as the face calls me to responsibility for it, it shatters my solitude and demands its place. It does not, however, question my fact of existence or my right to place. While it calls into question my authority, thereby subjecting me, it does so in a movement of respect: "As nonviolence it nonetheless maintains the plurality of the same and the other. It is peace" (TI 222/TI 203). In this, the face that shatters my solitude leaves my existence intact. The subject who emerges from the encounter is subjected, but whole; responsible to an other, but in that responsibility, whole in itself—whole, but compelled. In this, Levinas's description of the creation of the subject is neither humanist nor antihumanist, but decidedly post-humanist.

Malcolm Bowie (1991) tells the story like this:

> At three forty on the afternoon of 3 August 1936, Lacan began to deliver his paper on "The Looking-Glass Phase" to the fourteenth International Psychoanalytic Congress which was being held in Marienbad. The bibliographical guide placed at the end of the first edition of *Écrits* piously records the details of time and date and in so doing suggests that the paper was an event of unusual historical significance. For on this occasion Lacan made his formal entry into the psychoanalytic movement, propounding a notion of human selfhood that was to be discussed in professional circles for many years to come and that was, in a variety of new and inflected forms, to remain active in his own thinking for the rest of his career. [p. 17]

On the surface, it is written as the beginning of a great career, which it no doubt was. The story, however, is really not that simple, for while the 1936 presentation marked Lacan's entry into the psychoanalytic movement, it was a rather dubious entry, with a rather interesting history to follow. Ten minutes into his presentation, Lacan was cut short by Ernest Jones, then president of the International Psychoanalytic Association (IPA). So infuriated was Lacan by the interruption, not to mention the lack of enthusiastic response he had hoped for, that he left the conference the next day, something that was simply not done.[14] Thus was marked Lacan's entry into psychoanalysis's inner circles. And so began a history of turmoil and strife, leading to no less than Lacan's resignation from the Société Psychanalytique de Paris (SPP), the only psychoanalytic society in France officially recognized by the IPA. When Lacan's splinter group, the Société Française de Psychanalyse (SFP), requested formal entry into the IPA, it was granted only under the condition that Lacan be banned from training analysts. In response, Lacan founded his own school in 1964, the École Freudienne de Paris (EFP), which in 1967 introduced its own training program, to be disbanded in 1980. Clearly, Lacan's relation to the psychoanalytic establishment was anything but amicable.

The history of the "Mirror Stage" paper is itself no less interesting. After the 1936 conference, Lacan is reported to have "summed [the paper] up in a few lines in [an] article on the family published in 1938."[15] Eleven years later, Lacan delivered a revised version of the original paper to the sixteenth International Psychoanalytic Congress, the article being published in the 1949 proceedings of that assembly. During the years 1936–1949, the first phase of Lacan's psychoanalytic career, Lacan published several companion pieces to the Mirror Stage essay, including the important "Aggressivity in Psychoanalysis" (collected in Lacan

---

14. Or so Ernst Kris, one of the founders of American ego psychology—the interpretation of Freud Lacan was to fight his entire career—said to him. Cited in Roudinesco, *Jacques Lacan* (1997), p. 113.

15. Lacan, ibid.

1966). As Gallop tells us, though, when years later Lacan's *Écrits* was published, the reference to the 1936 paper appeared, even though the actual essay, in its 1949 form, was fifth in the collection. Moreover, when preparing the English translation of various of the *Écrits*, translator Alan Sheridan (1966/1997) somehow references both the first and the second version of the essay. However, such a reference is, in no uncertain terms, an impossible fiction. Gallop (1985) writes:

> The first entry in "Bibliographical Information in Chronological Order" in the French *Écrits* is "The Mirror Stage," but the fifth entry is "The Mirror Stage as Formative of the Function of the I." The latter entry follows "Aggressivity in Psychoanalysis." Sheridan condenses the two different "mirror stage" entries in his bibliographical note, at the same time making one slight alteration. He writes: "An English translation of the [1936] version appeared in *The International Journal of Psycho-Analysis*, vol. 18, part I, January, 1937, under the title, 'The Looking-glass Phase.'" The first entry in the French bibliography simply reads "Cf. *The International Journal of Psycho-Analysis*, vol. 18, part I, January, 1937, p. 78, where this paper is inscribed under the title 'The Looking-glass Phase.'" Upon consulting the 1937 journal, one realizes that the French bibliography is not just ambiguous, but ironic. The other papers from the congress are summarized there, but one finds nothing at all under the title "The Looking-glass Phase." No version, no translation, not even a summary, simply the words "J. Lacan (Paris), The Looking-glass Phase." [p. 75]

There is no version in the 1937 proceedings from the 1936 conference because, as it turns out, Lacan never submitted the paper for publication. There is no original surviving 1936 essay, then, because such an essay was never published. But, as Gallop (1985) continues, this didn't stop scholars from wanting to comment on the original essay. For instance, she tells us:

> In his book on Lacan, Jean-Michel Palmier states: 'we will begin the study of the work of Jacques Lacan with the two texts that

he devoted to "The Mirror Stage"' . . . 'The first writing of Lacan devoted to the Mirror Stage remains at certain points quite imprecise. The second, despite the habitual difficulties relative to the Lacanian style, is of an incomparable richness' . . . [thus] Palmier characterizes as quite imprecise something he in fact cannot have read[!]. [p. 76]

This story of the famous Mirror Stage essay is fascinating on a number of levels. It shows Lacan's own stubborn reaction to the lukewarm reception of the original paper. It also reveals the insufficient research of an overzealous interpreter. But perhaps most important, and most interesting, it embodies something of the intricacies of the ideas of the actual essay itself, and the revolutionary ideas contained in it. Although Lacan's career is said to "begin" with the Mirror Stage essay, the essay in its original form does not exist. Instead what we have is a later version of it. As such, we retroactively establish the content of Lacan's early career through his later work. Not only does this speak to the wonders of chronology, it speaks to the very mechanism Lacan sought to explain in the essay, the mechanism by which the I is created—retroactively, and by its other. The first Mirror Stage essay may be the beginning, but we only have the second, later essay, which, Gallop reminds us, retroactively establishes the ideas of the first, and creates the Lacanian "self" we come to study. But we seem to be ahead of ourselves. Perhaps we should back up a bit, and start at, say, *the beginning*.

For Lacan, no less than Freud, the beginning is hard to locate. Lacan's 1949 essay, "The Mirror Stage as Formative of the Function of the I," does mark an important contribution to psychoanalytic theory, and is the seed of his later developments.[16] And, as

---

16. Of course, Lacan later abandons these early theories in place of the more sophisticated "Real, Imaginary, Symbolic" triumvirate structure. In this, Lacan's own development mirrors Freud's move from the ego of the early works, such as the 1914 essay "On Narcissism," in Freud (1991), to the ego of the later works, such as the 1923 book, *The Ego and the Id* (1960). For a helpful account of these shifts in Freud's and Lacan's works, see Elizabeth Grosz, *Jacques Lacan: A Feminist Introduction* (1990).

we have said, the idea that the essay "began" Lacan's career isn't a simple one. But our problems are not simply historical, or even theoretical; they are also textual, for the essay itself problematizes even our attempts to begin to read it! We could begin where Lacan seems to begin the essay—with the infant, as yet incapable of bodily control. We could further begin with Lacan's observation of the child's confrontation with its image in the mirror. But we are perhaps best advised to begin where *psychoanalysis* itself begins—with the present of the analytic session as the scene of the Unconscious.[17]

The practice of doing psychoanalysis is said to begin with the patient entering analysis—the patient who is experiencing some problem or other and who seeks a cure. The analyst begins with the patient's speech, with the stories and postures, with the events spoken and unspoken. From there the analyst works backwards, toward the event of trauma that caused some repressive mechanism to force an idea into the Unconscious. Of course, in Lacan, unlike in Freud, the event of trauma is never reached. Instead of uncovering a singular happening, Lacanian analysis seeks simply to uncover the fact of trauma, and thereby the fact of castration/impotence. The scene of the fact of trauma is worked out in the transference, in which the patient projects onto the analyst the event until it is "worked through," meaning that the patient comes to realize her inability to control such events, and the repressive mechanisms of neurosis recede into a gentler posture of everyday censorship. In the case of reading the Mirror Stage paper, if we want to understand Lacan on his own terms—as analyst—then we would do best not to begin with his observations about the infant, but rather with his observations about the adult.

Lacan the analyst begins with the adult's experience (or "recollection") of "the fragmented body." He writes:

---

17. When referring to the Unconscious as topographical unit, that is, as a "part" of the mind, I will capitalize it. When using it as an adjective, I will not. However, when quoting from other sources, I will respect their conventions of capitalization. For instance, Lacan does not capitalize "unconscious" at all, and so I will leave his usage intact.

This fragmented body [*corps morcelé*—body in pieces], which term I have also introduced into our system of theoretical references, usually manifests itself in dreams, when the movement in analysis encounters a certain level of aggressive disintegration of the individual. It appears then in the form of disjointed limbs and of those organs represented in exoscopy, growing wings and taking up arms for intestinal persecutions, the very same that the visionary Hieronymus Bosch has fixed for all time in his paintings, in their ascent from the fifteenth century to the imaginary zenith of modern man. But this form is even tangibly revealed at the organic level, in the lines of "fragilization" that define the anatomy of phantasy, as exhibited in the schizoid and spasmodic symptoms of hysteria. [E 97/E 4]

First, we have the patient. The patient, immersed in the therapeutic encounter, has begun, according to Lacan, to encounter in analysis a "certain level of aggressive disintegration of the individual." Through her analysis, she has begun to realize that she is not the whole and unified self, in complete control of her ideas and actions, that she thought she was. This is, according to Lacan, the major step in psychoanalytic therapy—the giving up of control. Not giving up control to the analyst, as the ego psychologists would have it, but the giving up of control in itself. This is no easy task, however, because the society in which we live posits self-sufficiency and self-mastery as the norm, as the real, as the true. We are led to feel that we are unified "selves" in control of our thoughts and actions. How can we begin to give this up?

Concurrent with the dreams of the fragmented body, we are also given, according to analysis, dreams of unity—unity in which the battle of the body in pieces takes place:

> Correlatively the formation of the I is symbolized in dreams by a fortress, or a stadium—its inner arena and enclosure, surrounded by marshes and rubbish-tips, dividing it into two opposed fields of contest where the subject flounders in quest of the lofty, remote inner castle whose form (sometimes juxtaposed in the same scenario) symbolizes the id in a quite star-

tling way. Similarly, on the mental plane, we find realized the structures of fortified works, the metaphor of which arises spontaneously, as if issuing from the symptoms themselves, to designate the mechanisms of obsessional neurosis—inversion, isolation, reduplication, annulment, displacement. [E 97–99/E 5]

At the same time at which we find the patient dreaming of her body in pieces, we find the patient dreaming of herself as a fortress, a stadium—a whole, enclosed place—a "self." Within the walls of herself as arena, the patient finds herself divided into two opposing teams, each fighting for control of some inner castle, the deep inner recesses of the soul, fighting in herself for control of her innermost soul, struggling to control it. But the obsessional patient is not in control, and it is precisely this lack of control that she is fighting. Obsessional neuroses are attempts at control, displaced control, in which the patient organizes a part of her life that she can control precisely because there are so many parts of her life that she cannot control. And this is the essence of the dream. But notice again, the dream takes place within an arena, the enclosed and unified field of battle that is symbolic of the subject, and moreover that the battle is for another unified circle of selfhood, the inner arena, the innermost place of unity. The battle for mastery takes place within one unity and for another.

This is where to begin: with the patient battling for control of herself, she who finds her body at one and the same time a body in pieces and a unified stadium in which a battle is taking place—a battle for the person's very soul. In these events of the neurotic or hysteric patient, Lacan finds the germ of the very construction of the modern self to which we are all, as modern subjects, subjected. To make sense of where we are now, Lacan tells a story of the origin of our sense of self. This is the story of the mirror stage.[18] The

---

18. As is probably already clear, I am uncomfortable calling this a "stage," for if we begin in analysis only to go back to this supposed event of our childhood, it does not follow an actual stage-progression. I will say more on this below in discussing the three registers, but for now let it suffice that I will continue to refer to the mirror stage, as is customary, but not without reservations.

child, between the ages of 6 and 18 months, discovers itself as an image in the mirror. In finding its reflection, it is enraptured by the sense of wholeness and unity in the image, and in a series of gestures and postures, takes up the position of the image, upright and in control, reduplicating the image of itself in the mirror. The child is jubilant, for it finds in the mirror that which it itself is not (yet)—an entity that presents itself as unified and whole. The infant, having been born prematurely in that it lacks the motor skills and the coordinate capacities to control its limbs, its body, its actions, does not (yet) have the experience of unity and control it finds in the mirror. It is only a "body in pieces," not yet a unified "I." But it sees itself as a unity, as a total unified form, in the mirror, and so triumphantly claims its position and power. The image in the mirror becomes for the child the ideal-I that it wishes itself to become. At the same time, this total body form, this gestalt, is that which the child realizes itself not to be, even though according to the image in the mirror it is that unity. In this, the image of the body in the mirror becomes not only the unity that the child seeks to be, but also the *I* that the subject is supposed to be but is not yet. In this, the image in the mirror is both constituent and constitutive; the mirror is a mirror and the mirror is a stage.[19]

What the child sees in the mirror becomes that which it seeks to be. But that which it seeks to be is something that it is not, and so the identity it assumes for itself is a fictive one, for the child is still the body in pieces. It is this totalized form of the image in the

---

19. Whether or not Lacan believes that the actual event of the mirroring can take place without the mirror itself is in dispute. For instance, Elizabeth Grosz (1990) has argued that, as the child equally comes to identify with the image of the mother as unified gestalt, the mother can serve as a mirror; in the mother, the child comes to see that which it can become, and there equally it seeks to be that which it is as of yet not. However, Shuli Barzilai (1999) has made a strong case that for Lacan the mirror cannot be replaced by the mother. See Grosz (1990), Chapter 2, and Barzilai (1999), Chapter 4. While I tend to side with Barzilai on her strict reading of Lacan's texts, I also tend to side with Grosz on her interpretation of the possibilities within Lacanian discourse. However, neither thinker addresses the mirror stage from the perspective of analysis, which, I argue, is the only proper reading of the mirror stage, both as theme and as essay.

mirror that dictates how the child will direct itself in years to come, how it will come to view itself. It is this gestalt around which it will orient itself, and this gestalt will remain the Ideal-image—the *I* the child strives to be. But the child will never realize this image, because from the start the image is that which the child is not. As such, the very sense of "who the child is" is not only founded in alienation, but also is alienation itself:

> This form [the image in the mirror] situates the agency of the ego, before its social determination, in a fictional direction, which will always remain irreducible for the individual alone, or rather, which will only rejoin the coming into being of the subject asymptotically, whatever the success of the dialectical syntheses by which he must resolve as *I* his discordance with his own reality. [E 94/E 2]

The mirror stage is the event that thrusts the infant from the body in pieces to fictive gestalt, and as such from a very real nothing to a very false something never to become real:

> The mirror stage is a drama whose internal thrust is precipitated from insufficiency to anticipation—and which manufactures for the subject, caught up in the lure of spatial identification, the succession of phantasies that extends from a fragmented body image to a form of its totality that I shall call orthopedic—and lastly, to the assumption of the armor of an alienating identity, which will mark with its rigid structure the subject's entire mental development. [E 97/E 4]

Since the image that the child seeks for itself is that which it is not, Lacan concludes that when attempting to understand the original constitution of the I, we should start not from reality, but rather from fiction, not from the simple (re)cognition of the body in the mirror, but rather from the (mis)representation of the unity in the mirror: "from the *function of méconnaissance* that characterizes the ego in all its structures" [E 99/E 6]. The ego (the internalized mental picture of the "I"—that mapping of the body the *I* takes as its blueprint) is a psychical creation based on a fictionalized sense of unity, and as such the *I* is never the unity it believes itself to be, never the self it seeks, and can never be such. As Dany Nobus (1999a) puts it:

> From the idea that the "me" is a mirage, it is easy to infer that the self-consciousness associated with it cannot point the way to a truth self-understanding. Rather than considering the "me" as a mental component through which a human being comes to know and understand him or herself, Lacan regarded the "me" as a source of *méconnaissance*, that is to say of misunderstanding and failure to recognize. In Lacan's view, the "me" is not the representative of reality, as Freud conceived it, but a showpiece of illusory mastery, a simulacrum of individual control. [p. 117]

The mirror stage is the inaugural moment of what Lacan calls the Imaginary register.[20] In his later work the Imaginary is one of three registers of existence that explain the psychical growth of the subject.[21] The first register, the Real, is the pre-mirror-register existence of the child. In the Real, the world is but a mass of impulses and the child has no understanding of the split between self and other, between inside and outside, between subject and object. The second register, the Imaginary (which is the first to present itself in Lacan's writings, here in the Mirror Stage essay), is the register during which the child recognizes itself as distinct through the image it finds in the mirror. In the Imaginary register (so named because here the child is defined by the image it sees in the mir-

---

20. In much scholarship, the Imaginary is often referred to as a "stage," but this suggests that the registers are temporal stages, and to read them this way is to miss the fundamentally analytic, and thus nontraditionally temporalized, reading that Lacan offers of these three registers.

21. As is custom in much scholarship, I will often refer to the Symbolic register as the Symbolic order, but it should be noted that the Symbolic is the only register that can properly be called an "order" as it is the only register that orders and is ordered according to the social-linguistic logic that we familiarly associate with the term "order."

ror), the child is fundamentally engaged with its mother. The mother feeds, the mother clothes, the mother plays with the child, and it is to her that the child has its primary attachment. As such, the Imaginary register is inherently dual in structure, with little outside the child–mother pair holding any meaning. The third register, the Symbolic (which is in fact the only *actual* stage, the stage from which the other two are posited), is the stage at which the child moves from the duality of the Imaginary into the trifold structure of the social order, and in which the child takes up its position as a sexually differentiated social-linguistic being. In the Symbolic, the child must forego his or her primary attachment to the mother and choose a position as dictated by the oedipal prohibition.[22] The Symbolic assumption of sexual identity and subjecthood will remain affected by the Imaginary identification with the mother, however, and the misrecognition of the mirror stage will remain with the child as it moves from the Imaginary register to the Symbolic register: "This moment in which the mirror-stage comes to an end inaugurates by the identification with the *imago* of the counterpart and the drama of primordial jealousy . . . the dialectic that will henceforth link the I to socially elaborated situations" (E 98/E 5). Always binding itself to the image of the other, the child will always be defined by something outside its "self."

As I have stated, the three registers are often referred to as "stages" in Lacan scholarship; and moreover, the often-encountered desire to present the three registers as "stages" is problematic. Again, the only stage that *is* is the Symbolic. Both the Imaginary and the Real are effects of our Symbolic reading of the past. In

---

22. Again, the mirror stage is also a stage of primary attachment to the (m)other, who equally can serve as the image the child wishes to assume. In the Imaginary register, the child seeks to control its relation with the mother, and when the father intervenes and utters the word "no," the child must learn to displace its love for the mother onto other love objects. We will return to this both in Chapter 2 on sexual difference and in Chapter 3 on language, where we see the child's use of language as an attempt to displace control of the (m)other onto control of meaning.

analysis, the analyst and patient retroactively construct the mirror stage as the founding event; in the Symbolic, the Imaginary is retroactively constructed as a prior stage. The mirror stage itself posits a "before"; the Imaginary rests on the existence of the prior Real. But the Real is only a product of the Imaginary, and the Imaginary is only a product of the Symbolic, just as the fragmentation of the infant is only a product of the mirror stage, which is only a reading of adult fragmentation. In this, the Imaginary—and even more so the Real—are epistemic fictions. This is not to say that the prior events aren't real in the ordinary sense of the word. Certainly, every present is built on and out of a past. Still, in psychoanalysis, it is the present understanding of the past that is of the most significance, and so whether or not these events actually preceded the present is not of importance. It is always from the present that we view the events of the past, always from the Symbolic that we give meaning to the happenings of the Imaginary and the Real.

Lacan is describing in the Mirror Stage essay an encounter with an other that creates for the child a sense of "what it is to be." The Lacanian ego that comes out of the mirror stage is an ego "by the other." The *I* that emerges, then, is itself an other. Before this encounter with something other than itself (the mirror image), the pre-subject is incomplete, not-yet. After this encounter with that other, the pre-subject has a sense of who and what it is, who and what it is to be. This encounter, then, is the first formative encounter for the subject in Lacan, the second encounter being the oedipal encounter.[23] The *I* is nothing more than an imitation of the cohesiveness of the mirror image. The *I is* only insofar as it is a mimicry of something that it is not—the cohesive image in the

---

23. And we are not truly speaking of "subjects" yet, for in Lacan the subject only comes to be when the self moves out of the duality of the Imaginary into the trifold structure of the social order, when the father intervenes in the child's relationship with the mother. There, again, the sense of self the child assumes will be dictated by an other, only there it will not be the other in the mirror, but the "Other" (capital O) which represents the Law of the Father, the Phallus as transcendental signifier. We will take up this theme in Lacan in the following chapter.

mirror, the gestalt, the totalized body-form in control of itself. The "I" as we know it only comes to be in this encounter with the other, the other which dictates not only *that* the I is, but *what* the I is—a fictive taking up of a non-real image—an internalized attachment to an ego-structure that is based on something other than the child itself.

Of course, talk of self and other in this way is problematic, and we must be careful in so doing. For the infant, there is no such thing as self and other. In the Real all is one, and no distinctions are made. It is in coming to see the mirror image as other that the child learns what self and other are, that the child adopts these themes. But in this, the other that forms the child's sense of self is not outside the child, but is rather always already within the child, for the inside–outside split is based on the assumption of the split presented in the mirror stage. The other, then, is never outside, but in fact creates the very idea of inside and outside in forcing the child to take up an image of itself as self—as separate.

The idea of the I as the taking up of a non-real image (of the unity of the self) becomes even more radical when we consider the fact that the I in fact is taking up a very real image (the actual reflection of itself). Let us look at this understanding of the mirror stage as an event that marks the formation of the I, and go one step further, one step beyond the traditional interpretation extracted from that believed to be event, in order to understand all the better what the phrase "I is an other" means for Lacan. At its very heart, this phrase is in fact far more radical than has been commonly argued.[24] While we can understand the sense in which the unity that the child assumes as its *I* is not in fact its self but is only an image that appears, there is, I believe, something more at work here than a simple "adhesion to the other." For while what the child sees in the mirror is an other that it fantasmatically realizes it is not yet, more than that, the child sees not only that it is not that *yet*, but that at the very same time it *is* that supposed unity, for *there it is in the*

---

24. For a welcome change from interpretations that fail to account for the radicality in Lacan, see Bowie (1991, Chapter 2) and Gallop (1985, Chapter 3).

mirror. The child sees this and not only assumes that it can become that unity, but realizes that that which it seeks to become is in fact *it* because the unity is *its* image. In this the child's ego is, from the very start, "other than itself." The child not only *is not* what it sees, but what it sees is in fact *it*, so that the image that is an "other" is at the same time an image of its "body-self." The child is split from the very beginning in such a way that not only does the other define what the child thinks it should be, but the other (the image of her self) takes up the space of that which the child in fact is. What the child sees may be from the start something other than that which the child truly is, for it *is* only the body in pieces, but that other also claims to be itself because it is in fact the child's image—it is a picture that *presents* as it *represents*. The image in the mirror may be an other in that it is something that the child in any biological sense is not, but in claiming to be the child's own image, the mirror image so assumes itself as the child-itself, and so the child assumes itself to be that mirror image—that unity that the child is *not*, and yet *is*. Not only is the image an other to the child, the image as a *reflection* of its *body-self* is an other which is, prior to the anticipation of what it will become, even now "its *body-self*," and as such the child, and its image of its body as reflective image, is an "other to itself" even in its very sense of unity. From the first moment, then, in the Lacanian scheme, that *I* the child assumes to be its self truly *is* an other.

I is an other. It works on so many levels. Contrary to interpretations that see unity as a product of the mirror stage and fragmentation as the prior state of the child, the I as unity is not in fact the only thing that is created in the mirror stage; it is not simply the "fiction of the self" that is brought forth. Instead, the mirror stage at one and the same time also brings forth the *prior* understanding of the body as fragmented; the mirror stage creates the sense of non-unity in precisely the unity that it presents in the mirror. Before the idea of unity, the child does not understand itself as fragmented, as lacking control, as incomplete. It is only upon seeing completion that the child realizes that which it is not.[25] The mirror stage establishes both the infant's future *and its past*:

> The mirror stage would seem to come after "the body in bits and pieces" and organize them into a unified image. But actually, that violently unorganized image comes only after the mirror stage so as to represent what came before. What appears to precede the mirror stage is simply a projection or a reflection. There is nothing on the other side of the mirror. [Gallop 1985, p. 80]

And there never will be. For as long as the self first sees itself as what it will become in the mirror, that specter will constantly haunt its attempt at becoming. As Gallop is so deft at showing, the fact of the anticipation of wholeness of the self (as created in the mirror stage) ruins the possibility of actualizing any such project:

> Lacan earlier says that the infant "anticipates the maturation of his power." Yet . . . we see that anticipation is much more complicated than a simple projection into a future. For the anticipated maturation will never simply arrive. Not that the infant will not learn to walk, grow up, become capable of independent survival. But the very process of "natural maturation" is now affected by the anticipation. It at first appears that the infant is inscribed in an inevitable developmental chronology and merely "anticipates" a later moment in that development, but the "I," the subject that can say "my history," must defend against "natural maturation," must defend against natural chronology in favor of the future perfect [that which I will have become]. Any "natural maturation" simply proves that the self was not mature before, and since the self was founded upon an assumption of maturity, the discovery that maturity was

---

25. Again, we must be careful here. All these events are in fact preconscious happenings recognized and inscribed in fantasy. None of them are real in the mundane sense of the word. And yet, as analysis shows, the reality they hold for the subject is as real as any other reality. In this, even the fictive Imaginary and Real are powerfully real.

prematurely assumed is the discovery that the self is built on hollow ground. Since the entire past and present is dependent upon an already anticipated maturity—that is, a projected ideal one—any "natural maturation" (however closely it might resemble the anticipated ideal one) must be defended against, for it threatens to expose the fact that the self is an illusion done with mirrors. [Gallop 1985, p. 83]

Hence the dreams of fragmentation and cohesion. As soon as we confront the fact of our own fictivity, we revert back to what we were before the mirror stage—the I fighting to be whole. Or, more properly speaking, since there is no "prior to the mirror stage," we begin to act out the very scene of the mirror stage itself—the scene of the infant creating *both* its false sense of unity (the arena) and its retroactively realized impotence (the fragmented body). In her dreams, the patient returns to the mirror stage and reminds herself that she is creating herself both as fictively whole and fictively fragmented. She re-creates herself as striving to be the whole she is not, though both the whole and the not are equally fictive.

Gallop's interpretation is striking in its precision. In it we are easily able to see what this foundational moment of the Lacanian subject looks like, what the subject at its very imaginary heart is— pure fiction, always defended against. In this, it is clear why the Levinasian encounter with the other clearly bespeaks a "humanism of the other person" whereas the Lacanian encounter with the other clearly marks an "antihumanist" reading of the creation of the unified I. Gallop is quick to remind her readers that all too often we see in the past an anticipation of what is to come in the future when, in fact, it may not have actually been there. Although there is the experience of the infant as part of a universe it sees as one, and although there is a moment at which the infant learns to separate self and the other, and a later moment at which the child learns to assume a sexual identity, our understandings of these events are all created out of our current memories of the past, out of the psychoanalytic experience itself. Did they actually happen or not? This isn't even the question to be asking, for they are as real as they need to be, because we make them real. But that doesn't make them actual, doesn't make them ontological. Rather, they are effects, and that is all they need be. It seems the fact of "the mirror stage" itself is no exception to this reading. As the mirror stage itself is merely a reading effectuated by the present in dreams of fragmentation and unity, it, too, is an effect, and we are led back to the beginning where Lacan proclaims the fictive nature of the subject, and we realize that this assumption operates on far (and many) more levels than we can even begin to fathom. So we are not actually left with *nothing* behind the mirror, but really with the *mirror* behind the mirror, looking back onto itself ad infinitum.

The Levinasian subject and the Lacanian "I" are each foundationally inscribed by the intervention of the other, and yet they remain two radically differing visions of the self. The Lacanian I is a fiction imposed onto a child's reality based on the assumption of a unity that is not yet. The Levinasian subject is a self subjected to the otherness of the other, called to responsibility by the fact that the other is fundamentally not of the self, and therefore cannot be ignored. To better understand these two *competing* notions of the self, the Levinasian "humanism of the other person" and the Lacanian "antihumanism," we can briefly turn to two more texts, Lacan's "Aggressivity in Psychoanalysis," collected in Lacan (1966) and Levinas's "Substitution," in Levinas (1974). "Aggressivity in Psychoanalysis" was published in 1948, just more than a year before the second Mirror Stage report. It can be read as a further explication of some of the basic themes of that earlier and later report that gives specific attention to the concept of aggressivity. "Substitution," on the other hand, was written in 1967 and became the centerpiece of Levinas's second major work, *Otherwise than Being* or *Beyond Essence*, and can be read both as a shift in Levinas's thinking away from the metaphysical language of *Totality and Infinity*, thereby distancing itself from the earlier work, and as an attempt at a better explication of the non-phenomenality of the encounter with the other person, thereby being an extension of the earlier work.[26] By looking at our two texts side by side, we begin better to understand not only how each thinker construes the construction of the self, but also the stakes involved in such projects.

In *Totality and Infinity* the central concept was the intervention of "the face"; in *Otherwise than Being* it is the "approach" of the other that calls the self into "substitution." The approach and substitution are the events of the other as described in non-phenomenological terms. Where in the earlier work Levinas stressed the difficulty of describing the event of the face, marking it as the failure of philosophy, now Levinas attempts actually to *make* the move beyond phenomenology itself. Robert Gibbs (1992) writes:

> In *Totality and Infinity* [the] approach [of the other person] was termed "the face," but in *Otherwise than Being*, Levinas refers to it as "proximity." He analyzes the moment of encounter when someone is near to me, or perhaps better, draws me near . . . This approach of the other, this drawing near to me, this other becoming my neighbor, this approach of the face of the other is not thematizable. It is literally not a phenomenon and so cannot be described by the methods of phenomenology. Here [in "Substitution"] Levinas is reflecting on the very failure of phenomenology . . . The approach leads from what can be described and displayed phenomenologically, to the groundless, indescribable reality that is the other approaching me. [p. 205]

The other approaching me is "groundless." For Levinas this is the essential move. The proximity of the other cannot be reduced to a moment in time or to a piece of knowledge. It is not a phenomenon. As such, it is not primarily intentional or self-conscious. Rather, it is the event which is "always 'already in the past'" (AE 158/OTB 100). Levinas calls this always already in the past "an-

---

26. The charge of metaphysical language is one of the key points Derrida makes in "Violence and Metaphysics," in Derrida (1978). The move to radical phenomenology in *Otherwise than Being* can easily be read as a response to Derrida.

archy" and argues that the only way to describe it is to use "ethical language."

An-archy is for Levinas "not disorder as opposed to order" but that which "brings to a halt the ontological play which, precisely qua play, is consciousness, where being is lost and found again" (AE 159, 160/OTB 101). An-archy is the event that interrupts the ego in its solitude, "interrupting it, leaving it speechless. Anarchy is persecution" (AE 160/OTB 101). Ethical language is the non-ontological order in which we do not thematize the relationship with the other, but simply describe it without any attempt at philosophical reduction:

> The tropes of ethical language are found to be adequate for certain structures of the description: for the sense of the approach in its contrast with the knowing; the face in its contrast with a phenomenon.
>
> Phenomenology can follow out the reverting of thematization into anarchy in the description of the approach: ethical language succeeds in expressing the paradox in which phenomenology finds itself abruptly thrown . . . The trace in which a face is ordered is not reducible to a sign: a sign and its relationship with the signified are synchronic in a theme. The approach is not the thematization of any relationship as such, but is this very relationship which resists thematization as anarchic. [AE 192/OTB 120–121]

The an-archic approach of the other person is the movement that calls me into responsibility and being, and this being called forth out of hypostasized existence Levinas describes as "substitution."

Substitution is, literally, being in the place of the other person. The self is put in the place of the other person because the self finds itself "accused" by the other person, and, in that accusation, called to responsibility. The accusation of the self literally puts the self "in the accusative." It is the accusation of the self by the other person that makes the self what it is, that calls it not only to responsibility, but also to being. The accusation of the self marks the self's ability to take the nominative, to call itself "I," but the nominative *I* is always for and by its finding itself accused. Before the call to responsibility, there is no *I* proper. What makes the self the self, or, better yet, what creates the subject qua individual subject, is this subjection to the other person.

> The uniqueness of the self is the very fact of bearing the fault of the other person. In responsibility for the other person subjectivity is only this unlimited passivity of an accusative which does not issue out of a declension it would have undergone starting from the nominative . . . Everything is from the start in the accusative. [AE 177/OTB 112]

Before the accusation, there is only hypostasized being. In the accusation, the subject is formed. Thus, the first utterance of the I is a response to an accusation: "The word I means here I am" (AE 180/OTB 114).

In responding to the other person, the subject takes upon itself the suffering of the other. As accused, the self finds itself "accused of what the others do or suffer, or responsible for what they do or suffer" (AE 177/OTB 112). Substitution, then, is not simply the taking on of responsibility *for* the other person, but is the taking on of the responsibility *of* the other person. Calling oneself an I *is* "answering for everything and for everyone" (AE 180–181/OTB 114). As such, the subject finds itself fundamentally for-the-other prior to its possibly being anything else. In this, the subject finds its identity "inverted." It is interested in the other person more than and prior to its own interests; it literally puts itself in the other's place. This self that finds itself subjected, then, is not the conscious ego-self, but a primordial self upon which all later ideas of self are constructed. Levinas writes:

> This self [of substitution] is out of phase with itself, forgetful of itself, forgetful in biting in upon itself, in the reference to itself that is the gnawing away at oneself of remorse. These are not events that happen to an empirical ego—that is to say to an ego already posited and fully identified—as a trial that would

lead it to be "more conscious of itself" and make it more apt to "put itself in the place of others." What we are here calling "oneself" or "the other in the same," where inspiration arouses respiration, the very pneuma of the psyche, precedes this empirical order, which is already conditioned in a system—a part of being, of the universe, of the State. Here we are trying to express the unconditionality of a subject, which does not have the status of a principle . . . The self is Sub-jectum. [AE 182–183/OTB 115–116]

The parallels to Lacan are striking. The self is not an established ego prior to its encounter with the other. Rather, it is the other imposing its existence on the self that allows, even requires the self to emerge out of its solitude and take on an identity. But such an identity is for both Levinas and Lacan an identity of the other person. For both, the needs of the other are the needs of the self, the desire of the other is the desire of the self, but these mean fundamentally different things. In Levinas, I substitute myself *for* the other person, and thereby take on her suffering and responsibility. In Lacan, I construct my sense of self *from* the other, creating internal aggression, and thereby become his competitor.

Lacan's essay "Aggressivity in Psychoanalysis," collected in Lacan (1966), elaborates on several themes left underdeveloped in the Mirror Stage.[27] The topic here is not the formation of the I, but the role of aggressivity in psychoanalytic theory and practice. Lacan begins by arguing that aggressivity is a subjective experience (that is, the experience of a subject), quickly moving on to his first major point (the essay's second thesis): "Aggressivity in experience is given to us as intended aggression and as an image of corporal dislocation, and it is in such forms that it shows itself to be efficient" (E 103/E 10). Here we are on familiar ground—the image of the fragmented body. From a brief examination of these images as presented in, again, dreams, paintings, and even childhood play, Lacan moves to his third thesis, which is that in fact aggressivity is

---

27. Of course, to say this is something of a contradiction, since "Aggressivity" was published before the second "Mirror Stage" essay.

what motivates the psychoanalytic encounter. It is not until the fourth thesis that the argument of the essay begins to take shape. Now that Lacan has set out certain basic premises, he can turn to the issue at hand—aggression as primary in the human person. Lacan's fourth thesis is this: "Aggressivity is the correlative tendency of a mode of identification that we call narcissistic, and which determines the formal structure of man's ego and of the register of entities characteristic of his world" (E 110/E 16). Lacan now carefully retraces the steps of the mirror stage, and elaborates on one of its key ideas—that the creation of the ego in the child also creates an internal aggression that is formative of the condition of the subject:

> There is a sort of structural crossroads here to which we must accommodate our thinking if we are to understand the nature of aggressivity in man and its relation with the formalism of his ego and his objects. It is in this erotic relation, in which the human individual fixes upon himself an image that alienates him from himself, that are to be found the energy and the form on which this organization of the passions that he will call his ego is based. [E 113/E 19]

In order to understand what Lacan is talking about here, a brief return to Freud, the figure who is always looming everywhere in Lacan's texts, is necessary. Lacan saw his project as a "return to Freud," that is, a return to the meaning of Freud, which had become lost in the abuses of ego psychology. The central texts for Lacan were Freud's early ones, for it is there that Freud was at his most revolutionary. As we shall see, it is the early discoveries— the Unconscious, transference, the sexual life of children—that are so fundamental for Lacanian thought. And though Lacan also draws on the insights of the later texts, it is in those texts that Freud sought to write his insights into a stable psychoanalytic system—a move which, according to Lacan, led to Freud forgetting the radicality of his own claims. *The Interpretation of Dreams* and *Three Essays on the Theory of Sexuality* were two of the more important texts, as far as Lacan was concerned, in contrast to such too-systematic works as *The Ego and the Id*, in which Freud began to dull his own discomforting ideas.

However, even though *The Ego and the Id* is in many ways the foil for the early Lacan in essays such as the Mirror Stage, it is *The Ego and the Id* that most clearly *defines* the ideas that Lacan is here relying on to make his point about aggressivity. So, while Lacan may go to great lengths to recast the structural claims of *The Ego and the Id* and to critique its systematicity, some of its basic ideas are crucial for him to be able to do the work he does in his early essays.

Although *The Ego and the Id* is geared toward providing a new structural model of the self that Lacan ultimately does not follow (Ego–Id–Superego), replacing (or at least modifying) Freud's earlier construction (Unconscious–Preconscious–Consciousness), we can extract from it a helpful reading of the nature of the ego.[28] In this work, the ego is fundamentally a "coherent organization of mental processes."[29] These processes mark the idea of "self" and offer a home to what we call consciousness. The ego is formed through the infant's attachment to its body (what Freud earlier called primary narcissism). The infant organizes its mental and physical sensations around a coherent picture of its body. In Lacan, this picture is provided by the image in the mirror. In Freud (1960), this picture is provided by the infant's body itself:

> A person's own body, and above all its surface, is a place from which both external and internal perceptions may spring. It is seen like any other object, but to the touch it yields two kinds of sensations, one of which may be equivalent to an internal perception . . . The ego is first and foremost a bodily ego; it is not merely a surface entity, but is itself the projection of a surface. [pp. 19–20]

---

28. We will see, however, the importance the superego does play in Lacan's discussion of ethics.

29. Freud (1960), p. 8. The ego is also a site of contestation. Consciousness isn't easily mappable onto the id/ego/superego model, not only because Freud's theory undergoes so many changes, but also because at any one point along the way the pieces of the theory are themselves never easily compartmentalized.

The ego, then, is the projected picture of the surface of the body around which the infant organizes its conscious (and, depending on which Freud one reads, some unconscious) mental processes and its bodily sensations (libido).[30]

Returning to Lacan, the child invests itself in what is to become its ego through its narcissistic attachment to the image of the other as the image of itself. This investment, then, being an organization of mental processes and physical sensations, is, at least in part, libidinal, and therefore erotic. As we already know, for Lacan the taking up of an identity via the splitting of the subject through the image of the other is fundamentally alienating. Now Lacan tells us that in fixing itself upon an alienating image, the child's libidinal energies gravitate toward aggression. Why? The answer is simple: in identifying with the image of the other, the child also identifies with the desires of the other, and in so doing, the child becomes a competitor with the other, for in that identification the child now begins competing for the objects of the other's desire. Ultimately, as we shall see, no one's desire can ever be fulfilled, as desire is always desire for (1) the fictive unity promised in the mirror stage, and (2) the fictive power promised in the phallus. Thus from the beginning the other is not only that to which the child aspires, that whom the child wishes to be, but also that which the child wants to become, that whom the child wishes to conquer, and the child's erotic impulses are therefore from the beginning not only alienating, and therefore betraying, but also

---

30. Notice that I am using the neuter here. For Freud and Lacan, sexual difference emerges in the resolution of the Oedipus complex, and as such the preoedipal child is not only polymorphously perverse, but is originally bisexual. However, if the ego is a bodily ego, and if the ego is an organization not only of mental but also of physical sensations around a picture of the body, then bodily morphology must play some part in the construction of the ego. Therefore, while sexual difference (this is Lacan's term—Freud refers to the anatomical difference between the sexes) may not yet have emerged, sexually different bodies must still play a role in this construction. This is the standard feminist critique of Freud and Lacan. For fuller treatments, see Luce Irigaray (1985a and b, and Elizabeth Grosz (1994, Chapter 2).

competitive as well: "This form will crystallize in the subject's internal conflictual tension, which determines the awakening of his desire for the object of the other's desire; here the primordial coming together is precipitated into aggressive competitiveness, from which develops the triad of others, the ego and the object" (E 113/E 19).

Aggressivity in psychoanalysis, then, is: "a correlative tension of the narcissistic structure in the coming to be of the subject" (E 116/E 22).[31] Lacan goes on in the rest of the essay to connect aggressivity to oedipal relations as well as civilization as a whole, but for now we can see the basic point: the creation of the ego is both marked by an aggressive intrusion by the other (as we saw in the preceding section) and creates an aggressive response by the self who, with no sense of self outside of the desire of the other, comes to view the other as competitor.

Let us now return to Levinas. Where Lacan sees aggressivity and competition, Levinas sees responsibility and obligation.[32] Why the difference? What causes one to see one, and the other the other? The answers lie in part in the very mechanisms we have already outlined: Levinas is describing an an-archic non-event where Lacan is describing a retroactive understanding of the origin of the ego; Levinas's work operates on the level of a prophetic ethical metaphysics (in *Totality and Infinity*) and later a post-phenomenology (in *Otherwise than Being*) where Lacan's descriptive-analytical work operates on the level of the everyday self in engaged action, as well as with unconscious motivations.[33] For Levinas, the subjectivity

---

31. The term "subject" here is somewhat misleading, because primary narcissism marks the creation of the imaginary ego-ideal, not the subject, who only comes to be in the resolution of the Oedipus complex.

32. We will, of course, return to the meaning of an ethics of psychoanalysis in Chapter 4.

33. Prophetic has many meanings. In this context I mean both that Levinas's work comes out of a tradition of Judaic thought that takes seriously the social voice of the Hebrew prophets, and that Levinas's work views itself as a "call from on high"—a vision that gives voice to the original call of goodness of God's commandments.

of the self was not a subjectivity of intention, as intentionality belongs to the register of phenomenology, so Levinas broke out of phenomenology and intention into "ethical language" and "anarchy." Lacan, too, broke out of phenomenology, moving back to an earlier foundational moment, but Lacan's moment is not a prophetic call to responsibility, but rather a psychoanalytic reading of primary identification. Differences aside, each is presenting a picture of the self, and more specifically, of the self as created by/in the intervention of the other. But what *is* the fundamental difference? The answer lies in the question of what comes *before* (and hence, after) the other. For Levinas, the prior-to-the-other self may not yet be subject, but it is something. For Lacan, there literally is nothing on the other side of the mirror. Levinas's pre-other self may not be a fully formed ego, but in calling on this self, the other person calls a person who can view himself as such. When the other person approaches, there is an *I* to answer the call. This movement is not, for Levinas, one of alienation, but one of inspiration: "It is, however, not an alienation, because the other in the same is my substitution for the other through responsibility, for which I am summoned as *irreplaceable*. By the other and for the other, but without alienation: I am inspired. This inspiration is the psyche" (AE 181/OTB 114).

Not only is this movement an inspiration, it is a liberation as well, for the creation of the subject and its corresponding psyche (which, for Levinas, seems to represent the newly created intentionality of the subject), offers the self a freedom

> in the irreplaceable subject, unique and chosen as a responsibility and a substitution—a mode of freedom, ontologically impossible, breaks the unreadable essence. Substitution frees the subject from ennui, that is, from the enchainment to itself where the ego suffocates in itself because of the tautological way of identity, and seeks without ceasing the distraction of play and sleep in a thread of erosion. [AE 198/OTB 124]

But in all of these descriptions, there is still always something that is summoned. Although it may not be a subject, and may not be properly called *I* until it is accused, there is still *something* being accused, some unity being called into responsibility.

The Levinasian self, then, in the approach of the other, is freed of its self-enchainment, free to be responsible for the other—this is her original goodness; the Lacanian self, on the other hand, is aggressive, bound to a picture of self that comes from outside and both creates and betrays the infant's picture of itself as lived body—this is its original alienation. Although both Levinas and Lacan mark their "selves" through the other, it is clear that these are fundamentally different moments. Levinas's praise for antihumanism is not that it shows the fictivity of the subject, but that it displaces the importance of the subject qua individual, thereby making room for the move to a humanism of the other person. Lacan allows no such move precisely because for him the very idea of the self is fictive, and therefore the point is to learn how to live with this fictivity. These two alternate visions mark the foundation of what are to become their competing notions of ethical subjectivity. In Levinas the direction is already clear—toward a subject bound to the other person in responsibility based on a pre-temporal moment of being "called upon from on high" and "drawn near." For Lacan it seems that ethical subjectivity will rest on some recognition of an original alienation such that the person will be able to open herself up to the unconscious aggression she feels toward the other so that she will be able to free herself of the symptoms of repression. The Levinasian "ethical" seems to be directed toward uncovering itself as the very foundation of subjectivity, whereas the Lacanian "subject" seems to direct us toward an ethic of the knowledge of the Unconscious. As we proceed, we will further develop these ideas, building their visions into two more fully explained alternate options.

2

Sexed Subjectivity,
Symbolic Subjectivity

> *I think the absolutely contrary contrary, whose contrariety is in no way affected by the relationship that can be established between it and its correlative, the contrariety that permits its terms to remain absolutely other, is the feminine.*
>
> —Levinas, TA 77/TO 85

> *The fact that the phallus is a signifier means that it is in the place of the Other that the subject has access to it. But since this signifier is only veiled, as ratio of the Other's desire, it is this desire of the Other as such that the subject must recognize, that is to say, the other insofar as he is himself a subject divided by the signifying* Spaltung.
>
> —Lacan, E 693/E 288

Having laid the groundwork for their views of the subject, Levinas in his presentation of the original subjection of the one to the other, Lacan in his presentation of the Imaginary constitution of the one via the other, Levinas and Lacan move on to spell out more fully their visions of subjectivity. For both Levinas and Lacan, the subject is a social subject, one categorized in terms prescribed by the social/Symbolic order.[1] Additionally, for both Levinas and Lacan, sexual difference is the primary category in determining the subject as social/Symbolic production. However, sexual difference has very specific connotations for both Levinas and Lacan. It is not simply a separation of kind, but a hierarchizing of kind, built around language and power. Each writer presents a reading of sexual difference in a very different way, owing to and indicative of their opposing projects; where Lacan has a descriptive reading

---

1. Of course, for Levinas, "social" has two meanings: (1) the intersubjective order of the one and the other (ethics), with which we are concerned here, and (2) the order of the third (justice), which we will not deal with in this book.

of the imperative of sexed subjectivity, built on Freud's work on the origins of sexual differentiation, Levinas, in his early works, employs the language of ontology and metaphysics not only to *explain* the subject as sexually differentiated, but to *ground* and *give content to* the very notion of otherness at play in the ethical imperative. Moreover, Levinas's metaphysical subject depends on the sexually different other for its own survival and escape from the enchainment of its subjection. Levinas's early project, then, is both solidly grounded *within* and a grounding *of* a particular masculinist paradigm. Levinas's later writings eschew the metaphysics of his earlier ones, and thereby attempt to eschew their masculinism as well. Lacan's reading is, on many fronts, no less problematic than Levinas's early reading, for it fails to offer the possibility of an alternate vision of the subject as sexually hierarchized. Yet, Lacan offers a reading of sexual difference that, in its pure discursivity, challenges the ontology of Levinas's early work. Here we see more clearly where the gulf between Levinas and Lacan lies, for in examining the question of origin we once again find the post-humanist and the antihumanist readings at odds, a location that sets the scene for their differing treatments of the relationship between the subject and language. In examining these themes, we will see how these two thinkers once again take similar themes and develop them in different directions.

Having set out the basic structure of the subject as the one for the other, Levinas now inquires into the structure of the other person whom we encounter. We know what is entailed in that encounter, and how it is manifest for the self. But what about the other person? We are already told that the other person is "situated in a dimension of height and abasement . . . the poor, the strange, the widow, and the orphan, and, at the same time . . . the master called to invest and justify my freedom" (TI 281/TI 251). But who is that other person, and how are we to understand that otherness in relation to ourselves? And what happens after the approach of the other person? What are we to do after we are called into our infinite responsibility? These are questions Levinas resists answering concretely. Still, he offers us patterns and structures by which we can come to a better understanding of what lies in and beyond the otherness of the other person. To answer these questions we return to the early work where Levinas first set out the structure of the subject as "by" the other (though not yet "for" the other)—*Time and the Other*.

In Chapter 1, we left *Time and the Other* with Levinas's proclamation that "time is essentially a new birth" (TA 72/TO 81). That is, in the confrontations with death and the other person, time and subjectivity begin. But the confrontation with death seems to leave the subject paralyzed, unable to see beyond its own demise, unable to vanquish the inevitable. Here it is the other person who provides the subject the opportunity to overcome death as a limit and to mark it as a possibility, not of its impossibility, but of transcendence itself. Levinas writes that in "vanquishing death [one can] maintain, with the alterity of the event, a relationship that must still be personal" (TA 73/TO 81). This is the event that must be explicated—the relationship that allows the subject to vanquish death, that is, to transcend its own subjective limits. How is this to be done? What does such a relationship entail? Levinas asks:

> What, then, is this personal relationship other than the subject's power over the world, meanwhile preserving its personality? How can the subject be given a definition that somehow lies in its passivity? Is there in the human a mastery other than the virility of grasping the possible, the power to be able? If we find it, it is in it, in this relation, that the very place of time will consist. [TA 73/TO 81–82]

This relation with the other person, then, is the starting point in our attempt to overcome the limits of death.

The subject overcomes death not by erasing the otherness of the other person, reducing the other to the same. Such a reduction does in fact happen via sympathy, knowing the other "as another (my)self" (TA 75/TO 83). This is an event of everyday life, of the nonphenomenological plane, of the mundane and the nonphilosophical. But the other person is not simply an alter ego, another (my)self; he is otherness in the extreme, and not simply because of a spatial or conceptual gulf, but because of a metaphysical one. We cannot reduce the otherness of the other person to psychological or physiognomic difference. Rather, the otherness of the other person is alterity itself—that which both separates and is separate, that which differentiates and is different. The other person is, in the strictest metaphysical sense, that which "I myself am not" (TA 75/TO 83). The question then remains: What is the relationship with the other person that allows the transcending of the limits of death, that which limits the subject into itself? This situation can only be thought if alterity is thought in its purity, and so Levinas asks: "Does a situation exist where the alterity of the other appears in its purity?" (TA 77/TO 85). The answer for Levinas is "the feminine."

The feminine is the model par excellence of alterity for Levinas. Levinas sees sexual difference as neither a biological structure nor a structure of formal logic, neither a contradiction of binary opposition nor a division of primary fusion.[2] Instead, sexual difference is the precondition of alterity itself, the precondition for the ethical distance between subject and other. Specifically, it is the feminine that matters to Levinas here, because it is the feminine that represents alterity, and it is through the feminine that we can come to theorize alterity:

> What matters to me in this notion of the feminine is not solely the unknowable, but a mode of being that consists in slipping away from the light. The feminine is, in existence, an event different from that of spatial transcendence or of expression that goes toward light. It is a flight before light. Hiding is the way of existing of the feminine, and this fact of hiding is precisely modesty. So this feminine alterity does not consist in the simple exteriority of the object. Nor is it made up of an opposition of

---

2. This last option was Plato's explanation in *The Republic* (1987) and is one reading of Freud's (1962) theory of original bisexuality in *Three Essays on the Theory of Sexuality*, although we will see below that Freud's reading is actually far more nuanced than this.

wills. The other person is not a being we encounter that men-
aces us or wants to lay hold of us. The feat of being refractory
to our power is not a power greater than ours. Alterity makes
for all its power. Its mystery constitutes its alterity. [TA 79–80/
TO 87]

The feminine, then, is not a mode of alterity, something that stands
in juxtaposition to its "other"—the masculine—but rather is the
very model of alterity itself. That is, the other person's alterity is
not exteriority, is not the fact of another existent, but is "the event
of alterity" (TA 80/TO 87). Recall too that the other is that which
slips away from the light, that which transcends light and reason.
Here we see the same language used to describe the feminine. The
feminine is the failure of reason, that which escapes the light of
the same, and instead withdraws into its own existence, challenging our belief in power and control, and most of all, solitude. The
feminine is alterity, alienation, and otherness in all its purity.

The relationship of love with the feminine other is a relationship of failure. Love is an attempt at merging, but with the alter no
such merging is possible. All that is possible is the caress, an attempt at contact, never the touch, the actual contact, if the otherness of the other is to be preserved.[3] The subject moves to the other
in the caress out of a desire he knows can never be achieved—the
desire for unity. Levinas writes:

> The caress is a mode of the subject's being, where the subject
> who is in contact with another goes beyond this contact. Con-
> tact as sensation is part of the world of light. But what is ca-
> ressed is not touched, properly speaking. It is not the softness
> or warmth of the hand given in contact that the caress seeks.
> The seeking of the caress constitutes its essence by the fact that
> the caress does not know what it seeks. This "not knowing,"
> this fundamental disorder, is the essential. It is like a game with
> something slipping away, a game absolutely without project or

---

3. Levinas is using "caress" here as a technical term meaning the movement toward the other.

pain, not with what can become ours or us, but with something other, always other, always inaccessible, and always still
to come. The caress is the anticipation of this pure future,
without content. It is made up of this increase of hunger, of
ever richer promises, opening new perspectives onto the
ungraspable. [TA 82–83/TO 89][4]

The caress, then, is an anticipation of what is yet to come, of a pure,
unknowable future. In this it is a certain kind of desire, but the
caress is also the failure of love, the inability of the subject to transcend its enchainment to itself in the erotic relationship. One cannot through the caress grasp the other: "If one could possess, grasp,
and know the other, it would not be other. Possessing, knowing,
and grasping are synonyms of power" (TA 83/TO 90). So, where
love fails, something else must open up in its place.

   The failure of love to offer the self a mode of transcendence
through touch does not mean that the feminine will not still be the

------

   4. The next paragraph in the text is rather significant as an historical docu-
ment, for it is one of very few places in Levinas's texts where he speaks to Freud
directly. Levinas writes:

   This intentionality of the voluptuous—the sole intentionality of the
   future itself, and not an expectation of some future fact—has always
   been misunderstood by philosophical analysis. Freud himself says
   little more about the libido than that it searches for pleasure, taking pleasure as a simple content, starting with which one begins an
   analysis but which itself one does not analyze. Freud does not search
   for the significance of this pleasure in the general economy of
   being. My thesis, which consists in affirming voluptuousness as the
   very event of the future, the future purified of all content, the very
   mystery of the future, seeks to account for its exceptional place. [TA
   83/TO 89–90]

The attention to Freud here is quite uncharacteristic for Levinas, and while
Levinas here faults Freud for failing to take his investigation far enough, it is
striking to note that Levinas does here seem to be citing Freud for the attempt to
think what Levinas believes has been left unthought. Such a generous nod to the
Freudian project, even in the criticism that lies beneath the nod, speaks volumes
of the unappreciated connections there are to be made between Levinas and Freudian thought, including Lacan.

mode by which the subject does escape its subjection. Instead, it is *precisely* in this understanding of the feminine as alterity that Levinas can now offer a model for the way the subject escapes the confines of his monad without sacrificing the structure of otherness he holds so dear. How does the feminine offer a way of transcendence? Through the category of fecundity, and its correlate, paternity:

> Before a pure event, a pure future, which is death, where the ego can in no way be able—that is, can no longer be an ego— I seek a situation where nonetheless it is possible for it to remain an ego, and I have called this situation "victory over death." Once again, this situation cannot be qualified as power. How, in the alterity of a you, can I remain I, without being absorbed or losing myself in that you? How can the ego that I am remain myself in a you, without being nonetheless the ego that I am in my present—that is to say, an ego that inevitably returns to itself? How can the ego become other to itself? This can happen only in one way: through paternity. [TA 85/TO 90–91]

In paternity, which is only possible through the fecundity of the feminine other, the subject is able to connect with a subject who is at one and the same time an other and a self. In paternity, the subject is in the son and the son is a stranger to the subject. "I do not have my child," Levinas writes, "I am in some manner my child" (TA 86/TO 91). I am my child not through sympathy, the connection of the everyday that Levinas discards, but through *being*. In paternity, the subject creates a nontotalizing multiplicity of being, creating an alter ego that is both of the self and still entirely other. And in the life of the son, the father's being becomes multiple, existing beyond death, neutralizing the future impossibility before which all subjects stand.

The sketches offered in *Time and the Other* are highly illustrative of the possibility of transcendence in Levinas, but again it is in *Totality and Infinity* that these ideas receive their full elucidation, specifically in the elaboration of the erotic encounter as both within

and beyond the ethical encounter. Here the discussions of the caress, Eros, fecundity, fraternity, and filiality expand on the basic
structure set forth in the earlier work. Therefore, to enrich further
and spell out the position presented in *Time and the Other*, we now
turn to the later work.

In the final section of *Totality and Infinity*, Levinas offers an
exploration of what lies "beyond the face." Beyond the face we find
that the approach of the other person does not erase its otherness,
does not make it into the same: "[t]he relation with the other person does not nullify separation. It does not arise within a totality nor
does it establish a totality, integrating me and the other" (TI 281/
TI 251). Otherness remains, and the separation between self and
other stands firm. There is no systematic union, no dissolution of
one into the other. Each piece of the dyad remains whole and intact. This does not mean that there is no possibility of relation
between the two terms of the dyad. Something emerges through a
primordial relation. Levinas calls this something "the metaphysical event of transcendence" (TI 284/TI 254). This event is linked
to love, but not accomplished in it. Love is an event of pure immanence, in which the other person is "divested of all transcendence"
(TI 285/TI 254). However, the other person can appear as "an object
of need while retaining his alterity" (TI 285/TI 255). In this, love
aims beyond itself, at that which does not erase transcendence, and
it is this movement of love with which Levinas is ultimately concerned. Here, love does not subsume the other person, but rather
"aims at the other person" (TI 286/TI 256). In this, the alterity of
the other person is preserved, and the movement is a movement
toward, not an ingestion of the other person. The movement of Eros
as *fecundity* is a movement that does not lapse into totality.

The feminine again emerges as one and the same with the other
person for whom we reach in Eros:

> To love is to fear for another, to come to the assistance of his
> frailty. In this frailty as in the dawn rises the Loved, who is
> the Beloved. An epiphany of the Loved, the feminine is not
> added to an object and a Thou antecedently given or encoun-

tered in the neuter, the sole gender that formal logic knows. The epiphany of the Beloved is but one with her *regime* of tenderness. The *way* of the tender consists in an extreme fragility, in a vulnerability. [TI 286/TI 256]

The feminine is not simply a mode of representation of Eros, but rather is the very foundation of the erotic encounter. And, again, it is this movement toward the other person that Levinas calls "the caress." The caress is the ethical movement itself, the manifestation of responsibility. Like responsibility itself, the caress is a non-action, a passive response to the coming of the other. The caress reaches toward the other person not to possess her, but to comfort her: "Wholly passion, it is compassion for the passivity, for the suffering, for the evanescence of the tender" (TI 290/TI 259). As such, the caress is a mode of being-for-the-other-person, which, again, "is to be good" (TI 292/TI 261).

But the caress also extends into the realm of the erotic, as a movement toward the beloved, and Eros, while a mode of being for another, poses a difficulty for Levinas's an-archic foundationalism.[5] Eros, the love of the loved as beloved, is a kind of violation of the ethical commandment in that Eros excludes the possibility of sociality:

> The relationship established between lovers in voluptuosity, fundamentally refractory to universalization, is the very contrary of the social relation. It excludes the third party, it remains

---

5. By foundationalism, we mean the possibility of envisioning a basis upon which to construct and an origin to which we must turn when judging actions as ethical. By an-archic foundationalism, we signify the fact that the "foundation" (the encounter with the other) is not a phenomenon, not an experience, not a past–present, and as such cannot be inscribed in the orders of phenomenology or ontology. The foundation is, rather, what Levinas calls an "immemorial past" or an "an-archy"—a non-event "beyond being." Thus, whenever I refer to a Levinasian "foundation," it is always with the fact of an-archy in mind. The question of Levinas's an-archic foundationalism will be of significance in Chapter 4 and the conclusion, where we will examine these terms and ideas in much greater detail.

> intimacy, dual solitude, closed society, the non-public par
> excellence. The feminine is the Other, refractory to society,
> member of a dual society, an intimate society, a society with-
> out language. [TI 297/TI 264–265]

The feminine, then, as the recipient of the love of the lover, is at
one and the same time the instance par excellence of the other
person and the instance of an impossibility of the universalization
of the project of the an-archical ethical:

> The principle "you shall not commit murder," the very
> signifyingness of the face, seems contrary to the mystery which
> Eros profanes and which is announced in the femininity of the
> tender. In the face the other person expresses his eminence, the
> dimension of height and divinity from which he descends. In
> his gentleness dawns his strength and his right. The frailty of
> femininity invites pity for what, in a sense, is not yet, disrespect
> for what exhibits itself in immodesty and is not discovered
> despite the exhibition, that is to say, profaned.
>
> But disrespect presupposes the face. Elements and things re-
> main outside of respect and disrespect. It is necessary that the
> face have been apperceived for nudity to be able to acquire the
> non-signifyingness of the lustful. The feminine face joins this
> clarity and this shadow. The feminine is the face which sur-
> rounds and already invades clarity. [TI 294/TI 262]

At once both the model for the ethical and the snag that en-
tangles the possibility of the ethical, the feminine is a paradox, for
it is here that the feminine is both object of Eros and the alterity of
the ethical: the feminine is that which invites pity for what should
not be profaned. This is the meaning of the face as "feminine" and
of the feminine as "the face." And it is precisely in this paradox
that Levinas finds a way to move forward back into universality
without sacrificing the insular duality of Eros. This is realized in a
fuller spelling-out of an already presented Levinasian concept:
fecundity.

Whereas Eros violates a mode of being for the other person as a universal imperative, limits itself in the intimate society of two, and excludes itself from the social, the relationship to the feminine gives way to the transcendence of the self in the other, and hence to the social:

> I love fully only if the other person loves me, not because I need the recognition of the other person, but because my voluptuosity delights in his voluptuosity, and because in this unparalleled conjuncture of identification, in this *trans-substantiation*, the Same and the Other are not united but precisely—beyond every possible project—beyond every meaningful and intelligent power, engender the child. [TI 298/TI 266]

The engendering of the child is an act of transcendence of the self. In fecundity, the father discovers in his child both himself and an other: "My child is a stranger (Isaiah 49), but not simply to me, for he *is* me. He is for me a stranger to myself. Not only my work, my creature . . . At once my own and non-mine, a possibility of myself but also a possibility of the other, of the Beloved" (TI 299–300/TI 267). This child is the possibility of an other person who is myself, the reality of myself in an other. This "trans-substantiation" allows the self to give fully to the other so as to manifest the responsibility for the other as not simply the protection of but also the production of his life. And fecundity begets fecundity, as the child becomes the father:

> Transcendence is time and goes toward the other person. But the other person is not a term: he does not stop the movement of Desire. The other that Desire desires is again Desire; transcendence transcends toward him who transcends—this is the true adventure of paternity, of the trans-substantiation which permits going beyond the simple renewal of the possible in the inevitable senescence of the subject. Transcendence—the for the other person—the goodness correlative of the face, founds a more profound relation: the goodness of goodness. Fecundity engendering fecundity accomplishes goodness: above and

beyond the sacrifice that imposes a gift, the gift of the power of giving, the conception of the child. [TI 302/ TI 269]

Eros has established itself, then, as the mode by which the subject moves beyond its dyadic relationship with the other person into a social relationship with the third. This is not through an other beyond the two, but through an other person who emanates from the two. Eros, then, is both a fusion and a movement beyond fusion, both a joining and a further separation, for it creates in its connection the possibility of an other beyond. In this, Eros establishes in the subject a new sense of subjectivity, for in the child the I is drawn back to itself and its possible continuation in the other person who is both other than and yet still myself. Eros challenges traditional notions of subjectivity as the singular subject apart from other existents. Now, subjectivity is bound up in an other who is not like myself, but who is myself, without sacrificing his otherness. As such, we create a society structured not simply by multiplicity instead of singularity, difference instead of fusion, but equally by transcendence instead of separation, continuation instead of death: "Fecundity attests to a unity that is not opposed to multiplicity, but, in the precise sense of the term, engenders it" (TI 306/TI 273).

According to Levinas, transcendence is, of course, when classically conceived, a self-contradictory term. How can the I transcend itself and remain itself? How can something both exist and go beyond existence? Historically, pluralism has only ever been thought among subjects, not within them; and yet, this is precisely what Levinas is here attempting—a new mode of thinking the subject as plural. While it seems contradictory to his monadic project to move in this direction, this again shows Levinas as constantly challenging our preconceived philosophical ideas, as the philosopher against philosophy attempting to create something truly new and unique, arguing against both the totalizing force of the one and the equally totalizing force of the one like others among many:

For it is in effect as a characteristic of the very ipseity of the I, the very subjectivity of the subject, that the erotic relation is to be analyzed. Fecundity is to be set up as an ontological category. In a situation such as paternity, the return of the I to the self which is set forth in the monist concept of the identical subject is found to be completely modified. The son is not only my work, like a poem or an object. Nor is he my property. Neither the categories of power nor those of knowledge describe my relation with the child. I do not have my child; I am my child. Paternity is a relation with a stranger who while being an other person—"And you shall say to yourself, 'who can have borne me these? I was bereaved and barren . . .'" (Isaiah, 49)—is me; a relation of the I with a self which yet is not me. In this "I am" being is no longer Eleatic unity. In existing itself there is multiplicity and transcendence. In this transcendence the I is not swept away, since the son is not me; and yet I *am* my son. The fecundity of the I is its very transcendence. The biological origin of this concept in no way neutralizes the paradox of its meaning, and delineates a structure that goes beyond the biologically empirical. [TI 310/TI 277]

This new vision of subjectivity is one that attempts to move beyond the logical and the empirical, and in so doing challenges our very methods of assessment as well as understanding.[6]

Levinas no doubt places great importance on the feminine in his project, but does this do justice to the feminine, and does such a treatment of the feminine do justice to the greatness of his project? The simple answer that has often been offered to both of these

----

6. The epistemological question is a significant one, and becomes a focal point of Derrida's (1978) "Violence and Metaphysics." How are we to know the unknowable, and how are we to thematize the unthematizable? As soon as we attempt to do so, have we not become complicit with the very idea we attempt to undercut? As such, can Levinas's indictment of philosophy ever escape the philosophical, and can infinity be rescued from totality? What is Levinas's metaphysics if not an exercise in ontology, and what is Levinas's empiricism if not a pure metaphysics? Derrida's adept exploration of these questions is one of the most profound treatments of Levinas yet to appear.

questions is no. However, the situation is not so simple. Clearly, the presentation of the feminine is problematic. For instance, whereas Levinas does attempt to distance his treatment of the feminine from patriarchal forces ("I do not want to ignore the legitimate claims of the feminism that presupposes all the acquired attainments of civilization" (TA 79/TO 86)), he still engages in a characterization of the feminine that can only be read as masculinist. The fact that the subject is, for Levinas, always the masculine subject does not seem incidental. Could he just as easily have presented his theory from the feminine perspective, speaking of the masculine as alterity, and working toward the engendering of the daughter and the sorority of sisters in the world? Considering the investment in the feminine as "mystery" itself, it seems highly unlikely that such a rewriting would be possible. On closer examination, certain shifts in focus emerge. At least in these early works, the role the feminine plays is grounded in a certain reading of the ontological qualities of the feminine, and no reversal is possible. There is little choice but to read this as a particular and essential bias. Whereas in *Time and the Other*, Levinas is somewhat cryptic in his positing of Eros as essential (it is a place where alterity can be explicated in its "purity," but is never posited as a necessary but instead only as an incidental piece of the investigation, one used precisely for its strategic value as opposed to its intrinsic place in the project), in *Totality and Infinity*, the role of Eros is clear. Eros is not only *a* "plane both presupposing and transcending the epiphany of the other person in the face," but also is *the* place where "subjectivity is posited in these functions [love and fecundity]" (TI 284/TI 253). That is, Eros is the plane on which subjectivity becomes plural. No longer simply a place of description, now Eros has become the mechanism by which the subject transcends himself. This does not mean that the project must be given up. On the contrary, although such a rewriting is not possible, it may be possible to avoid this entire chapter of the Levinasian corpus while still retaining (and perhaps even enhancing) the radical potential of his thought. This is precisely the move that we found in *Otherwise than Being*, where Eros is given up in favor of substitution, and where the feminine is no longer posited as alterity personified. As we have seen, the plurality of the subject is achieved in substitution without sacrificing the concreteness of Eros. Substitution is not the only alternate view that Levinas offers. As we shall see, by further abstracting the confrontation with the other person, and in so doing thereby moving us toward a confrontation with otherness in the person as the trace of God, he will also offer a different way of thinking alterity and transcendence through a certain kind of theology that does not fall back into masculinist thinking. While the move from fecundity to fraternity remains entangled in a masculinist paradigm, Levinas's ideas of substitution and the trace of God move him forward.[7]

For Lacan, sexuality, which is neither merely a biological nor merely a social category but rather a psychical and linguistic one, marks the prescription of the Symbolic order, a predetermined system of meaning to which the child must ascend and which the child must introject in order to access fully his place in society as a "subject." Access to subjectivity in Lacan is access to language, and access to language is the ability to take up a position in relation to language's master signifier—the phallus. In choosing a position in regard to the phallus, the child in Lacan becomes sexed, and the sexed child is the subject. But as in the earlier founding move of the assumption of the image in the other, here, too, the child takes up a position determined not by some inner "self," but rather by an other. Recall, though, that in psychoanalysis the other is not the same as the outside. The markers inside–outside are fictions created in the mirror stage; however, in the psyche, every outside is inside. As such, the creation of something by "an other" does not mean "from without" but rather is meant to challenge the very idea of within–without, and in so doing to challenge the very idea of a unified internal "self" that can be separated from a unified external "other." In our reading of Lacan on sexed subjectivity, then, we must address three interrelated concepts: the Oedipus complex, the

---

7. We will return to the trace of God in Chapter 4 of this work.

phallus, and the Symbolic order. In focusing on one of his most widely read essays, we come to see Lacan at his most sophisticated, and his most revolutionary, and begin to uncover what differentiates Lacan's view of sex and the subject from Freud's view.

The Oedipus complex is one of Freud's most important contributions to theories of subjectivity, and one of his most contested. Whereas the actual description of the Oedipus complex undergoes various reworkings, the basic idea remains the same throughout Freud's corpus. The Oedipus complex, in its active form, is the child's (both the boy child's and the girl child's) original desire for the mother; in its passive form, it is the child's (again, both the boy child's and the girl child's) desire for the father.[8] The mother is the child's original love object, as the mother is the child's source of nourishment, and so is the child's first source of pleasure. Throughout childhood, the child's sexuality undergoes various "stages" of development, substituting object for object, aim for aim. With the onset of puberty, the child emerges into a new phase of its sexual development, in which the demands of social normativity take center stage. In desiring its mother, the child comes to see the father as a rival, and a conflict emerges in which the child must resolve his or her place in relation to the parents. The boy is forced to resolve his active Oedipus complex when confronted with the perceived threat of castration.[9] Freudian doctrine describes the threat of castration as discovered in the boy's viewing the apparent castration of the little girl or the mother, in his coming to see that she lacks the penis. The boy comes to believe that the father has taken away the penis as punishment for a transgression of the

---

8. Freud also labels these the "masculine" and the "feminine" forms of the Oedipus complex. Elsewhere, Freud conceptualizes the terminology of the Oedipus complex to include a positive (love of the parent of the opposite sex) and a negative (love of the parent of the same sex) form. For the various formulations, see his 1924 essay "The Passing of the Oedipus Complex" and his 1925 essay "Some Psychological Consequences of the Anatomical Distinction Between the Sexes," both collected in Freud (1963); and see Freud (1960).

9. How the boy child resolves his passive Oedipus complex is a topic that remains unexplained in Freud.

law, in this case the law prescribing the mother as being for the father and not for the son, and the prohibition against incest is upheld in the boy's giving up the mother to the father out of fear of castration and in deference to the father's law. Such a resolution takes place through the realization that the boy can find his own woman to become his, as the father has done with the mother, and so the boy takes up a position in the socially prescribed order as "man"—the bearer of the penis who will take the woman for his own. The girl starts out on the same trajectory as the boy, but goes through a different process of resolution. According to Freudian doctrine, the girl, upon discovering the anatomical difference between the sexes, comes to envy the boy his penis, and realizes herself already to be castrated, eventually coming to learn that the mother, too, is castrated. In the girl's eyes, the mother's lack of the penis and the father's possession of it serves as the reason the mother desires the father, as a means to make up for her own (the mother's) lack. In realizing this, the girl also realizes that she can never be the object of the mother's love, as the girl herself lacks the penis the mother desires. This in part pushes the girl to desire to herself become an object of the father's affection. In addition, following the mother, the girl, too, wishes for his (the father's) penis, in order to make up for her own lack. These two things, then, combine to push the girl away from her love of the mother toward a love for the father (her passive Oedipus complex). In this, the girl gives up her desire to possess the mother as love object (a choice to be "man") and instead chooses to become the love object of the man—the "woman" position via the socially prescribed description of the woman as for the man.[10] Of course, the girl has no strong

---

10. The debates that go on over Freud's reading of the production of men's and women's sexual identity are interesting, but rarely fruitful. The standard feminist critique of Freud's misogyny holds little force when we come to understand that Freud is describing a process of maturation as an analytic observer, and that moreover he realizes quite fully that few children go through this process smoothly or exactly. His description is indeed one of the seamless movement to "normal" sexual identity as prescribed by the social order. In other words, Freud is describing how good little girls become good little girls and how

impetus to give up her desire to be loved by the father to be loved by
another man in his place. Thus, she has no strong impetus to resolve
her Oedipus complex. So, Freud concludes that where for the boy
the castration complex resolves the oedipal dilemma, for the girl the
resolution of the oedipal dilemma puts an end to the castration complex. In this, the girl fails to internalize the social "law of the father,"
and so develops a weaker superego than the boy does.[11]

Lacan builds on Freud's reading of the Oedipus complex in
structuring his own theory of sexed subjectivity. For Lacan, the
resolution of the Oedipus complex marks the child's ascension
into the Symbolic order that will govern his or her entire life from
that point on. Although Lacan's writings rarely focus on a fixed
topic in the way that Freud's did, it is the "Phallus" essay that
most clearly outlines what Lacan had to say on the subject of
Oedipus and subjectivity.[12] Lacan begins the essay with a brief
statement on Oedipus's correlative, the castration complex:

> We know that the unconscious castration complex has the func-
> tion of a knot: (1) in the dynamic structuring of symptoms in

---

good little boys become good little boys. He readily realizes that few children
actually move through this process as he describes it. Moreover, he readily realizes that he is describing a socially prescribed norm, not a biologically determined
one. As well, it is essential to realize that Freud's use of the term "normal" is
descriptive and not prescriptive. Normal means nothing less than "socially accepted as" normal—and nothing more. In addition, Freud goes to great lengths
to describe the mechanisms at work by which the child does not successfully
achieve the norms set out by society, and his descriptions do serve as fruitful
models for inquiry.

11. Whether or not the boy or girl actually succeeds in taking on his or
her socially prescribed role is quite another story. Homosexual identity is for Freud
a psychosexual refusal of the socially chosen role—for example the girl's refusal
to give up her love for the mother or the boy's refusal to take up the place of the
father. Still, the road to "normal" sexual identity is clearly laid out for the child,
and society advises the assumptions of its prescribed norms.

12. Lacan first addresses the Oedipus complex in his 1938 essay "Les complexes familaux dans la formation de l'individu: Essai d'analyse d'une fonction en
psychologie" (Lacan 1974), but it is not until his writings of the 1950s that he
begins to bring into clear focus his own interpretation of one of Freud's most
important concepts.

the analytic sense of the term, that is to say, in that which is analyzable in the neuroses, perversions, and psychoses; (2) in a regulation of the development that gives its ratio to this first role: namely, the installation in the subject of an unconscious position without which he would be unable to identify himself with the ideal type of his sex, or to respond without grave risk to the needs of his partner in the sexual relation, or even to accept in a satisfactory way the needs of the child who may be produced by this relation.

There is an antinomy here, that is internal to the assumption by man of his sex: why must he assume the attributes of that sex only through a threat. [E 685/E 281]

The ascension of man to his ideal type is subsumed under a threat: desire the mother and I, the Father, will castrate you. The little girl, of course, resolves her penis envy through the oedipal threat, coming to accede—without fear of castration, which is for her already a reality—to the Symbolic order dictated by the Father.[13]

Now, you will notice here that I have begun to capitalize "Father" where before I did not. What I am pointing to now is the Lacanian explication of what lay implicit in Freudian doctrine: Oedipus is a social phenomenon to which the adult comes to realize he has acceded. Subjectivity is always already sexed. And it is not the real father that is important, but the Law he represents, the oedipal prohibition—the Law of the Father. At any rate, this is the basic order of events surrounding the creation of the Lacanian subject.

As always, Lacan, like Freud, situates these realizations within the reality of the patient in analysis. Lacan writes: "It is only on the basis of the clinical facts that any discussion can be fruitful. These facts reveal a relation of the subject to the phallus that is established without regard to the anatomical difference of the sexes, and which, by this very fact, makes any interpretation of this relation especially difficult in the case of women" (E 686/E 282).

---

13. One of the best readings of Lacan on gender is Charles Shepherdson's (1994) essay "The Role of Gender and the Imperative of Sex."

And this is where the confusion begins. Two things are being established by Lacan here: first, the disjuncture between the penis and phallus, and second, the difference between how "men" and "women" relate to the phallus. For many, these two things seem difficult to reconcile, and so begins the confusion of the interpreter, the one who must take seriously Lacan's protestations that the phallus is not the penis and yet must come to terms with the fact that Lacan sees the phallus as privileged, the one who understands the disjuncture between sex and gender begun by Freud and continued by Lacan but who still mistakenly reads in psychoanalysis a biological origin, if not destiny.

What is one to do? Lacan offers:

> The problem may be treated under the following four headings:
>
> (1) from this "why", the little girl considers herself, if only momentarily, as castrated, in the sense of deprived of the phallus, by someone, in the first instance by her mother, an important point, and then by her father, but in such a way that one must recognize in it a transference in the analytic sense of the term;
>
> (2) from this "why", in a more primordial sense, the mother is considered, by both sexes, as possessing the phallus, as the phallic mother;
>
> (3) from this "why", correlatively, the signification of castration in fact takes on its (clinically manifest) full weight as far as the formation of symptoms is concerned, only on the basis of its discovery as castration of the mother;
>
> (4) these three problems lead, finally, to the question of the reason, in development, for the phallic stage. We know that in this term Freud specifies the first genital maturation: on the one hand, it would seem to be characterized by the imaginary dominance of the phallic attribute and by masturbatory jouissance and, on the other, it localizes this jouissance for the woman in the clitoris, which is thus raised to the function of the phallus. It therefore seems to exclude both sexes, until the end of this stage, that is, to the decline of the Oedipal stage, all instinctual mapping of the vagina as locus of genital penetration. [E 686–687/E 282]

Lacan briefly mentions the existence of various attempts to think through these issues by members of the psychoanalytic establishment (Ernest Jones, Helene Deutsch, Karen Horney, Melanie Klein), but concludes that the answer to the question of how to solve these paradoxes lies in Freud's anticipation of modern linguistic theory. That is, in Freud we come to see the possibility of reading the phallus as signifier: "It is Freud's discovery that gives to the signifier/signified opposition the full extent of its implications: namely, that the signifier has an active function in determining certain effects in which the signifiable appears as submitting to its mark, by becoming through that passion the signified" (E 688/E 284). The phallus is the signifier that governs the subject's assumption of sex: the phallus tells us what we are, and we become it. We become it in that the phallus not only governs what we do, but acts through us—specifically in language. And this is the Lacanian intervention in psychoanalysis—the introduction of linguistic theory into the psychoanalytic scene:

> This passion of the signifier now becomes a new dimension of the human condition in that it is not only man who speaks, but that in man and through man it speaks, that his nature is woven by effects in which is to be found the structure of language, of which he becomes the material, and that therefore there resounds in him, beyond what could be conceived of by a psychology of ideas, the relation of speech. [E 688–689/E 284]

So the assumption of a sexed subject position is the assumption of a linguistic position in and through a master signifier. Subjectivity is a sexed linguistic position—a relation to the signifier "phallus." And this phallus is not only the mechanism through which man speaks; man is the mechanism through which it speaks. The interrelation between sex and language may be contingent, but it is absolutely unavoidable.

This ordering of the subject through the signifier is of extreme significance, for it continues Lacan's antihumanist project and explains the very origins of the various forms of psychic discord about which psychoanalysis is concerned. The problem that is initiated in the phallus is the difference between demand and desire, the difference between the Imaginary and the Symbolic. Demand is the Imaginary counterpart of need, the translation of the child's impulses and instincts onto the mirror scene. In demand, the child seeks satisfaction of its needs via the (m)other, the one who has the unity and presence the child wants and, therefore, the one who can deliver it:

> Demand in itself bears on something other than the satisfactions it calls for. It is a demand of a presence or of an absence—which is what is manifested in the primordial relation to the mother, pregnant with that Other to be situated within the needs it can satisfy. Demand constitutes the Other as already possessing the "privilege" of satisfying needs, that is to say, the power of depriving them of that alone by which they are satisfied. This privilege of the Other thus outlines the radical form of the gift of that which the Other does not have, namely, its love. [E 690–691/E 286]

Thus, the demand for unity, for the presence that is absent, for the absence that is present, is the demand for the Other, the demand for love. The Other, here, is that which the child finds as its ideal in the (m)other. It is not the (m)other herself, but that other which she represents. But as we already know, this demand for unity in, through, and by the other is one that can never be satisfied, as the absence the child wishes to fill can never be filled, for the unity of presence he desires is but a defended fiction. Thus, love, the demand upon the Other for the (m)other to fill the child's longing, can never be realized, and demand already falls short of need (the Real's companion to demand).

Of course, demand still remains within the realm of the Imaginary, the dyad of the child–(m)other. What we have here, in the assumption of sexuality, is the move into the Symbolic, the triangulated structure of child–(m)other–Father.[14] In the oedipal scene,

---

14. Evans (1996, pp. 127–130) argues that it is improper to speak of the Imaginary as a dyad and the Symbolic as a triad, stating that it is precisely Lacan's

the child displaces its demand for the (m)other and instead takes up its socially determined position as sexed subject that desires either the husband or the wife (depending on the sexed position the child assumes in relation to the phallus—that is, man or woman). Desire displaces demand as the Father replaces the (m)other. Again, it is not the real father that enters the picture, but the Symbolic Father (Freud calls this "the name of the father"). The Symbolic Father is bearer of the social prohibition against incest stated in the Oedipus complex. The child must accede to the Father's Law (the incest prohibition). Whereas the real father can be the representative of the Symbolic Father, it is the signifier Father, not its referent, that is significant in the Symbolic order. The real father need not be present for this to happen: his existence is only incidental. Thus, the oedipal conflict (and the subsequent assumption of a sexed subject position) happens in all families, within or outside the nuclear structure, where the social norms of the phallus are in effect; in other words, this is a situation common to all societies of the modern industrialized West. Whereas Freud had been accused of a certain imperialism in his theories, Lacan goes to great lengths to situate Oedipus and psychoanalytic theory within a particular historical moment. In so doing, the argument for its universal presence *within that moment* is considerably strengthened.

And thus Lacan gives us the definition: "desire is neither the appetite for satisfaction, nor the demand for love, but the difference that results from the subtraction of the first from the second, the phenomenon of their splitting" (E 691/E 287). Desire is that which fills the gap between the need for instinctual enjoyment and the demand that this need be filled by the (m)other; it is the child's

---

intervention to present the Imaginary as a triad and the Symbolic as a quad. That is, according to Evans, for Lacan the Imaginary is not simply the relation of the child and the (m)other, but the relation of the child and the (m)other and the ideal of presence the (m)other represents to the child—that is, the Imaginary phallus, while the Symbolic is a place where the Father enters the picture and the child must take up a subject position in relation to the fourth term, the Symbolic phallus—the signifier that guarantees the child a relationship of desire.

turning elsewhere to satiate the need that was left empty by demand. But in this, desire is always already determined by the Other. Whereas demand is a demand for the (m)other to fill the void of which she has made the child aware, desire goes one step further: desire is not only the desire for an other (mate), but is a desire by the Other. That is, the very position the child must assume to become subject is the position determined and given by the Symbolic order, a position in relation to the phallus. In this, while demand is for and because of the other, desire is for and through the other. Not only is its reality determined by the other, but also its very content is something the child assumes for himself, not something the child finds within some purely internal and separate "self." And as the Other is an ideal that can never be attained, desire will always remain unfulfilled. So long as the subject believes that desire is somehow rooted in and originates from a unified sense of self, it will continue to believe that desire can be fulfilled, and in so believing will constantly set itself up for failure and disappointment.

In addition to going back to the relationship between the Symbolic and the Imaginary, the search for unity in the Symbolic also goes back to the relationship between the Imaginary and the Real. Recall that in the mirror stage, the child forms its fictive sense of self. But more is happening in the mirror stage, as well, for it is in the encounter with the (m)other that the child comes to form the very concepts of "self" and "other," of inside and outside. Prior to the mirror stage, in the Real, the child has no sense of subject and object: all is present *for* the child and *as an extension of* the child. It is only in coming to see something that it cannot be, in that confrontation with the unity in the mirror, that the child begins to realize that there is any disjunction between self and other. Before the mirror stage, in the Real, the infant does not in fact see itself as incomplete.[15] In the earliest stages of infancy, everything is entirely complete, as a unified mass. For the infant, there are no inside and outside, no self and other; there is only the world in its entirety as

---

15. To speak of a "before" is misleading, for as we shall see, the Real is always a retroactive positing of an un-real space.

the extension of the infant's body. All is object, all is subject, and the infant does not distinguish between the two. It is because of the realization of otherness in the mirror stage that the child learns to separate subject and object, learns to see inside and outside. As such, the mirror stage is not only the moment of otherness creating the sense of self; it is also the moment of otherness creating the very self–other split in the first place. And so, the *I* taking up a misrecognized image of a unified self is radical in that it not only creates self, but also creates the very division between self and other. As such, the Imaginary introduces the child into the very dyad of subject–object. The Symbolic, on the other hand, is the well of meaning on which the child draws when she enters the triangulated social realm (the realm of the Father, the third). For the child, taking up a position as a sexed subject means drawing on that material available to her and introjecting it into her sense of self (ego). And the most prominent material upon which the child draws is its position as sexed—its relation to the phallus. The child must assume a subject(iviz)ed relation to the object-signifier "phallus."

We are still left with the questions, what is the phallus, and why is it so important (that is, why is it the master signifier)? Lacan is adamant in telling us what the phallus is not. "The phallus is not a fantasy, if by that we mean an imaginary effect. Nor is it as such an object (part of, internal, good, bad, etc.) in the sense that this term tends to accentuate the reality pertaining in a relation. It is even less the organ, penis or clitoris, that it symbolizes" (E 690/ E 285).

Moreover, continuing the Freudian subversion of the assumed connection between biological sex and social gender, Lacan even associates the phallus with the mother as well as the father. In the Imaginary, it is the mother who is imbued with power, specifically the power to give love, and so for the child it is the mother who is associated with the phallus. And it is only when the child learns that the mother does not have the phallus that the child looks elsewhere, giving the father the position of power once belonging to the mother. But the father does not possess the phallus any more than the mother does, for his own power is only a socially prescribed role in which he has come to place himself as the object of the mother's desire and in which he has learned to desire the mother himself (for the father, too, was once a child who acceded to the Symbolic order). As such, it seems that the phallus is the desire of the Other to which the child accedes; that is, the phallus is the prescription of sexed subjectivity as sexed desire, and thus is the signifier around which both boy and girl take their places as man or woman. It is in this that Lacan is able to offer his famous distinction between being and having the phallus:

> The demand for love can only suffer from a desire whose signifier is alien to it. If the desire of the mother is the phallus, the child wishes to be the phallus in order to satisfy that desire. Thus the division immanent in desire is already felt to be experienced in the desire of the Other, in that it is already opposed to the fact that the subject is content to present to the Other what in reality he may have that corresponds to this phallus, for what he has is worth no more than what he does not have, as far as his demand for love is concerned because that demand requires that he be the phallus. [E 693/E 289]

But what is all the more striking is, again, the fact that being or having the phallus is only a fiction, because desire can never be fulfilled. Of course, the illusion must continue, if we are to continue to be sexed subjects. Thus we are given "the intervention of a 'to seem' that replaces the 'to have' [and the 'to be'], in order to protect it on the one side, and to mask its lack in the other" (E 694/E 289).

Why do we continue to be sexed subjects? One answer is that, so long as the phallus exists, it will continue to govern, and so long as it continues to govern, it will continue to exist. This is the Lacanian paradox: the phallus is a self-perpetuating fiction, and thus the Symbolic orders a self-perpetuating system. And this is where the charge of conservatism enters. Though simply describing and not endorsing a system, and though exposing the system as a Symbolic order that is only fictively real, Lacan has shown how the system maintains itself without giving any indication as to how it might be subverted. However, a stronger answer to this question emerges when we recall the paradigm out of which Lacan is working—Freudian psychoanalysis. In forgetting Freud, we forget the basic assumptions upon which Lacan always relies. And so, to understand Lacan, we must force ourselves to return constantly to Freud. Why must we continue to be sexed subjects? For Freud, the question really is, Why are we sexed subjects at all? And the answer to that question lies in understanding the process by which our egos are formed.

According to psychoanalysis, the infant constructs its ego when it learns to differentiate itself from others through the series of identificatory relations Lacan calls the mirror stage (Freud calls this primary narcissism). In doing so, the infant is engaged in a process of reordering its biological instincts by investing itself in its pleasure-giving body. This investment in its body as "self" (distinct from, yet shaped by the internalized other) marks the creation of the child's drives (the drives can be seen as the Imaginary counterpart to the instincts, which belong to the register of the Real, though, as we shall see, the drives are fundamentally ordered by the Symbolic). As the drives are, like the instincts, centered on the body as a source of pleasure, they are libidinal (sexual). Thus, the differentiation of self and other that occurs in the mirror stage is a differentiation that takes place as the child inscribes libidinal meaning on the body—that is, this differentiation is a sexual differentiation ("this is my pleasure-giving body, not yours"). The emergence of sexual difference as a psychical-social phenomenon (the man–woman split) occurs in the Oedipus complex, but this later split is always founded on the earlier split, this prior moment. Thus, the fantasmatic appropriation of the Symbolic phallus rests on the prior investment in the status of the body as self in the Imaginary (and thus on the Imaginary phallus).[16] In the

---

16. Evans (1996) offers a very sophisticated reading of the phallus in which he distinguishes between the Real, the Imaginary, and the Symbolic phallus. According to Evans, the Imaginary phallus is that which, in the Imaginary, the child sees as the object of the (m)other's desire. In our reading, then, the child would

resolution of the Oedipus complex, the child takes up a social-linguistic position in relation to the Symbolic phallus—that is, as a boy or a girl. Sexual difference, then, is this positioning with regard to the Symbolic phallus. But there is no Symbolic phallus without the Imaginary phallus, and in this the Symbolic is founded on the retroactive construction of the Imaginary, on the prior construction of the child's ego-self in the sexual body-investment of the mirror stage.

The specific function of the phallus as Symbolic phallus is a historically determined one, but the fact of sexual investment is not. It is important to understand this distinction in order to defend Lacan from charges of conservatism and sexist phallocentrism. For while it is on the issue of the phallus that Lacan receives the most charges of conservatism, we must remember that it is also here where Lacan is at his most radical. For one thing, the understanding of the child as a sexual being is a radical one and is not tied to any specific historical understanding of sex and social positioning. More important for our understanding of Lacanian psychoanalysis as antihumanist, the insistence on the phallus as signifier is the insistence on the continuation of alienation, the pronouncement of the fact that the castration complex is never in fact completely resolved, and the argument that sexual identities are effects of the Symbolic. If there is a split between signifier and signified, the assumption of a position in regard to the phallus is always tenuous. If sexual identification is always tenuous, we are reminded that we never in fact move completely beyond castration and Oedipus. We never fully resolve the dilemmas of childhood, even in the assumption of our sexed subjectivities. That is, we never succeed in making ourselves whole. This is Lacan's point. The project of psychoanalysis is not the project of ego-completion, but rather the realization of ego-impotence, and the phallus is one way in which Lacan can make this point. In further establishing the subject as a product of pure alienation, in which the construction

---

displace her own desire to be the object of the (m)other's desire (and thus of her own desire) onto her own body.

of the subject is not simply the act of some individual cut off from an inner self, but is rather the specific delineation of self and other by which the very idea of self and its content are first formed, we are led not only to a rethinking of contemporary theories of subjectivity, but also to a rethinking of analytic practice itself. For, to Lacan, "man cannot aim at being whole (the 'total personality' is another of the deviant premises of modern psychotherapy), while ever the play of displacement and condensation to which he is doomed in the exercise of his functions marks his relation as a subject to the signifier" (E 692/E 287).

In moving from Levinas to Lacan in separate treatments of the subject of sexed subjectivity, it has been difficult to resist the temptation to compare the two. They are on so many levels connected, on so many levels similar. I have withheld comparison until now because to compare them prematurely might lead one to see only commonality when so much difference does exist. They each present visions in which subjectivity is essentially sexed. They each argue that procreation is the primary means by which the subject seeks to conquer its own inevitable demise. But sexual identities have significantly different origins for the two thinkers, and these different origins are of the utmost significance in further illuminating their opposing and competing views of subjectivity. Levinas recognized the problem of the ontological bent of his earlier work and shifted away from it later. In so doing Levinas moved closer to Lacan. To illuminate this shift, we return to Levinas's second major work, *Otherwise than Being*, specifically looking at Chapter 3, "Sensibility and Proximity." However, we must note that, in moving closer, Levinas did not meet but only approached Lacan. To keep sight of their essential differences, then, we also turn to a different text of Lacan (and again one of his most difficult works), his later *Encore* (1975). By looking at these two texts side by side, we can see each author's mature statement of his view on subjectivity and sexuality, presented here in order to trace common and divergent themes in their works, as well as to better set the stage for a discussion of their views on subjectivity and language in Chapter 3.

Recall that *Otherwise than Being* can be read as an attempt to rewrite the themes of *Totality and Infinity* without metaphysical language. Here metaphor replaces (pseudo)phenomenon; the trope replaces the (non)event. And, as substitution replaced the caress, so too will fecundity give way to a more mature statement. But at the same time that a metaphysics is eschewed, a pre-ontological reality remains—a something prior, a grounding of the ethical act. And the feminine remains a central term in this description of the primordial giving of self to other, ethical subjugation. The metaphor changes from wife to mother—or more properly, to maternity and the maternal body. But the true change is in the positionality of the feminine metaphor. Where in *Totality and Infinity* the feminine stood as a testament to the other's distance from me, in *Otherwise than Being* the maternal is the metaphor for my *own* nearness to the other, and it is this nearness that engenders the sensibility that marks the subject's giving of self to other, and marks this state of giving as the foundational mode of the subject's coming to be.[17]

For the later Levinas, the body is explained in and through the concept of subjective sensibility—that form of being which brings the self toward the other and freezes the self in its absolute passivity: "The one-for-the-other has the form of sensibility or vulnerability; pure passivity or susceptibility, passive to the point of being an inspiration, that is to say, precisely, alterity in the same, the trope of the body animated by the soul, psyche in the form of a hand that gives even the bread taken from its own mouth. The psyche is here the maternal body" (AE 109/OTB 67).

The psyche as maternal body is the psyche's giving over of itself to and for the other. However, signification itself is only possible in an incarnate body. The only self who can be subject is the self who speaks from the body, for it is in and through the body that the self threatens the existence of the other, in and through the body

---

17. This is a difference between *Totality and Infinity* and *Otherwise than Being* that is too often overlooked in secondary literature. One happy exception is Catherine Chalier's (1991) "Ethics and the Feminine."

that the self takes up that piece of being that belongs to the other, and it is only in and through the body that the self can be weak before the other, for vulnerability is always incarnate: "Signification is only possible as incarnation. The animation, the very pneuma of the psyche, alterity in identity, is the identity of the body exposed to the other, becoming 'for the other,' the possibility of giving" (AE 111/OTB 69). But I am the one who gives, for I am the one who is naked, exposed, vulnerable before the other:

> The subject called incarnate does not result from a materialization, an entry into space and into relations of contact and money which would have been realized by a consciousness, that is, a self-consciousness, forewarned against every attack and first non-spatial. It is because subjectivity is sensibility—an exposure to others, a vulnerability and a responsibility in the proximity of others, the-one-for-the-other, that is, signification—and because matter is the very locus of the for-the-other, the way that signification signifies before showing itself as a said in the system of synchronism, the linguistic system, that a subject is of flesh and blood, a man that is hungry and eats, entrails in a skin, and thus capable of giving the bread out of his mouth, or giving his skin. [AE 124/OTB 77]

The subject is thus vulnerable before the other, and it is precisely this vulnerability that allows him to be able to be "for-the-other." Without his own existence at stake, he could not conceivably be for the other, for he would not be able to substitute himself for the other. Substitution only holds meaning if it is in fact my very life that I am willing to give for the other by standing in his place, and I can only give this if I am threatened, vulnerable.

Again, I can only be vulnerable if I am incarnate. In this, not only is incarnation necessary, but it is also original, originary, prior to thought or action. It is the very ground of my being, the very foundation of my subjectivity. And in this I am always already subjected, always already for-the-other. Before being the Cartesian ego, I am a bodily subject:

A notion of subjectivity independent of the adventure of cognition, and in which the corporeality of the subject is not sepa-
rable from its subjectivity, is required if signification signifies
otherwise than by the synchrony of being, if intelligibility and
being are distinguishable, if essence itself signifies only on the
basis of an ascription of meaning that devolves from the-one-
for-the-other, the signifyingness of signification. Subjectivity of
flesh and blood in matter is not for the subject a "mode of self-
certainty." The proximity of beings of flesh and blood is not
their presence "in flesh and bone," is not the fact that they take
from a look, present an exterior, quiddities, forms, give images,
which the eye absorbs (and whose alterity the hand that touches
or holds, suspends easily or lightly, annulling it by the simple
grasp, as though no one contested this appropriation). Nor are
material beings reducible to the resistance they oppose to the
effort they solicit. Their relationship with a mouth is not an
adventure of knowledge or of action. Subjectivity of flesh and
blood in matter—the signifyingness of sensibility, the-one-for-
the-other itself—is the preoriginal signifyingness that gives
sense, because it gives. Not because, as preoriginal, it would
be more originary than the origin, but because diachrony of
sensibility, which cannot be assembled in a representational
present, refers to an irrecuperable pre-ontological past, that
of maternity. [AE 125–126/OTB 78]

Sensible subjectivity, then, is that pre-original past, that mode of
being in which I am always already for-the-other: "incarnation is
not a transcendental operation of a subject that is in the midst of
the world it represents to itself; the sensible experience of the body
is already and from the start incarnate" (AE 123/OTB 76). And
maternity is that mode of subjectivity in which we stand not only
vulnerable to the other, but also obsessed by the other.[18]

My being obsessed by the other is my desiring to hold myself
responsible for him. But the other no longer revolves around some
ontological difference, no longer rests in his mode of being as differ-

---

18. On maternity, Lisa Walsh (2001) has offered a truly excellent reading
in a recent article.

ent from mine. He remains apart, but this difference is not thematized through gender. Rather, it remains within the realm of bodily separation. While I am like the other person, the other person is not like the feminine; rather, she is like the neighbor, the stranger, the widow, or the orphan—the one before whom I am vulnerable in my ability to enjoy, the one before whom my eating means her starving, the one with whom I am obsessed, taking responsibility for her nudity, her poverty, her suffering. In the face of the other, I again see the trace of my responsibility, my being called, and I respond before I can even question the question:

> A trace of itself, given over to my responsibility, but to which I am wanting and faulty, as though I were responsible for his mortality, and guilty for surviving, the face is an anachronous immediacy more tense than that of an image offered in the straightforwardness of an intuitive intention. In proximity of the absolutely other, the stranger whom I have "neither conceived nor given birth to," I already have on my arms, already bear, according to the Biblical formula, "in my breast as the nurse bears the nursling." He has no other place, is not autochthonous, is uprooted, without a country, not an inhabitant, exposed to the cold and the heat of the seasons. To be reduced to having recourse to me is the homelessness or strangeness of the neighbor. It is incumbent upon me. [AE 145/OTB 91]

The feminine has given way to the stranger, the illusion of the self-sufficient pre-subject to maternity, and a new ground for the ethical relation emerges. Having moved beyond the need for metaphysics and ontology, Levinas has moved beyond the solidification of subjectivity in gender, and is now able to put aside the feminine, instead using maternity as a trope, and the post-humanist vision of his work now emerges fully and completely. The subject is not bound to any notion of metaphysics or ontology, is neither self-conscious nor self-determined.

In eschewing the last remnants of metaphysics and ontology from his programmatic statement on the creation of the subject, Levinas has indeed come very close to Lacan. And yet it is here again that the two will part ways. For Levinas, the subject is now more than ever a subject by and for the other. Still, the subject is a self, a unity that offers itself to the other. It does come to know itself, does come to control itself, to an extent, and as such is not the antihumanist subject of Lacan. More important, the subject's coming to be in the giving over of itself to the other is rooted in a pre-originary moment that Levinas describes in his later works as maternity, thus endorsing a notion of the human outside and before discourse. Lacan will have none of this. His understanding of the subject remains thoroughly within the realm of the discursive and the constructed, and thus the antihumanist.

In order to determine the extent to which Levinas's and Lacan's visions of the ethical subject are at odds and the extent to which they can be reconciled, we need to get a bit clearer on just exactly where Lacan is moving that Levinas is not on the topic of subjectivity as sexed. Much of what we know about Lacan comes to us from the publication of his yearly seminars.[19] Beginning (officially) in 1953 (unofficially in 1951) and continuing until 1979, only two years before his death in 1981, Lacan held weekly seminars, organized around a different topic each year, in which most of his teaching occurred. Many famous intellectuals attended his seminars at one time or another, from his disciples to his dissenters, thinkers from Jacques-Alain Miller, his son-in-law and heir to the Lacanian orthodoxy, to feminist revisionaries such as Luce Irigaray, to, interestingly, renowned Levinas scholars such as Alphonso Lingis. The beginning of the Seminars coincided with Lacan's infamous 1953 Rome Discourse, to which we will turn in the next chapter. As the years progressed, so, too, did Lacan's thoughts and teachings. The topic of sexuality was one that became an increasingly explicit preoccupation in Lacan's teachings over the years, and by 1972 Lacan decided to devote a great deal of time to the topic in the seminar entitled *Encore* (1975), translated as *On Feminine Sexuality: The Limits of Love and Knowledge* (1998). Bits and pieces of

---

19. For a brief but very useful discussion of the seminar and the history of its publication, see Roudinesco (1997), pp. 413–427.

this seminar have been available for some years in English, but it was only in 1998 that a full English translation emerged, a significant development in Lacanian scholarship, finally making one of his most famous seminars available to a wider range of readers.[20]

In this seminar, Lacan, as always, surprises his readers. Reading it in its entirety one is struck by the sense of purpose and direction weaving through it. Lacanian geometry (his use of symbols, equations, and diagrams to outline his theories) is ever-present in the work, as is Lacan's dense and intricate linguistic style. Still, a theme emerges—one that is vaguely familiar yet powerfully new. What we find is that in this seminar Lacan proposes to interrogate the supposed gulf between the body and sex, between the material and the discursive, between incarnation and the psyche. As does Levinas, Lacan sees a marked intersection between the body and the relation to the other. However, whereas for Levinas there is a coincidence of need and gift, for Lacan the body can never fulfill— it is always imbued with meaning that is foreign to it, inscribed in an order in which it does not originally belong. That is, the idea of a purely internal sense of self as biologically sexed is false and additionally rests on a false dichotomy between self and other, because meaning, particularly a subject's understanding of its "self" and its "body," is always achieved by and through an other.

These are the themes of the seminar, then, and in setting out the trajectory of the seminar, Lacan seems to be promising an explication of some of the themes outlined in the "Phallus" essay. The

---

20. This is one of Lacan's most difficult works, but it is also one of his richest. In this section I will focus only on certain of Lacan's discussions of sexuality and the body, but it would be a mistake to think that this seminar only takes on these themes. It is a much richer work with far more in it than my presentation here suggests. The structure of this book will not allow me to treat the seminar in full and give it the completeness of attention it deserves. Nor will I be able to offer a complete reading of Seminars VII and XI, which I will deal with in Chapter 4. I beg the reader to remember that this book is not meant to be a comprehensive introduction to Lacan, and so I hope that she or he will forgive my all too focused attention to particular themes in the seminars at the expense of fuller readings. For particularly excellent engagements with Seminar XX, see Fink (1995) and Barnard and Fink (2002).

seminar, in typical Lacanian fashion, is far more complicated, and far more fragmented than any of the *Écrits*. In examining his claims in this seminar, however, Lacan, as always, stays true to psycho-analytic method; the starting point, any starting point, seems difficult to locate, but we find it if we recall that it is not in the past. It is always in the present, in the experience of analysis, and in the things analysis teaches us about how the lived social present constructs our misunderstood-to-be pre-social past.

The problematic of the seminar is set out from the start—the question of the sexual relationship and how it can in fact "be" when our very conception of sex, as sexed characteristics, as sexed bodies, is not the founding moment of our sexed subjectivity. Here the phallus of Lacan's earlier essay is ever more the fraud, now not so much the image, even less the organ, but rather the symbol around which desire is ordered (and recall, as we argued in Chapter 1, desire is the founding moment of the subject, for it is in the emulation of the love object (the [m]other) that the child creates her image of self). Bruce Fink (1995) states it nicely when he writes:

> In its quest for love and attention, a child is sooner or later confronted with the fact that it is not its parents' sole object of interest. Their multiple, and no doubt multifarious, objects of interest all have one thing in common: they divert the parents' attention away from the child. The parents' attention is what has the highest value in the child's universe: it is the gold standard, so to speak, that value against which all other values are measured. All objects or activities which attract their attention away from the child take on an importance they might otherwise never have had. Not surprisingly, one signifier comes to signify that part of the parents' desire which goes beyond the child (and by extension, their desire in general). Lacan refers to it as the "signifier of desire," and—as "man's desire is the Other's desire"—it can also be referred to as the "signifier of the Other's desire." It is the signifier of that which is worthy of desire, that which is desirable. [pp. 101–102]

This signifier is, of course, the phallus.[21]

The phallus as a mark of the Other's desire symbolizes to the reader the significance sex takes on in contemporary Western culture. Sex of course is an ambiguous term. It can refer to various forms of biology, genitalia, acts of sexual coupling, sexual orientation, gender identity, and gender attribution, as well as having wider meaning when considering the family unit and beyond. Lacan takes more care in his language than to simply speak of "sex" without realizing the ambiguity. Using his language with care, Lacan goes on to tell us more of what he does and does not mean in referring to all things sexed and sexual as he writes:

> The body's being is of course sexed, but this is secondary, as they say. And as experience shows, the body's jouissance, insofar as that body symbolizes the Other, does not depend on those traces . . .

> Assuredly, what appears on bodies in the enigmatic form of sexual characteristics—which are merely secondary—makes beings sexed. Undoubtedly. But being is the jouissance of the body as such, that is, as asexual, because what is known as sexual jouissance is marked and dominated by the impossibility of establishing as such, anywhere in the enunciable, the sole One that interests us, the One of the relation "sexual relationship." [S XX 11, 12–13/S XX 5, 6–7]

---

21. Fink (1995) goes on to make an important point:

Psychoanalytic practice suggests, as do other practices, that in Western culture in general, that signifier is the phallus. Though many claim that that is no more than a preconceived notion, psychoanalysis claims that it is a clinical observation, and as such is contingent. It is verified time and time again in clinical practice, and thus constitutes a generalization, not a necessary, universal rule. There is no theoretical reason why it could not be something else, and there perhaps are (and have been) societies in which some other signifier plays (or played) the role of the signifier of desire. [p. 102]

So many interesting claims are being made here that it is worth our while to stop and look closely. The body as sexed is secondary to analytic reading. Biology of course exists, in many different forms—sexual organs, chromosomes, hormones, to name but a few. But this is not what matters most, nor what concerns the analyst in her looking at sexual desire. Instead what matters is something else, something that concerns jouissance and concerns the question for the "One" of the sexual relationship.

For Lacan, a person's "sex," meaning his or her position in relation to the phallus, is not reducible to the body. While we become "sexuated" most commonly along lines that split the world into two biological sexes, the psychical sexes that we assume are not necessarily tied to our biology. As Fink (2002) writes, "sexuation is not biological sex: what Lacan calls masculine structure and feminine structure do not have to do with one's biological organs but rather with the kind of jouissance that one is able to obtain" (p. 36). That is, in Lacanian psychoanalysis there is room for the transsexual, for the female man and the male woman.[22]

---

22. Fink (2002) goes on to acknowledge that one might be inclined to thereby associate sexuation with gender identification, but warns against that, as "gender," he tells us, is a recent English-usage term. I would tend to agree from a textual and historical standpoint, but from a constructive standpoint would argue that we need to move beyond either the second-wave feminist sex/gender distinction or the Lacanian biological sex/psychical sexuation distinction, as each is insufficient. In contemporary gender theory many of us are now operating under a threefold schema of sex—(biological)/gender identity (psycho-social)/gender performance (psycho-social). In this schema, gender identity would correspond to psychical sexuation. Thus, while Fink elsewhere (1995, p. 194, footnote 24) makes the intelligent distinction between male/female as referring to biology and man/woman and masculine/feminine to psychoanalytic determination, we would do better to use male/female to refer to biology, man/woman to refer to psycho-social gender identity, and masculine/feminine to refer to psycho-social gender performance. In other words, Fink, following a Lacanian reading, cannot sufficiently distinguish between the terms man and masculine, assuming that to be a man (regardless of biology) is to take up a masculine structure, while we would do better to make room for the feminine man as one who can take up a particular kind of relation to the phallus (as a man) but still take on feminine gender attributes, and to make room for the masculine woman as one who can take up a

The material body qua biological body remains distant from the psychical body.[23] Instead, sexuation is a symbolic positioning in reference to the master signifier. Surely the psychical assumption of a sexed identity (man/woman) takes its reference to and from a biological body, but it is not the biological body that determines psychical sexuate identity. Again, as in the earlier work, discourse reigns supreme over metaphysics or biology, and Lacan remains truer to the discursive than Levinas.

What does this have to do with knowledge, though? Well, knowledge and desire are closely linked, as we shall see more clearly in Chapter 4. For now suffice it to say that we desire he whom we think is whole, and he whom we think is whole is whole, in part, because we think he has the knowledge of how to satisfy and possess that which he, and in turn we, desire. Knowledge is consumption, just as is love. So, if Lacan sees sexuation as a positioning via the phallus, in specific an ordering of our desire, what is our desire to possess the phallus if not a desire to obtain wholeness, to become the One?

We can already see some differences between Lacan and Levinas on sex and the body. However, the situation gets even more complicated. In Seminar XX, Lacan makes one of his most famous and misunderstood claims—that woman does not exist. He tells us:

> That is what analytic discourse demonstrates in that, to one of these beings qua sexed, to man insofar as he is endowed with

---

particular kind of relation to the phallus (as a woman) but still take on masculine gender attributes. In both cases, biology is still not determinative. Thus, in the threefold schema we move beyond both Freud and Lacan and into new terrain without sacrificing the basic psychoanalytic insights we gain from them. That is, while Lacanian discourse makes room for the transsexual, we here make room for the transgendered and the genderqueer. For more on this debate, see, again, Shepherdson (1994) and the very fine continuation of his ideas in Eliot and Roen (1998). For more on my take on gender identity and gender theory today see Fryer (2003b).

23. This seems to me to be an advance over Freud who, though not in the least a biological determinist, still saw a deeper connection between gender identity and biology.

the organ said to be phallic—I said "said to be"—the corporeal
sex or sexual organ of woman—I said "of woman", whereas in
fact woman does not exist, woman is not whole—woman's
sexual organ is of no interest except via the body's jouissance:
"Analytic discourse demonstrates—allow me to put it this
way—that the phallus is the conscientious objection made by
one of the two sexed beings to the service to be rendered to
the other." [S XX 13/S XX 7]

So here things will continue to be complicated, for what does it
mean for woman not to exist? Well, it certainly does not mean that
women, as body-subjects in the world, do not exist. Nor can it mean
that the female body does not exist. Nor can it even mean that the
"feminine structure" of the psyche does not exist. So what does it
mean? Lacan continues: "Analytic experience attests precisely to
the fact that everything revolves around phallic jouissance, in that
woman is defined by a position that I have indicated as 'not whole'
with respect to phallic jouissance" (S XX 13/S XX 7). In part, woman
does not exist in that she is "not whole" with respect to phallic
jouissance. That is, as the phallus is at least in part the mark of the
male/masculine, woman cannot ascend fully to the Symbolic because the master signifier is not hers. Thus she will always fail
because she is not only alienated, but, from the perspective of the
master signifier of the Symbolic, she is not real.[24] But if one goes
further, lack, the inability to be whole, is not a position that only
afflicts woman; it is not only *woman* who is not "whole" with respect to the phallus! As Lacan tells us: "I will go a little further.
Phallic jouissance is the obstacle owing to which man does not
come, I would say, to enjoy woman's body, precisely because what
he enjoys is the jouissance of the organ" (S XX 13/S XX 7). Castration permeates the masculine psyche as much as the feminine.

———————————

24. Again, Fink (1995) puts it well when he writes, "Socially speaking,
Lacan's assertion that there is no signifier of/for Woman is, no doubt, related to
the fact that a woman's position in our culture is either automatically defined by
the man she adopts as partner or is defined only with great difficulty. In other
words, the search for another way of defining herself is long and fraught with
obstacles" (p. 116).

The dialectic of whole and not-whole, which drives Lacan's later work on sexuation, is quite interestingly played out.[25] Why is it that both man and woman are distant from the wholeness they seek in sexual relationship? Because from the beginning sexual relationship is based on the search for an unattainable unity—a unity with the Other. But, as we know, any unity with the Other will only result in an uncovering of the aggression the subject already feels in reference to himself, for it is the Other that has given him his own false sense of unity, his own false sense of oneness. Here love and aggression and knowledge and unity are all bound up in the same struggle. Thus Lacan asks, "What is involved in love? Is love—as psychoanalysis claims with an audacity that is all the more incredible as all of its experience runs counter to that very notion and as it demonstrates the contrary—is love about making one? Is Eros a tension toward the One?" (S XX 12/S XX 5). Love, sex, union—these things are part and parcel of the self's struggle for unity, for a desire to return to a phantasmatic unity of the self based on a prior union with the mother before any split has taken place, a phantasy to return to the womb. But this unity and this union are but fictions in the life of the infant, and the drive toward sexual union is doomed to failure. Thus, the jouissance that is sought in sexual union is always just out of reach, always unattainable. Lacan writes, "jouissance is marked by the hold that leaves it no other path than that of phallic jouissance," and, as phallic, it is always mediated by a Symbolic order that, however real, rests on a Real that is not (S XX 14/S XX 8). The signified that the phallus supposedly represents is never to be properly had.[26] If, as Lacan asserts, the Real is the impossible, then the phallus, as the symbolic representation of the Real, is also the impossible.

---

25. Fink (1995) labels this a dialectic of part and whole; see ibid., p. 98.

26. Again, a reading of Fink (1995) is useful, for he makes clear the distinction between the phallus as wholly symbolic and the *objet petit a* as the cause of desire that supposedly lies in the real, that *signified* that the phallus in part is meant to represent. See Fink (1995, 2002). We will return to the *objet petit a* in Chapter 4.

In addition to exploring the themes of sexuation and the phallus, Lacan also wishes to explore the broader question of the relation between body and the *word*, and in so doing uncovers some of the inner and under workings of what Levinas left buried in having moved away from the feminine in his later works. To engage in this investigation, Lacan addresses the problem of ontology, warning against misinterpreting *being* as primary:

> Ontology is what highlighted in language the use of the copula, isolating it as a signifier. To dwell on the verb "to be"—a verb that is not even, in the complete field of the diversity of languages, employed in a way we could qualify as universal—to produce it as such is a highly risky enterprise.

> In order to exorcise it, it might perhaps suffice to suggest that when we say about anything whatsoever that it is what it is, nothing in any way obliges us to isolate the verb "to be." [S XX 33/S XX 31]

Ontology, in other words, is a production of language, and therefore is one of its effects. Ontology is not prediscursive, but, rather, post-discursive. As such, when we ontologize, thinking of what "is" in a prediscursive reality, we are in fact operating always already from discourse, from a linguistic position that we cannot escape, that we cannot get beneath. In effect, for the linguistic subject, there is no prediscursive reality—language is first, all else follows. As Lacan writes: "How is one to return, if not on the basis of a peculiar discourse, to a prediscursive reality? That is the dream— the dream behind every conception of knowledge. But it is also what must be considered mythical. There is no such thing as a prediscursive reality. Every reality is founded and defined by a discourse" (S XX 33/S XX 32). And if language is before being, then so, too, is it before sexual difference. "A man is nothing but a signifier. A woman seeks out a man qua signifier. A man seeks out a woman qua—and this will strike you as odd—that which can only be situated through discourse, since, if what I claim is true—namely, that woman is not-whole—there is always something in her that escapes discourse" (S XX 34/S XX 33).

As such, language not only prefigures but forms sexual difference: "The signified is not what you hear. What you hear is the signifier. The signified is the effect of the signifier" (S XX 34/S XX 33). In practice, then: the phallus comes first, the object of desire that it represents, second; the sexuate identity comes first, the biological body onto which it is described, second; the subject comes first, the self, second.[27]

Lacan is engaged in a project aimed at displacing the body from its privileged place in some forms of Freudian discourse, and, by extension, a project aimed at displacing ontology from its privileged place in philosophy. Thus, by extension, we find Lacan in close proximity to Levinas. Like Levinas, Lacan sees in sexual difference a place in which ontology takes root. And like the later Levinas, Lacan realizes the inherent problem in this. Unlike Levinas, however, Lacan is not interested in the project of discovering ethical foundations (even an-archical ones) at this point, so that Lacan is able to move down a stricter path in his critique of being. Where Levinas makes room for something beyond language, an otherwise-than-being, Lacan keeps language on the primary plane. This allows Lacan a descriptive element all but silent in Levinas: Lacan can describe the assignation of form to word, of content to sign—that is, the binding of signifier and signified in the one producing the other. This permits Lacan to describe the problematic of masculinism through a reading of the phallus; and in this he is able to explain the problematic at work in *Totality and Infinity*, the one from which Levinas found himself forced to move away. Levinas might have been right to move away from this masculinism, but he was unable to explain why and how he was in it in the first place, and thus was unable to justify his moving away from it. Interestingly, the fact that Lacan can explain masculinism also leads, in a sense, to his

_____

27. This idea of the retroactive positing of the Real as prior and real will be of central importance in Chapter 4 and the conclusion.

being able to stay within it. As a descriptive theorist, Lacan recognizes that we still live in a masculinist world, and thus he insists on a radical disjunction between sexuated persons. Perhaps Levinas, in an all-too-quick attempt to distance himself from his own masculinism, then, gave up something that was worth preserving— a recognition of the dominance of masculinist discourse and the impossibility of completely escaping it in our world. Lacan, in effect, explains why the figure of the feminine as other had to be put aside in the mature Levinas, while further explaining why denouncing the idea of ontological difference is not enough.

Clearly Lacan is more thoroughly the antihumanist in thinking through the issue of subjectivity as sexed. In a deeper commitment to the discursive production of categories of the human, all connections to a previous humanism are swept aside. Levinas is more attenuated in his dismissal of humanism. In both the remnants of ontology in his early writings and in the phenomenologically based reading of the trope of maternity as a prediscursive connectivity and receptivity to the other in his later writings, Levinas emerges as post-humanist.

Certain issues have now become more clear, while others have become more cloudy. Of course the ontological play of *Totality and Infinity* had to be let go. Of course Levinas and Lacan can both agree that the biology of the body is not the way to begin a theorizing, either of sex or of ethics. The question is, can Levinas still justify the privilege of the other in the other person? Can there still be a notion of the ethical that is founded on something outside, something beyond? Or is language as foundational as Lacan makes it out to be? If Lacan is right, is not Levinas simply skirting the issue by trying to create a notion of the ethical otherwise-than-being when in fact any foundation is still caught up in the attempt to justify a ground before language? If Levinas is right, can Lacan really justify his adherence to the priority of the Symbolic? Here Levinas and Lacan are at their most divergent, and to better understand this divergence, we turn directly to the question of language in Chapter 3.

3

Linguistic Subjectivity and the Speaking Subject

*The entity that appears identical in the light of time is its essence in the al-
ready said . . . The very exposition of Being, its manifestation, essence qua
essence and entities qua entities, are spoken. It is only in the said, in the epos
of saying, that the diachrony of time is synchronized into a time that is re-
callable, and becomes a theme . . .* But is the power to say in man, however
strictly correlative to the said its function may be, in the service of being?
*If man were only a saying correlative with the logos, the subjectivity could
as well be understood as a function or as an argument of being. But the signification of saying goes beyond the said. It is not an ontology that raises up
the speaking subject; it is the signifyingness of saying going beyond the essence that can justify the exposedness of being, ontology.*
—Levinas, AE 65–66/OTB 37–38

*The psychoanalytic experience has rediscovered in man the imperative of
the Word as the law that has formed him in its image. It manipulates the
poetic function of language to give to his desire its symbolic mediation. May
that experience enable you to understand at last that it is in the gift of speech
that all the reality of its effects resides; for it is by way of this gift that all
reality has come to man and it is by his continued act that he maintains it.*
—Lacan, E 322/E 106

The subject only comes to be because of its relationship with the
other. But the other is more than simply the other person; the other
is also the subject's subjection to the order of sexual difference that
gives it meaning and direction. But sexual identity is not the only
way in which the social pervades the life of the subject. Language
and the subject's relation to it emerge as fundamental in the determination of subjectivity. In fact, as we have seen, for Lacan it is
precisely through language that sexual identity is produced in the
subject. Having seen how subjectivity is inherently sexed—for
Levinas in his use of sex to describe the notion of otherness and
responsibility, for Lacan in his presentation of the subject as sexed

from the start and in our every understanding of it—we now move to a fuller explanation of what the sexed subject *is* by turning to language and the linguistic systems that undergird the very existence of their thought. The linguistic order emerges into their respective systems of thought as that by which for Levinas the subject becomes situated, grounded, and that by which for Lacan the subject, again, comes to be. In this, the subject finds itself subjected to laws and orders that are other—a system of meaning in which the subject places itself. Yet, it is in this linguistic order that the subject creates for itself moments of resistance to the dominance of the totality of being. For both Levinas and Lacan, the linguistic order is a site of conformity and resistance, a site of totality and infinity. However, the linguistic order has very specific meanings for both Levinas and Lacan. Whereas for Lacan the linguistic is primarily a symbolic order, and an order of meaning and signification, for Levinas the linguistic has a special relation to the ontological, a special relationship to Being itself. For Levinas, then, the resistance of the subject to the linguistic is a resistance of the singular in the face of the universal, a resistance of the one *for* the other in place of the one *and* the other as parts of the whole. In this, the subject who emerges as constituted by but resistant to the totality of language is a posthumanist subject, bound to the other but still whole in itself, resistant in its power to resist. For Lacan, however, the linguistic order is the end in itself, is its only justification; language is the first and last word. Resistance, according to Lacan, can only come from within the system itself, in the holes in language, and in the overdetermining power of the system itself. In this, the linguistic order indeed constructs in the subject a split, a breach. Here, Lacan's linguistic subject is at its most antihumanist, for in refusing to be a self, a unity in and of itself, it also refuses to be a unified *subject*, for its one and only master also orders that subject in contradictory directions. By examining these moments in Levinas and Lacan, we will again gain greater insight into their singular projects and further understand the ways in which they differently order their shared investments in certain basic ideas—

in this case the importance and primacy of language in structuring the subject and its subjectivity.

The face of the other person is always the call of the other; approaching is always a summoning. Responsibility is a being called into responsibility. From the outset the ethical subject is one bound by language, bound by the linguistic call of the other, the accusation and imperative "Thou shalt not kill (me)." This emphasis on the importance of the linguistic nature of the call of responsibility is present from *Totality and Infinity* onward. However, it is not until *Otherwise than Being* that language receives Levinas's full attention, as a particular issue that needs to be elucidated as a central feature of his critique of philosophy. Perhaps it is the moving away from metaphysics that compels Levinas to a more conscious look at language. Indeed, language, and specifically "ethical language," becomes the central mode through which he defines his understanding of the ethical—substitution, the hostage, expiation, all become the tropes through which Levinas articulates his program. Our focus here, however, is slightly different. We are not simply concerned with the turn to language as the means by which Levinas presents his critique. We are concerned with Levinas's specific evaluation of language as it relates to philosophy and to the ethical, as it relates to Being and to beings, as it relates to totality and to infinity. In the fascinating juxtaposition between the saying and the said we gain further insight into the Levinasian project, and see again the further shift away from the metaphysical language of the earlier works. And in so doing, we see the Levinasian subject emerge in more detail, now not simply as a subject struggling against totality and toward infinity, now not simply as a subject who emerges as ethical before it is ontological, but also as a subject immersed in a linguistic system, and as such as a linguistic subject struggling to put forth her responsibility before and behind the system of language/Being that structures her; she is a subject who, through language, is at one and the same time part of and rebelling against the system that does and does not contain her.

Chapter 2 of *Otherwise than Being*, entitled "Intentionality and Sensing," begins the second section of the work, "The Exposition."[1] True to form, Levinas begins this expository section with the pseudo-Heideggerian question: What is the role of being in philosophy and our critique of philosophy? He writes: "A philosopher seeks, and expresses, truth. Truth, before characterizing a statement or a judgment, consists in the exhibition of being. But what shows itself, in truth, under the name of being? And who looks?" (AE/OTB 23). And, from the beginning, Levinas answers in decidedly anti-Heideggerian terms. As for what being shows, Levinas writes:

> What shows itself under the name being? This name is not unequivocal. Is it a noun or a verb? Does the word being designate an entity, ideal or real, that is, or this entity's *process of being*, its *essence*? And does this word *designate*? No doubt it does designate. But does it only designate. For if it only designates, then, even taken as a verb, it is a noun. And the process captured by the designation, even if it is a movement, shows itself, but is immobilized and fixed in the *said*. Does this mystery of being and entities, their difference, disturb us already? . . . If this difference shows itself in the said, in words (which are not epiphenomenal), if it belongs to *monstration* as such, it belongs on the same plane as being, whose hide-and-seek game is indeed essential. But if monstration is a modality of signification, we would have to go back from the *said* to the *saying*. The said and the non-said do not absorb all the saying, which remains on the side of, or goes beyond, the said. [AE 43–44/ OTB 23]

The discussion here is reminiscent of Heidegger's (1992) discussion in *Being and Time*, but Levinas goes further. For one thing, where Heidegger sees the lack of understanding in what the word

---

1. The reading that follows is an interpretation of language in Levinas as it relates to ethical subjectivity. For a discussion that focuses on Levinas's use of "saying" and "said," see Colin Davis's treatment in *Levinas: An Introduction* (1996, pp. 74–79).

"being" designates, Levinas sees something beyond designation itself. Additionally, Levinas interprets this question of designation as a properly linguistic question. And here is where Levinas will begin to take the discussion someplace new, for while he has already shown the insufficiency of Heideggerian ontology in *Totality and Infinity*, it is *Otherwise than Being*'s focus on language that marks Levinas's shift away from metaphysics into new territory.

Levinas continues: even as the question of "what" points to something beyond itself, this question remains within the realm of meaning, and as such within the realm of being:

> The question enunciates a "what?" "what is it?" "what is it that it is?" Concerning what is it wants to know what it is. The "what?" is already wholly enveloped with being, has eyes only for being, and already sinks into being. Concerning the being of what is, it wants to know what it is. The question—even "what is being?"—then questions with respect to being, with respect to what is precisely in question. The answer required is from the start in terms of being, whether one understands by it entity or being of entities, entity or being's essence. The question "what" is thus correlative of what it wishes to discover, and already has recourse to it. Its quest occurs entirely within being, in the midst of what it is seeking. It is ontology, and at the same time has a part in the effectuation of the very being it seeks to understand. If the question "what?" in its adherence to being is at the origin of all thought (can it be otherwise, as long as thought proceeds by determinate terms?), all research and all philosophy go back to ontology, to the understanding of the being of entities, the understanding of essence. Being would be not only what is most problematical; it would be what is most intelligible. [AE 44/OTB 23–24]

Again, the critique of ontology at its strongest. If the question "what" is caught up in Heidegger's understanding of how phenomena show themselves, then the question "what" is caught up within the ontological gesture. And so, the focus on the question "what" is insufficient, for it continually leads back into the Heideggerian labyrinth of being, continually refers us back to the question of ontology—"what *is*"—and, in turn, to the question of *fundamental* ontology—"What is *being*?" Interestingly, Levinas makes the claim that this question is not the least understood, as Heidegger would have it, but rather the very condition of understanding. Being is intelligibility itself. But for Levinas, there is more there, more here, more than being. And it is to this more, to this something beyond, that Levinas wishes to look.

For Levinas, being, even in its primordiality, is not the first cause:

> The manifestation of being, the appearing, is indeed the pri-
> mary event, but the very primacy of the primacy is in the pres-
> ence of the present. A past more ancient than any present, a
> past which was never present and whose anarchical antiquity
> was never given in the play of dissimulations and manifesta-
> tions, a past whose other signification remains to be described,
> signifies over and beyond the manifestation of being, which thus
> would convey but a moment of this signifying signification. [AE
> 45/OTB 24]

As we inquire into the what, we point *beyond* but still remain fundamentally *within* being, and so we realize the need to look beyond the what to the who; it is there that the interval that separates same and other will become most clear. And the question "who?" inevitably leads us back to the question of subjectivity. But the question remains caught within the other as the same, within totality instead of the infinite. Still, even as we remain on the hither side of being, we are always pointing to a something beyond, to a something otherwise:

> In the diachrony which turned up under our pen above, with
> regard to the progressiveness of manifestation, one can suspect
> there is the interval that separates the same from the other, an
> interval that is reflected in manifestation. For manifestation,
> which one might have thought to be by right a fulgurating in-
> stant of openness and intuition, is discontinuous, and lasts from
> a question to the response. But this leads to surprise the Who
> that is looking, the identical subject, allegedly placed in the

openness of Being, as the crux of a diachronic plot (which remains to be determined) between the same and the other. [AE 45/OTB 24–25]

This interval that separates, this discontinuous manifestation is the question of "who" exceeding the question of "what" as same and other begin to take different paths, the one irreducible to the other.

In interrogating subjectivity, we will find this disturbance, for the subject as the one for the other, the one by the other, is, as such, an otherness that disturbs and disrupts our idea of self, our singular consciousness, and puts the same into question. Levinas writes:

> Subjectivity is the other in the same, in a way that also differs from that of the presence of the presence of interlocutors to one another in a dialogue, in which they are at peace and in agreement with one another. The other in the same determinative of subjectivity is the restlessness of the same disturbed by the other. This is not the correlation characteristic of intentionality, or even that of dialogue, which attests to essence by its essential reciprocity. The folding back of being upon itself, and the self formed by this fold, where the effect of being remains correlative with being, also does not go to the crux of subjectivity. [AE 46–47/OTB 25]

Subjectivity now is the impossibility of self-sameness, a disruption within the self that disallows a fully present intentionality of consciousness. Being cannot explain all of what it is to be a subject, for the question of "who" exceeds the question of "what" and being, open to beings, is not open to an otherness beyond being itself.

The subject that we discover here is not the subject of Kant and Hegel, not the subject of Plato and Heidegger. Rather, the subject is one who moves beyond knowing to a different modality, a subject who cannot subsume the other in the same.[2] Something other than the same lies in subjectivity, a beyond, a difference, and in the subject we will see more than being and its singular totality:

---

2. John Drabinski (2001) has a particularly instructive reading of subjectivity in Levinas's *Otherwise than Being*.

Being then would not be the construction of a cognitive subject, contrary to what idealism claims. The subject opening to the thought and truth of being, as it incontestably does, opens upon a way quite different from that which lets the subject be seen as an ontology or an understanding of being. Being would not derive from cognition. This not coming from cognition has a quite different meaning than ontology supposes. Being and cognition together signify in the proximity of the other and in a certain modality of my responsibility, this response preceding any question, this saying before the said. [AE 47/OTB 26]

Subjectivity cannot be explained as simple cognition, for cognition is the reduction of the other to the same. Something beyond the cognitive happens in the subject, in its being "for-the-other." It is the structure of the subject as for-the-other, the structure of subjectivity as responsibility, as substitution, which points to this beyond. Here we will find this "otherwise-than-being" that the title of the book promises, and here we will see something beyond Heidegger and philosophy, in all their totalizing glory. The saying is not reducible to the said, the other to the same, the otherwise to being:

Being signifies on the basis of the one-for-the-other, of substitution of same for the other. Both being and the vision of being refer to a subject that has risen earlier than being and cognition, earlier than and on this side of them, in an immemorial time which a reminiscence could not recuperate as an a priori. The "birth" of being in the questioning where the cognitive subject stands would thus refer to a before the questioning, to the anarchy of responsibility, as it were on this side of all birth. We will try, with the notion of the saying without the said, to expose such a modality of the subjective, an otherwise than being . . . in this very finitude (of the subject), taken as an outcome of the-one-for-the-other structure characteristic of proximity, we already catch sight of the excellence, the height and the signification, of responsibility, that is, or sociality, an order to which finite truth—being and consciousness—are subordinate. [AE 47–48/OTB 26]

The saying and the said: in these Levinas sets out to expose the modality of the otherwise-than-being, the possibility of a subject who, in its very finitude, in its very limiting by the other, points to and takes part in something beyond, in something different. Notice the metaphors that Levinas here employs—proximity and excellence, with excellence as height and signification. The language is both similar to and different from the language of the earlier works. The modality of the subjectivity of the other is not only over and above us, but now also near, proximate. This proximity we have to excellence, the excellence of the other, is our "birth" as subjects, our birth into our an-archic responsibility, and it is in the linguistic possibility of saying before, beyond, and without the said that this responsibility comes to light.

To get to the difference between the saying and the said, which we will define below, Levinas first takes us through that which leads us to the understanding of the subject as linguistic: temporality.[3] Where Levinas argued that it was in the move from the question "what?" to the question "who?" that we made the move to the possibility of a beyond being, strictly speaking the question "who?" remains caught within the grasp of being, as does the question "what?" for the "who-ness" of the who is still a question of cognition and consciousness, of knowing. Only the same can know, and the same is the realm of the one, of being. As Levinas writes: "The question 'who is looking?' is also ontological. Who is this *who*? In this form the question asks that 'the looker' be identified with one of the beings already known" (AE 48–49/OTB 27). By focusing on this question and in turn being turned back to being, the attempt to move beyond would fail. However, for Levinas, time acts as a mechanism of disruption through which subjectivity moves beyond the simple narrative line, and as such moves beyond the same and the one, precisely because the narrative exposure of truth in being is contradictory, and thus implies a rupture in being itself. This

---

3. As temporality will be one of the subjects of Chapter 4 of this work, we will make only a few preliminary remarks about its role in Levinas's argument here.

being is time, and time is in turn the foundation of the beyond. Levinas writes: "The manifestation cannot occur as a fulguration in which the totality of being shows itself to the totality of being, for this 'showing itself to' indicates a getting out of phase which is precisely time, that astonishing divergence of the identical form itself!" (AE 50–51/OTB 28). In time, in the getting out of phase, being cannot recover its totality, and so it opens up a space for the beyond in the rupture of its self-sameness (over time). He writes:

> The getting out of phase of the instant, the "all" pulling off from the "all"—the temporality of time—makes impossible, however, a recuperation in which nothing is lost. There is a disclosing of being; disengaged from its identity, from itself (what we are here calling a getting out of phase) and rediscoveries of truth; between what shows itself and the aim it fulfills there is monstration . . . There is remission of time and tension of the recapture, relaxation and tension without a break, without a gap. There is not a pure distancing from the present, but precisely re-presentation, that is, a distancing in which the present of truth is already or still is; for a representation is a recommencement of the present which in its "first time" is for the second time; it is a retention and a projection, between forgetting and expecting, between memory and project. Time is reminiscence and reminiscence is time, the unity of consciousness and essence. [AE 51/OTB 28–29]

Levinas proceeds to a detailed critique of Husserl on time, in which the basic conclusion is that Husserl reduces time to events, and in so doing makes way for the Heideggerian reduction of being to a noun.[4] Even as a questionable reading of Husserl (horizonality is never a question of simple presence of events in Husserl), Levinas is able to move the conversation forward, for in exploding the presence of time, Levinas takes us further into the idea of a beyond being. To do so, Levinas wants to

---

4. This is, of course, a fair characterization of neither Husserl nor Heidegger. Still, one can see how Levinas could have read his teachers as making these claims.

view time as a flowing, as a verb that resists reduction to the noun.[5] He writes:

> The verb [to be] understood as a noun designating an event, when applied to the temporalization of time, would make it resound as an event, whereas every event already presupposes time. Time's modification without change, the putting of the identical out of phase with itself, teems behind the transformations and the endurance, and, as aging, even within endurance. And yet a verb perhaps comes into its very verbalness by ceasing to name actions and events, ceasing to name. It is here that a word "has its own ways," unique of their kind, irreducible to symbolization which names or evokes. The verb *to be* tells of the flowing of time as though language were not unequivocally equivalent to denomination, as though in *to be* the verb first came to function as a verb, and as though this function refers to the teeming and mute itching of that modification without change that time operates. [AE 60–61/OTB 34]

Time is now not simply the flowing of one event into another. Rather, time is the possibility of a flowing beyond events themselves, a flowing where phenomena are put "out of phase" and the sameness of being is disrupted as the present remains always out of our grasp. The verb "to be" is beyond the be-ing of being.

Language is that which will provide the mechanism by which the verbness of being can emerge and time can stand as the site of the otherwise than being. According to Levinas, "Language is . . . not reducible to a system of signs doubling up beings and relations; that conception would be incumbent on us if words were nouns. Language seems rather to be an excrescence of the verb. And qua verb it already bears sensible life—temporalization and being's essence" (AE 61/OTB 35). Language is more than a system of signs, more than a collection of nouns. While language must include these things, it cannot be reduced to them. Rather, language is the

---

5. Here the key issue is time as a verb, for Husserl, of course, viewed time as "flowing" through retentive and protentive horizons.

possibility of activity, of action beyond events—language is the verb. But language is also the site of the same, also the site of signification, of giving meaning. Levinas tells us:

> But language is also a system of nouns. Denomination designates or constitutes identities in the verbal or temporal flow of sensation. Through the opening that temporalization works in the sensible, disclosing it by its very passing, assembling it by retention and memory . . . the word identifies "this as that," states with meaning: "this as that." In their meaning entities show themselves to be identical unities . . . Identification is kerygmatical. The said is not simply a sign or an expression of a meaning; it proclaims and establishes this as that . . . Before all receptivity an already said before language exposes or, in every meaning of the term, signifies (proposes and orders) experience, giving to historical languages spoken by peoples a locus, enabling them to orient or polarize the diversity of the thematized as they choose. [AE 61–62/OTB 35–36]

Identification is the word become flesh, as significating experience. Thus, in language entities show themselves as phenomena, as entities with an essence that can be proclaimed and uncovered.

Language is both sign and temporalization, both noun and verb. It is here, in this duality of language, in its status as the site of the same, of meaning and signification, and in its site as rupture through the temporal flowing of the verb, that language emerges as the definitive mode of the subject's taking part in both being and its otherwise, in both the said and the saying. Levinas writes:

> Language qua said can then be conceived as a system of nouns identifying entities, and then as a system of signs doubling up the beings, designating substances, events and relations by substantives or other parts of speech derived from substantives, designating identities—in sum, designating. But also, and with as much right, language can be conceived as the verb in a predicative proposition in which the substances break

down into modes of being, modes of temporalization. Here
language does not build up the being of entities, but exposes
the silent resonance of the essence. [AE 69–70/OTB 40]

Language is not simply a system for the re-presentation of objects
of our thought. It is also a system in which something else is in
fact signified. Language is the system of the said, the noun, but not
that only. It is also, and more profoundly, the system of the saying, the verb.

Perhaps here we need to back up and better define our terminology. For Levinas, the "said" and the "saying" are roughly defin-
able as, respectively, the noun and the verb, as the stabilizing "what"
that is being said and the disruptive "act" of saying something. And
it is in this act of saying that we move beyond the ontological and
point to an otherwise-than-being, and this otherwise-than-being will
be that which signifies our subjectivity. We will become subjects in
the verb and in the other, not in the noun and in the same. To begin,
Levinas writes:

> But is the power to say in man, however strictly correlative to the
> said its function may be, in the service of being? If man were only
> a saying correlative with the logos, the subjectivity could as well
> be understood as a function or as an argument of being. But the
> signification of saying goes beyond the said. It is not an ontology
> that raises up the speaking subject; it is the signifyingness of say-
> ing going beyond the essence that can justify the exposedness of
> being, ontology. [AE 66/OTB 37–38]

If saying were only correlative with the said, then language would
not go beyond being. But language does go beyond being in the
saying that exceeds the said, in the fact of the speaking subject.
Ontology is not the foundation of the speaking subject, nor is ontology the subject's ultimate goal. It is that which lies beyond being
that stands as the alpha and the omega of the subject and its saying. Because the saying exceeds and precedes the said, the subject
exceeds and precedes being.

This does not mean that the saying is not tied to the said—the saying does *in part* signify the said. It does share in the ontology of signification:

> In correlation with the said . . . the saying itself is indeed thematized, exposes in essence even what is on the *hither side of ontology*, and flows into the temporalization of essence. And this thematization of saying does indeed bring out in it characteristics of consciousness: in the correlation of the saying and the said the said is understood as a noema of an intentional act, language contracts into thought, into thought which conditions speaking, thought that in the said shows itself to be an act supported by a subject, an *entity* as it were put in the "nominative," in a proposition. The saying and the said in their correlation delineate the subject–object structure. [AE 79/OTB 46]

The saying does expose the essence of being on this side of the ontological question, on the side of being. And here we return to both Heidegger and Husserl, for being is an act of consciousness grasping its object, a correlation of the act of thinking and the object thought. Thus there is a subject–object relation for the subject qua Husserlian subject. There are characteristics of consciousness in the saying. This does designate language as the re-presentation of objects for intersubjective exchange. But the saying still does something more.

What more does the saying do? It points elsewhere. Where it points is to the subject as for-the-other, as ethical:

> Over and beyond the thematization and the content exposed in it—entities and relations between entities shown in the theme—the aphonasis signifies as a modality of the approach to another . . . This saying, in the form of responsibility for the other, is bound to an irrecuperable, unrepresentable, past, temporizing according to a time with separate epochs, in a diachrony. An analysis that starts with proximity, irreducible to consciousness of . . . and describable, if possible, as an inversion of its intentionality, will recognize this responsibility to be a substitution. [AE 80/OTB 47]

The saying, over and beyond the said, signifies an approach to another. In saying we speak to, we approach the other, and in so doing we open ourselves up to the other's preexisting demands on us. Our saying as an opening up to the other is not an intentional grasping, but an openness to the other's demands on us, an openness to the other's response as a call to our prior responsibility. We do not try to comprehend the other; rather, we substitute ourselves for the other in approaching her and speaking.

As a relation with the other, the saying does not signify an action, an activity on the part of the subject. Rather, as substitution, the saying signifies a passivity, an absolute receptivity—an openness to the being of the other. The saying gives up its hold on the said, gives up its place as subject over an object, and instead presents itself as subject before a subject, and as such as subjected to the other. In the saying, the subject emerges as responsible:

> The act of saying will turn out to have been introduced here from the start as the supreme passivity of exposure to another, which is responsibility for the free initiatives of the other. Whence there is an "inversion" of intentionality which, for its part, always preserves before deeds accomplished enough "presence of mind" to assume them. There is an abandon of the sovereign and active subjectivity, of undeclined self-consciousness, as the subject in the nominative form in an aphonasis. [AE 81/OTB 47]

The saying introduces the subject as passive in the face of the other, as no longer sovereign, but instead as abandoned to the other's power. The approach of the other therefore engenders the response of the subject in the saying as passive receptor to the needs of the other. Levinas calls this the "de-posing of the subject" (AE 81/OTB 48). And the de-posing of the subject manifests itself as the subject's exposing itself to the other. As such, saying, linguistic communication in the predicative, is irreducible to the nominative of the said:

> Saying is communication, to be sure, but as a condition for all communication, as exposure. Communication is not reducible

to the phenomenon of truth and the manifestation of truth conceived as a combination of psychological elements; thought in an ego—will or intention to make this thought pass into another ego—message by a sign designating this thought—perception of the sign by another ego—deciphering of the sign. The elements of this mosaic are already in place in the antecedent exposure of the ego to the other, the non-indifference to another, which is not a simple "intention to address a message." The ethical sense of such an exposure to another, which the intention of making signs, and even the signifyingness of signs, presupposes, is now visible. [AE 82/ OTB 48]

Communication is not the exchange of truth, understood as the correlation of sign and object; rather, communication is exposure to the other, exposing oneself to the demands of the other. This non-indifference to the other is the ethical nature of exposure in the saying. Levinas continues: "Saying is a denuding, of the unqualifiable *one*, the pure *someone*, unique and chosen; that is, it is an exposedness to the other where no slipping away is possible" (AE 85/OTB 50). In exposing itself in the saying, the subject denudes itself, and in so doing allows itself to be signified as the unique one-for-the-other—the chosen. In this denuding, the subject cannot escape its chosenness; it alone is responsible for the other.

The saying is an other mode of temporality, an other way of viewing the world, in which the immemorial past is enacted in the non-presence of the now.[6] In the saying the subject points beyond itself and suggests something otherwise than its essence, its meaning, its signs and words. Although the said is what gets said, it is the saying that stands out in the act of saying; and the saying is constitutive of ethical subjectivity, is that which makes the subject the ethical. The saying is that which gives the subject the possibility, even the necessity, of reaching beyond itself, of being for-the-other. Through the saying, the subject can substitute itself for the other,

6. We will return to the idea of the immemorial past in Chapter 4.

and, in this, can come to be as subject, as subjected, as ethical. For Levinas, then, the ethical subject is the linguistic subject; and the linguistic subject, the ethical one.

We have already seen how the Lacanian subject is a sexed subject, and how subjectivity is inherently tied up in the sexual order. However our view of Lacanian subjectivity is incomplete without more detailed attention to the Symbolic order, in which we discover that the subject is first and foremost the subject *in language*. If the Mirror Stage essay introduced onto the psychoanalytic scene what was later to be termed the Imaginary, it is in the 1953 essay "The Function and Field of Speech and Language in Psychoanalysis," collected in Lacan (1966), that its counterpart, the Symbolic, gets its first explication. As such, this essay is easily marked as the all-important counterpart to the Mirror Stage. And like the Mirror Stage essay, "The Function and Field of Speech and Language in Psychoanalysis" has a rich and complex history. This essay, most often referred to as the "Rome Discourse," is without doubt a turning point in Lacan's writing career, and as such stands with the Mirror Stage as one of the two Lacanian texts that can truly be called seminal. Here Lacan offers the argument that the subject is a speaking subject, and that psychoanalysis is a theory of the speaking subject. In this section we will explicate Lacan's reading of the Symbolic through an examination of language and its relation to subjectivity—that is, language as a site of the structuring order of society, as the locus of our relation to the Phallus, as the enactment of the Law that governs the social and commodifies sexual difference, as the site of hidden meaning, and as the structure of the Unconscious. In so doing we can begin to extract from Lacan the foundations for an ethic of knowledge of the Unconscious as a possible outgrowth of the psychoanalytic encounter.

In the Rome Discourse, three things emerge as distinctively Lacanian: (1) the psychoanalytic focus on language; (2) the triadic structure Real – Imaginary – Symbolic; and (3) the Lacanian style. The question of the Lacanian style, the refusal of simple argumentation, the playing with philosophical logic, the highly didactic and arcane style of speaking and writing, the difficulty and obscurity of the text, have already haunted us in our attempts to read the Phallus. But even when Lacan is dealing with subjects seemingly straightforward, such as "language" or "speech," his style is no less difficult, no less challenging, and no easier to penetrate.

The real breakthrough of the Rome Discourse is the focus on the centrality of language in psychoanalytic discourse. Language, of course, is not a new theme in psychoanalysis; psychoanalysis is, after all, the "talking cure." Freud discovered psychoanalytic theory in the language of his patients, in the slips of the tongue, in the use of language to structure his patients' thoughts, defenses, symptoms, and, in the linguistic interpretation of dreams, located it in the slippage of meaning from one sign to another. Freud (1977) writes:

> Nothing takes place in psycho-analytic treatment but an interchange of words between the patient and the analyst. The patient talks, tells of his past experiences and present impressions, complains, confesses to his wishes and his emotional impulses. The doctor listens, tries to direct the patient's processes of thought, exhorts, forces his attention in certain directions, gives him explanations and observes the reactions of understanding or rejection which he in this way provokes in him. The uninstructed relatives of our patients, who are only impressed by visible and tangible things—preferably by actions of the sort that are to be witnessed at the cinema—never fail to express their doubts whether "anything can be done about the illness by mere talking." That, of course, is both short-sighted and an inconsistent line of thought. These are the same people who are so certain that patients are "simply imagining" their symptoms. Words were originally magic and to this day words have retained much of their ancient magical power. By words one person can make another blissfully happy or drive him to despair, by words the teacher conveys his knowledge to his pupils, by words the orator carries his audience with him and determines their judgments and decisions. Words provoke affects and are in general the means of mutual influence among men. Thus we shall not depreciate the use of words in psycho-

therapy and we shall be pleased if we can listen to the words
that pass between the analyst and his patient. [p. 17]

Clearly, words are of the utmost importance for Freud. Speech,
linguistic exchange, is the very foundation of psychoanalysis. But
it is in Lacan where the question of language gets its fullest attention, where language emerges as not simply a means to an end, but
rather as the very foundation not only of analysis, but also of subjectivity itself. And thus it is Lacan's main contribution to psychoanalysis to make it a theory of language. With regard to analysis
and to the theoretical basis of psychoanalysis as a science, Lacan
reminds us that "whether it sees itself as an instrument of healing,
or training, or of exploration in depth, psychoanalysis has only a
single medium: the patient's speech" (E 247/E 40). Therefore, in
true Freudian fashion, it is with the patient's speech that we will
begin in order to see what Lacan has to say about the talking cure.

As speech is what constitutes the analytic relationship, it is
essential to understand that for Lacan speech is inherently relational, intersubjective. He writes: "I shall show that there is no
speech without a reply, even if it is met only with silence, provided
that it has an auditor: this is the heart of its function in analysis"
(E 247/E 40). For analysis to work, the analyst must not only realize the importance of speech, but must also understand how speech
functions, how language operates in the spoken exchange. As Lacan
states: "But if the psychoanalyst is not aware that this is how the
function of speech operates, he will simply experience its appeal
all the more strongly, and if the first thing to make itself heard is
the void, it is within himself that he will experience it, and it is
beyond speech that he will seek a reality to fill this void" (E 247–
248/E 40).

Moving beyond speech to a "reality" leads both the analyst and
the patient to a false search for "truth." But analysis is not about
truth per se, although as we shall argue below it is about truth on
some level. Rather, analysis seeks understanding—understanding
of the nature of subjectivity, understanding that the subject was in

fact formed primarily through an exchange with the other. This is what analysis uncovers—the function of the Imaginary in structuring the Real and an understanding of the way in which the subject comes to find itself situated in the Symbolic:

> Does the subject not become engaged in an ever-growing dispossession of that being of his, concerning which—by dint of sincere portraits which leave its idea no less coherent, of rectifications that do not succeed in freeing its essence, of stays and defenses that do not prevent his statue from teetering, of narcissistic embraces that become like a puff of air in animating it—he ends up by recognizing that this being has never been anything more than his construct in the imaginary and that this construct disappoints all his certainties? For in this labor which he undertakes to reconstruct for another [the analyst], he rediscovers the fundamental alienation that made him construct it like another, [the [m]other] and which has always destined it to be taken from him by another. [the Father]. [E 249/E 42]

Thus the subject in analysis is meant to realize, to come to terms with, the fact of its alienation and the fictivity of its constructed sense of self. In so doing the subject will be able to realize the goal of analysis, "the advent of a true speech and the realization by the subject of his history in his relation to a future" (E 302/E 88). And it is only in the intersubjective relationship, in analysis, that the subject can come to these realizations; through the task of reconstructing for an other the subject comes to realize itself as an other.

The danger of analysis is the all-too-easy event of either the patient or the analyst reverting back to a search for truth, perhaps in the reification of the images of the Imaginary uncovered in analysis. Attaching objective status to analytic discoveries only further situates the subject in the false unity created by the Imaginary. Lacan writes: "The danger involved here is not that of the subject's negative reaction, but rather that of his capture in an objectification—no less imaginary than before—of his static state or of his 'statue,' in a renewed status of his alienation" (E 251/E 43). On the contrary, analysis must maintain the sense of uncertainty in the patient if it is to be successful, if any progress is to be made. And no one knows this better than the analyst. It is therefore with the analyst that the burden lies. And if the analyst is to be successful, he must himself avoid the search for truth, the search for something objective lying beyond the patient's speech:

> To impute to regression the reality of an actual relation to the object amounts to projecting the subject into an alienating illusion that does no more than echo an alibi of the psychoanalyst.

> It is for this reason that nothing could be more misleading for the analyst than to seek to guide himself by some supposed "contact" experienced with the reality of the subject. [E 252/E 44]

The analyst must be vigilant in his task, careful not to fall into the lures of his own Imaginary. Additionally, the analyst must not only realize for himself, but must also impute to the patient the fictive but real nature of all their findings—nothing is true in the sense of being an experience of some "reality of the subject," but everything is real for the subject, no matter if it corresponds (in a strict philosophical sense) to an external reality. Everything internal matters.

In uncovering the internal life of the patient, analysis is aimed at teaching the patient the prevalence of the Unconscious as a guiding force in his life. And it is through analysis that the subject can come into contact with her Unconscious. Lacan writes: "The unconscious is that part of the concrete discourse . . . that is not at the disposal of the subject in re-establishing the continuity of his conscious desire" (E 258/E 49). But how is one to uncover the Unconscious? After all, the Unconscious is unavailable to the patient; it is, as Lacan states, "that chapter of my history that is marked by a blank or occupied by a falsehood: it is the censored chapter" (E 259/E 50). Lacan reminds us that the Unconscious leaves its marks and so can, to some extent, be rediscovered:

> the truth [of the unconscious] can be rediscovered; usually it has already been written down elsewhere. Namely:
> —in monuments: this is my body. That is to say, the

hysterical nucleus of the neurosis in which the hysterical symptom reveals the structure of a language, and is deciphered like an inscription which, once recovered, can without serious loss be destroyed;

—in archival documents: these are my childhood memories, just as impenetrable as are such documents when I do not know their provenance;

—in semantic evolution: this corresponds to the stock of words, and acceptations of my own particular vocabulary, as it does to my style of life and to my character;

—in traditions, too, and even in the legends which, in a heroicized form, bear my history;

—and lastly, in the traces that are inevitably preserved by the distortions necessitated by the linking of the adulterated chapter to the chapters surrounding it, and whose meaning will be re-established by my exegesis. [E 259/E 50]

In the traces, the analyst can help the patient rediscover what has been repressed, what has been lost, and in so doing can help the patient come to terms with a past that is structuring a present around a fiction.

Whereas Lacan's treatment of analytic speech is instructive and original, it is in moving from the act of analytic speech to the question of language where Lacan makes the contributions that are properly known as "Lacanian."[7] In looking at the language that structures the "what" of analysis, Lacan turns our attention to the question of dreams, and in turn back to Freud. He writes:

---

7. We by no means want to underemphasize the importance Lacan places on analytic speech. One of the insights in Lacanian discourse that this book wishes to offer is its adherence to a central Freudian doctrine—that all theorizing is done out of the psychoanalytic session, and hence that everything begins and ends in and with analysis. It is, I believe, the inattention to Lacanian theory as rooted in analysis, fueled by a skipping over of the places where Lacan refers to the analytic scene, which so easily leads to many of the common misreadings of Lacan. For instance, reading the mirror stage and its consequents as actually "happening" in the life of the child, a questionable interpretation of an early infantile event, comes from reading the Mirror Stage essay without paying attention to Lacan's discussion of the patient in analysis and his dreams of fragmentation and struggle.

> If for a symptom, whether neurotic or not, to be admitted in
> psychoanalytic psychopathology, Freud insists on the minimum
> of overdetermination constituted by a double meaning (sym-
> bol of conflict long dead over and above its function in a *no less*
> *symbolic* present conflict), and if he has taught us to follow the
> ascending ramification of the symbolic lineage in the text of the
> patient's free associations, in order to map it out at the points
> where its verbal forms intersect with the nodal points of its
> structure, then it is already quite clear that the symptom resolves
> itself entirely in an analysis of language, because the symptom
> is itself structured like a language, because it is from language
> that speech must be delivered. [E 269/E 59]

Language is the origin of speech, and the foundation of dreams,
for dreams function symbolically, with images attempting to convey meanings, but with conflicted and multiple meanings being
conveyed, indeterminate and overdetermined at one and the same
time. The symbol does not convey its intended meaning directly,
being subjected to the processes of condensation and displacement.
Meaning, then, must be discerned in the gaps, in the slips, in the
associations. And it is these hidden meanings that give the symbol
its function and form:

> something [must emerge that] completes the symbol, thus mak-
> ing language of it. In order for the symbolic object freed from its
> usage to become the word freed from the *hic et nunc*, the differ-
> ence resides not in its material quality as sound, but in its eva-
> nescent being in which the symbol finds the permanence of the
> concept.
>
> Through the word—already a presence made absence—absence
> itself gives itself a name in that moment of origin. [E 276/E 65]

Through the word, then, meaning is conferred on the psychic symbol. And in the symbol we come to Lacan's idea of the Symbolic.
As Laplanche and Pontalis (1973) see it:

> Lacan's use of the notion of the Symbolic in psycho-analysis
> seems to us to have two aims:

a. To compare the structure of the unconscious with that of a language, and to apply to the former a method which has borne fruit in its application to linguistics.

b. To show how the human subject is inserted into a preestablished order which is itself symbolic in nature in Lacan's sense. [p. 440]

We have touched on the first aim, and we will return to the notion of the Symbolic, and the Unconscious, as "structured like a language" in the next section of this chapter when we look at Lacan's other important essay on linguistics and psychoanalysis, his 1957 essay "The Agency of the Letter in the Unconscious," collected in Lacan (1966). Here, we want to focus on the second aim: to show how the Symbolic is the placing of the subject into a preestablished order. For Lacan, all speech is ordered by language, by a prior system of signification that gives it meaning and order. As speech is ordered by language, so, too, is the speaking subject: "It is the world of words that creates the world of things—the things originally confused in the *hic et nunc* of the all in the process of coming-into-being—by giving its concrete being to their essence, and its ubiquity to what has always been . . . Man speaks, then, but it is because the symbol has made man" (E 276/E 65).

Now we see what Lacan means by the Symbolic: the Symbolic is not simply the power of one thing to represent an other; it is also the order in which the person becomes the subject—the order of language. That order of language is the well of the "meaning of the symbol" upon which the subject can and will draw in creating a self-understanding, in creating an "identity." All identity is identification, and it is the Symbolic that offers the meanings with which the subject can identify. And, as we have already seen in Chapter 2, that order of language, that "repository of meaning," is governed by one overarching theme—sexual difference as determined by the law of the Father.[8] We return to Oedipus:

---

8. The phrase "repository of meaning" to describe the Symbolic was kindly suggested to me by Elizabeth Weed.

This is precisely where the Oedipus complex—in so far as we continue to recognize it as covering the whole field of our experience with its signification—may be said, in this connection, to mark the limits that our discipline assigns to subjectivity; namely, what the subject can know of his unconscious participation in the movement of the complex structures of marriage ties, by verifying the symbolic effects in his individual existence of the tangential movement towards incest that has manifested itself ever since the coming of a universal community. [E 277/E 66]

The Oedipus complex emerges as the basic structure around which society is ordered, and it is language itself that makes Oedipus real in the Symbolic. In our bowing to the order of sexual difference and its prohibitions, Oedipus is actualized as primordial Law:

> The primordial Law [Oedipus] is therefore that which in regulating marriage ties superimposes the kingdom of culture on that of a nature abandoned to the law of mating. The prohibition against incest is merely its subjective pivot, revealed by the modern tendency to reduce to the mother and the sister the objects forbidden to the subject's choice, although full license outside of these is not yet entirely open. [E 277/E 66]

The Law now presents itself as the structure of subjectivity, and hence of language, our means of ascending into subjectivity, for it is only through language that we can become speaking subjects. Language gives us the language of Oedipus, its laws and prohibitions, in its very structure: "This law, then, is revealed clearly enough as identical with an order of language" (E 277/E 66). In this Lacan has now shown us the means by which the subject is produced in the order of language, the Symbolic. The Symbolic rests on the retroactive creation of the Imaginary, to be sure, for it is only with recourse to the Unconscious that language can impose its power on the subject. But it is the Symbolic that orders the subject, the Symbolic that makes the rules—the rules that are always to be broken in and by the Imaginary.

As is the production of the Imaginary, the production of the Symbolic subject is achieved via the other on at least two levels. On the first level, language is an other to the subject, as it exists as an order into which he is initiated, an order passed down from parent to child, from father to son:

> Symbols in fact envelop the life of man in a network so total that they join together, before he comes into the world, those who are going to engender him "by flesh and blood"; so total that they bring to his birth, along with the gifts of the stars, if not with the gifts of the fairies, the shape of his destiny; so total that they give the words that will make him faithful or renegade, the law of the acts that will follow him right to the very place where he is not yet and even beyond his death; and so total that through him his end finds its meaning in the last judgment, where the Word absolves his being or condemns it. [E 279/E 68]

Every move the subject makes is subject to an order that precedes her; every attempt at rebellion against the system is, as much as is every act of complicity, already determined by the order itself. The Symbolic is the ever-present, the overarching, the fact that cannot be escaped, and however the child comes to it, she is always already structured by it, this other, this Law. Which is not to say that there is no freedom, no creativity, no individuality. On the contrary, the Symbolic not only allows but also encourages the individual; it is in the individual that the Symbolic can have its strongest power, for the individual is alone in his resistance to the Symbolic.

On the second level, the Symbolic is an other to itself. The child moving from the intersubjective identification with its mirror image into a triangulated social situation governed by law and language does so not according to laws emerging from some fictive self *outside* of language, sexual difference, and the Symbolic, but according to those of the other. The construction of the subject in the Symbolic, then, rests on the prior construction of the I in the Imaginary. In this, the Symbolic rests on the Imaginary. Recall that the patient in analysis becomes frustrated with the process of the talking cure, frustrated with language. In asking the origin of such frustration, Lacan sets out the basic idea so fundamental to the construction of the subject—the originary alienation of self by other in the construction of the Imaginary—only now he situates this alienation within the subject's new place in the Symbolic. Looking back on this passage from earlier:

> Shall we ask instead where the subject's frustration comes from? . . . Is it not . . . a matter of a frustration inherent in the very discourse of the subject? Does the subject not become engaged in an ever-growing dispossession of that being of his, concerning which—by dint of sincere portraits which leave its idea no less incoherent, of rectifications that do not succeed in freeing its essence, of stays and defenses that do not prevent his statue from tottering, of narcissistic embraces that become like a puff of air in animating it—he ends up by recognizing that this being has never been anything more than his construct in the imaginary and that this construct disappoints all his certainties? For in this labor which he undertakes to reconstruct for another, he discovers the fundamental alienation that made him construct it like another, and which has always destined it to be taken from him by another. [E 249/E 41–42]

Here we come to see the dependence of the Symbolic on the Imaginary. And given that the Imaginary is only ever discovered from the perspective of the subject already in language, so, too, is the Imaginary dependent on the Symbolic. The two are in a constant, tension-filled interdependent relation. There is no one without the other.

Having laid out his theory of psychoanalysis as grounded in speech and his theory of the subject as located in language, Lacan now integrates these two ideas in a theory of psychoanalytic technique as the coming to terms with the subject's situatedness. As he tells us: "Bringing psychoanalytic experience back to speech and language as its grounding is of direct concern to its technique" (E 289/E 77). And the proper field of psychoanalytic work is to offer the patient an understanding of his place in both the Imaginary and the Symbolic orders. Such a realization expels the mirages of unity and control from the subject, instead offering her a new understanding of her own constructedness: "Let me simply say that this is what leads me to object to any reference to totality in the individual, since it is the subject who introduces division into the individual, as well as into the collectivity that is his equivalent. Psychoanalysis is properly that which reveals both the one and the other to be no more than mirages" (E 292/E 80).

To make the subject aware of such division, and in turn of such fictions as "identity" and "self," the analyst must introduce the subject to his unknown, and specifically, his unconscious desire:

> We always come back, then, to our double reference to speech and to language. In order to free the subject's speech, we introduce him into the language of his desire, that is to say, into the *primary language* in which, beyond what he tells us of himself, he is already talking to us unknown to himself, and, in the first place, in the symbols of the symptom. [E 293/E 81]

To engender the cure, the analyst works with the symbols given to him in the language of the patient. Only by looking at the actual words can the analyst get beneath the words to the meaning they symbolize—only by looking at language as a system of unconscious signification can it attain any meaning. And the analyst does this by pressing the patient about the symbols present in his speech: "There is therefore no doubt that the analyst can play on the power of the symbol by evoking it in a carefully calculated fashion in the semantic resonances of his remarks" (E 294/E 82).

This evocation results in a twofold process: the affective response and the symbolic response. In the affective response, the patient experiences the repeated feelings of love and aggression toward the analyst and his interpretation; in the symbolic response, the subject is forced to look at her speech as symbolic, as having meaning, and in so doing allows herself as subject to begin to understand the role of the Unconscious in its relationship to a linguistic system.[9] Lacan writes: "For in its symbolizing function speech is

---

9. The affective and the symbolic are the two elements of transference, aspects that we will explore at length in Chapter 4.

moving towards nothing less than a transformation of the subject to whom it is addressed by means of the link that it establishes with the one who emits it—in other words, by introducing the effect of the signifier" (E 296/E 83). In seeing herself as an effect of the signifying system of language, the subject comes to see herself as defined by the discourse of the other and as defined by her Unconscious; in this we come not only to see the Symbolic as the field of the Other, but also as the field of the Unconscious.

The speech exchange between the analyst and patient is meant to provoke the patient to these realizations. It is less the *interpretation* the analyst offers than the *idea* of interpretation that pushes the patient to his realization. In this, language as a system itself is not simply a system of exchange of meaning, but is rather more fundamentally a system of exchange intended not to inform but rather to evoke, to solicit a response from the other:

> For the function of language is not to inform but to evoke.
>
> What I seek in speech is the response of the other. What constitutes me as subject is my question. In order to be recognized by the other, I utter what was only in view of what will be. In order to find him, I call him by a name that he must assume or refuse in order to reply to me. [E 299/E 86]

It is in speech that we find language ("Speech is in fact the gift of language" [E 301/E 87]), and in language that we find subjectivity. Moreover, in finding subjectivity, we find ourselves as subjects constructed by this exchange of language, and as such we find ourselves in the discourse of not only a past and a present but also a future to which the past and present always point: "I identify myself in language, but only by losing myself in it like an object. What is realized in my history is not the past definite of what was, since it is no more, or even the present perfect of what has been in what I am, but the future anterior of what I shall have been for what I am in the process of becoming" (E 299–300/E 86).

And so we again come to the final goal of analysis: "Analysis can have for its goal only the advent of a true speech and the

realization by the subject of his history in his relation to a future"
(E 302/E 88). And this realization is the realization of the Unconscious. Language, then, is the first and last cause in psychoanalysis—that which makes us subjects, and that by which we realize
ourselves as subjects. And it is only in speech that a subject can
become properly aware of her Unconscious—that is, ethical.

We have presented the basic trajectory of the subject in both Levinas
and Lacan. Now what we need to begin to ask is what these theories might offer us in the construction of a theory of the ethical
subject. We have seen how, for both Levinas and Lacan, language
is an essential component of a system of thought in which the subject finds itself ordered by a system of laws and meanings—by an
other. Moreover, for both Levinas and Lacan, language itself has
an other. Again, the similarities are striking. However, whereas for
Levinas this other is beyond the order of meaning set out in the
linguistic system, for Lacan this other is in language itself, in the
Symbolic order, for the Symbolic is the place where we access
the Unconscious, that "other site of meaning" which, because it is
in conflict with both consciousness and with itself, causes the patient conflict; the Unconscious, therefore, is the order to which the
patient is seeking access. Where Levinas sees a conception of the
ethical beyond language, and therefore beyond ontology, Lacan sees
the Unconscious as both prefiguring and figured by the Symbolic
order, as both the prior to and the retroactive effect of the construction of the subject in the Symbolic.[10] Now, by reading Levinas and
Lacan side by side, we will continue to see not simply how they
both diverge from interpretations of the linguistic order as unified
and complete, but also how, with each moving in a different direction—one toward a non-ontological response to the other person
in language, the other toward an uncovering of the knowledge of

---

10. On the concept of "prior to" we must look at Lacan's treatment of the
drive, a psychoanalytic concept that he deals with in the Seminar, Book XI, *The
Four Fundamental Concepts of Psychoanalysis* (1973/1981), to which we will turn
in Chapter 4.

the hidden recesses of the Unconscious—they may offer resources for a theory of the ethical subject.

We begin with Levinas.

First, let us further consider the exact relationship between language and subjectivity and, in turn, between language and the ethical. For Levinas, language as a system of meaning and signs is inherently bound up in the order of being. But if there is a beyond to being, it is expressed to us in that which lies beyond language as a system of signs, instead directing our focus to speech as the possibility of communication; that is, the beyond comes to us in the saying, not the said.

In the 1967 article "Language and Proximity," collected in French in Levinas (1967) and in English in Levinas (1993), Levinas presents an earlier version of some of the themes later to be explicated in *Otherwise than Being*.[11] Having laid out his theory of discourse as connected to sensibility and being, Levinas asks if perhaps there is not something that lies behind discourse: "One may indeed wonder whether, behind discourse, there does not lie hidden a philosophical thought distinct from discourse and refractory to its prestiges and pretensions, and whether there it does not aim at the singular which discourse cannot express without idealizing" (EDE 222/CPP 113).

What is interesting in this formulation, and in this article, is the prominence that Levinas ascribes to the idea of the "singular" and the possibility of a "singularity without universality." For Levinas, language is a system of universal meaning, where the truth for one is the truth for all because all take part in the same system. The way out of this paradigm is by positing a singularity that is not taken in by the universalizing gesture of being, not subsumed into the totality of language as a system of signs. The space where that singularity exists is in the verbal interchange, in speaking as contact. Levinas writes:

---

11. I will move *very* quickly here, as most of what we find in "Language and Proximity" we have already discussed at the beginning of this chapter. I only want to use this text here to highlight a few key points that will help illuminate the differences between Levinas and Lacan on language and subjectivity.

> For us the difficulty lies elsewhere: the hypothesis that the re-
> lationship with an interlocutor would still be a knowing reduces
> speech to the solitary or impersonal exercise of a thought,
> whereas already the kerygma which bears its ideality is, in ad-
> dition, a proximity between myself and the interlocutor, and
> not our participation in a transparent universality. Whatever
> the message transmitted by speech, the speaking is contact.
>
> One must admit then that there is in speech a relationship with
> a singularity located outside of the theme of the speech, a sin-
> gularity that is not thematized by the speech but is approached.
> [EDE 224/CPP 115]

The linguistic encounter, then, is the encounter with a singularity
that cannot be reduced to membership in a universal. And that
singularity is the approach of the other person:

> Proximity is *by itself* a signification. The subject has gone into
> the openness of the intentionality and the vision. The orienta-
> tion of the subject upon the object has become a proximity, the
> intentional has become ethical . . . The *ethical* does not desig-
> nate an inoffensive attenuation of passionate particularisms,
> which would introduce the human subject into a universal order
> and unite all rational beings, like ideas, in a kingdom of ends.
> It indicates a reversal of the subjectivity which is open upon
> beings and always in some measure represents them to itself,
> positing them and taking them to be such or such . . . into a
> subjectivity that enters into contact with a singularity, exclud-
> ing identification in the ideal, excluding thematization and rep-
> resentation—an absolute singularity, as such unrepresentable.
> This is the original language, the foundation of the other one.
> [EDE 225/CPP 116]

For Levinas, then, it is this original approach of the other that in
fact founds language and therefore grounds the very possibility of
exchange. Levinas calls this approach, this "saying," a "sign": "This
saying no doubt precedes the language that communicates propositions and messages: it is a sign given from one to another by prox-

LINGUISTIC SUBJECTIVITY AND THE SPEAKING SUBJECT **147**

imity about proximity" (EDE 231/CPP 121). This approach, this proximity, is the original moment, the pre-original language, in which signification is rooted, in which language takes hold:

> A sign is given from one to the other before the constitution of any system of signs, any common place formed by culture and sites, a sign given from null site to null site. The fact that a sign, exterior to the system of evidences, comes into proximity while remaining transcendent, is the very essence of language prior to every particular language.

> This understanding passing from singularity to singularity is able to create for itself the verbal or non-verbal signs of a particular language. [EDE 231–232/CPP 122]

The saying acts as a sign of my being for-the-other. So, through the ethical encounter, through the linguistic approach of the other, language is not only transcended, but language itself also comes to be.

We have now established a coherent, though not complete, picture of the Levinasian theory of the subject. In the preceding chapters, we have presented the basics of what the subject is and how it is constituted. Now we must ask, what does this theory of the ethical offer to a vision of ethical subjectivity? First, it offers a way out of the system of rules and meanings that language as a system imposes on us, a system to which we are inherently tied and that has time and again failed us. And, as Levinas rightly argues, all attempts to think the ethical within the confines of this system have ended in totality. But now, in seeing a beyond not only to being, but to language, and in taking the ethical out of the realm of the onto-philosophical and bringing it into the realm of the ethico-philosophical, we can approach the question from the level on which we operate—the interpersonal encounter. The "ethical encounter," according to Levinas, is still no phenomenal event to which we can all turn and that we are all able to see; but its impact remains, and its foundational power emerges as grounded in the encounter with the other person. Levinas, in his presentation of the saying and the said, then, begins to open a path in which sub-stitution can emerge as the foundation of our very subjectivity: the one-for-the-other is prior to any sense of the self, and in the act of approach—whether we call it the face, proximity, or the saying—the other establishes me as bound, as responsible, as held hostage, such that before I can enter into any contractual system of language and exchange, I am always already for-the-other.

How does this all compare with Lacan on the question of lan-guage? In turning psychoanalysis back to the Unconscious, Lacan succeeds in turning Freudianism back to its roots; in connecting the Unconscious to language and the Symbolic, Lacan makes his most radical argument. In Lacan, as we have seen, we find the Unconscious explicitly connected to language, and in turn to the Symbolic—the only order in which we actually live. In "The Agency of the Letter in the Unconscious, or Reason since Freud," Lacan sets out the basic formula: "what the psychoanalytic experience discovers in the Unconscious is the whole structure of language" (E 495/E 147).[12] What does this mean? For Lacan it means several things. First and foremost it means that the Unconscious is a sys-tem of representational meaning. To demonstrate this, Lacan draws on Saussure and the algorithm Sign = s/S (signified over signifier). Inverting this formula—and instead writing S/s (signifier over sig-nified)—Lacan emphasizes the importance of the signified as cre-ating its referent, and in turn the priority of language over being. In stressing this, Lacan argues for "the notion of the incessant slid-ing of the signified under the signifier," and in this, the slipperi-ness of language in general, and meaning in specific (E 502/E 154).

How does this argument about language and the sign connect to the Symbolic as the site of the Unconscious? In the second sec-tion of the Agency article, Lacan returns to Freud's texts and begins to show what he means by saying the letter is "in the unconscious"

---

12. Again, I will move somewhat quickly here, as I only want to highlight the key points that will help drive home the difference between Levinas and Lacan on the question of language and subjectivity.

(E 509/E 159). Repeating the prevalence of the Unconscious in the psyche, Lacan states: "The psychoanalytic experience does nothing other than establish that the Unconscious leaves none of our actions outside its field" (E 514/E 163). And it is this prevalence of the Unconscious that leads Lacan to his indictment of the Cartesian cogito:

> Is the place that I occupy as the subject of a signifier concentric or excentric, in relation to the place I occupy as subject of the signified?—that is the question.
>
> It is not a question of knowing whether I speak of myself in a way that conforms to what I am, but rather of knowing whether I am the same as that of which I speak. And it is not at all inappropriate to use the word "thought" here. For Freud uses the term to designate the elements involved in the unconscious, that is, the signifying mechanisms that we now recognize as being there.
>
> Is it nonetheless true that the philosophical *cogito* is at the center of the mirage that renders modern man so sure of being himself even in his uncertainties about himself, and even in the mistrust he has learned to practice against the traps of self-love? [E 516–517/E 165]

This attack on the self-certainty of the cogito, based on the slipperiness of the signifier over the signified ("the S and the s of the Saussurian algorithm are not on the same level, and man only deludes himself when he believes his true place is at their axis" [E 518/E 166]), leads Lacan to the following formula: "I am not wherever I am the plaything of my thought; I think of what I am where I do not think to think" (E 517/E 166). It is this indictment of Cartesian self-transparency, of the possibility of complete self-knowledge of a unified whole, that marks Lacanian antihumanism at its strongest. In the face of the Unconscious, there is no cogito.

From this we have an idea of how the Unconscious operates as language and in so doing disrupts our attempts at, and misdirected beliefs in, understanding and meaning as unified and as transparent. To say that language comes from an other is to say that language comes from something beyond the subject's illusion of control; to say that the Unconscious manifests itself in relation to the Symbolic is to say that the Unconscious is located in the Symbolic precisely because it is an effect of signification. According to Evans (1996):

> In arguing that speech originates not in the ego, nor even in the subject, but in the Other, Lacan is stressing that speech and language are beyond one's conscious control: they come from another place, outside consciousness . . . [and] the unconscious is the effect of the signifier on the subject, in that the signifier is what is repressed and what returns in the formations of the unconscious . . . . All references to language, speech, discourse, and signifiers clearly locate the unconscious in the order of the Symbolic. [pp. 133 and 218]

In being an effect of signification, the Unconscious is retroactively rooted in the Imaginary and the Real, for it is in the Real that the instincts are located and in the Imaginary that they are ordered into sexual drives, and it is in the gaps between the Symbolic and the Imaginary, between desire and demand, and between the oedipal law and the child's sexual ordering of ego-self, that the Unconscious comes to be formed. The Unconscious is manifest in these gaps, these chasms; it is the collection of representations of the mind that are refused by consciousness, and that later return in the repressed materials that disrupt the order and cohesion of the conscious mind. So for Lacan it is *in* language and *by* language that the Unconscious comes to be; and it is the Unconscious itself that escapes consciousness—the register in which we *mistakenly* think meaning lies, the register in which we *mistakenly* think language is located.

What does this mean for a theory of the ethical subject? Lacan asks: "Is what thinks in my place, then another I?" (E 523/E 171). Clearly the answer is no, for the very idea of "another I" further supports the structure of unity that Lacan is seeking to undermine. It is not simply that there is an other I in my place: the Unconscious is not simply another I. The conclusion we draw from this is rather that the very *idea* of the I as a transparent unity must be discarded. "I" am split, and in that split I am in conflict, and in that conflict lies my subjection and my subjectivity. I am an other to myself—this is the central theme that cannot be forgotten. Lacan writes:

> If we ignore the self's radical ex-centricity to itself with which man is confronted, in other words, the truth discovered by Freud, we shall falsify both the order and the methods of psychoanalytic mediation; we shall make of it nothing more than the compromise operation that it has, in effect, become, namely, just what the letter as well as the spirit of Freud's work most repudiates. [E 524/E 171]

Because of this, the "radical heteronomy that Freud's discovery shows gaping within man can never again be covered over without whatever is used to hide it being profoundly dishonest" (E 524/ E 172). So, the question we must ask and answer is this:

> Who, then, is this other to whom I am more attached than to myself, since, at the heart of my assent to my own identity it is still he who agitates me?

> His presence can be understood only at a second degree of otherness which already places him in the position of mediating between me and the double of myself, as it were with my counterpart.

> If I have said that the unconscious is the discourse of the Other (with a capital O), it is in order to indicate the beyond in which the recognition of desire is bound up with the desire for recognition.

> In other words this other is the Other that even my lie invokes as a guarantor of the truth in which it subsists. [E 524/E 172]

This Other is the Symbolic. The Other is the ideal around which we order our images of the Imaginary other, and this ideal comes from the repository of meaning that is the Symbolic, which we access through language. But the Other never "is," and the other, to whom I ascribe power, can never be the Other, who actually wields power. In this, we are caught up again in the endless process of alienation, for that to which we aspire is always something that we never from the start actually were.

Clearly our two thinkers are now starting to diverge, perhaps beyond the point of compatibility. Language functions in very different ways and signifies two very different orders for Levinas and Lacan.[13] For Lacan, the Unconscious, structured like a language, is still constituted by the Symbolic, and the Symbolic is the first and last register. Levinas, however, wants to offer us a beyond that is *not* formed by the Symbolic. What do we gain in following him down that path? And what do we lose? Are there things that Lacan offers us in his reading of the primacy of the Symbolic and the impossibility of going beyond it that we lose if we follow Levinas down his path? Before we can begin to answer these questions, we must complete our readings of the two thinkers. However, at this point our side-by-side readings are no longer useful, for Levinas and Lacan now move in radically different directions. Instead, we now turn to each thinker in isolation, allowing each to stand on his own, to make his own statement, so that we may begin to see each in his full radicality. Only then will we be able to bring them back together in conversation. Our conversation will at that point be markedly different than our conversations up to now, for then

---

13. One similarity is worthy of particular note here. For both Levinas and Lacan, the other plays an important role in the saying of language. In ethical subjectivity, the saying of the subject requires the presence of an other person to whom the subject says; in the analytic situation, speech requires the presence of the analyst as the one who hears and interprets. Thus, for both thinkers, language is inherently intersubjective. I am particularly grateful to an anonymous reviewer for bringing this similarity to my attention. It is not my insight, and so I don't feel comfortable elaborating on it to any significant degree, but it is very worthy of note. It is worth pointing out, of course, that even as intersubjective, language is for Lacan still a preexisting Symbolic order that is neither otherwise than being nor an-archic, but rather holds sway as a socio-linguistic foundation, whereas for Levinas the activity of speaking signifies a preexisting an-archic non-order beyond and before language—the an-arché of ethical responsibility.

we will see the contradictions and disagreements between the two thinkers in full. It is my contention, however, that it is precisely at that point that we not only can, but indeed must bring them together, and that is precisely what we will do. Now we must ask the question, What lies beyond language, beyond being? And once we have answered that, we can further ask, What does this mean for a theory of ethical subjectivity? It is to these questions that we now turn.

4

Ethical Subjectivity: God, An-Archy, the Subject, and Desire

> *Here there is, in the ethical anteriority of responsibility—for-the-other, in its priority over deliberation—a past irreducible to a hypothetical present that it once was. A past without reference to an identity naively—or naturally—assured of its right to presence, in which everything supposedly began. Here I am in this responsibility, thrown back toward something that was never my fault or of my own doing, something that was never within my power or my freedom, something that never was my presence and never came to me through memory. There is an ethical significance in that responsibility—without the remembered present of any past commitment— in that an-archic responsibility . . . there is a diachrony of a past that cannot be gathered into re-presentation.*
> —Levinas, EN 177/EN 170–171

> *The phallus is nothing more than a signifier, the signifier of this flight. Life goes by, life triumphs, whatever happens. If the comic hero trips up and lands in the soup, the little fellow nevertheless survives. The pathetic side of this dimension is, you see, exactly the opposite, the counterpart of tragedy. They are not incompatible, since tragi-comedy exists. That is where the experience of human action resides. And it is because we know better than those who went before how to recognize the nature of desire, which is at the heart of this experience, that a reconsideration of ethics is possible, that a form of ethical judgment is possible, of a kind that gives this question the force of a Last Judgment: Have you acted in conformity with the desire that it is you? . . . Opposed to this pole of desire is traditional ethics.*
> —Lacan, S VII 362/S VII 314

Subjectivity is a condition of being bound to the other. What is this other? Where does it lie? And how does it structure us? In particular, how does it make us ethical? We have just seen how, for both Levinas and Lacan, language plays a central role in structuring subjectivity, as the system to which the subject must accede. But where Lacan sees subjection to the Symbolic order, Levinas sees the possibility of the excess of the ethical, what he calls the "good beyond being." We ended the last chapter noting that this difference took our thinkers further apart than before, and in so doing we set the stage for this final chapter of textual analysis. Now we turn our attention directly to ethics and the ethical, asking what makes the subject ethical for Levinas and Lacan. As our thinkers have so sharply parted ways, we will, as previously stated, look at them solely in isolation from each other. In this we will best see the uniqueness of each of their projects. Additionally, we will further set the stage for the conclusion of this work, where I will bring them back together, this time in a more direct dialogue, in a more direct attempt to read them not simply alongside, but rather with one another, perhaps even attempting to see what it would look like to utter the "and."[1]

Levinas's subject is formed in the confrontation with the other, subjected to either an order of sexuality or to a system of gendered positions that embody and mark it as subject to this other, and situated in a linguistic system that presupposes this subjection as an ethical responsibility of the saying prior to the said. Have we arrived yet at a full picture of the ethical subject according to Levinas? Not quite, for we have two final themes to explore, two final themes that emerged at this point through which we can understand what this ethical subject will finally look like. First, as beyond being, this idea of the ethical is marked by something transcendent. Second, as beyond being, this idea of the subject as ethical is an an-archic foundation.[2] It is to these two themes that we will now address our inquiry. We begin with transcendence.

---

1. In a very insightful article, Ken Reinhard (1995) explores the difficulty of using the conjunction "and" when discussing Levinas and Lacan, and instead, following Lacan's reading of Kant and Sade, uses the conjunction "with" to explore how the two might be thought alongside one another. See Reinhard, "Kant with Sade, Levinas with Lacan," pp. 785–808.

2. I am extremely cautious with my use of the word "foundation." The very point of calling responsibility an-archic is to remove it from traditional conceptions of foundations. The an-archic is "outside of time," is "subject to an other order," is "otherwise than being," is "immemorial." If, as we explore these ideas, these markings, we remember that the an-archic is not in any traditional sense of the word a "foundation," then perhaps we can still use this word for our own purposes.

The problem of transcendence—its meanings, its very possibility—lies at the heart of Levinas's corpus. Not only does Levinas see in transcendence the possibility of a beyond, an otherwise-than-being, Levinas sees in transcendence the very structure of the subject as grounded by this beyond, this otherwise. So, in order to spell out fully Levinas's conception of the ethical subject, we must take this detour through his work on transcendence. And what better way to explore Levinas's conception of transcendence than to explore his conception of absolute transcendence, the idea of God who comes to mind?[3]

We have already argued that *Otherwise than Being* can be read as a revision of *Totality and Infinity* influenced by Jacques Derrida's (1978) reading of the earlier work in his essay "Violence and Metaphysics: An Essay on the Thought of Emmanuel Levinas." Even more concretely, however, we can turn to Levinas's 1975 essay "God and Philosophy," collected in Levinas (1982/1998), as his attempt to respond directly to Derrida's reading of his work. "God and Philosophy" opens with a reference to Derrida's basic criticism of Levinas: "Not to philosophize is to philosophize still." This is the claim Levinas sets out to disprove in this essay. Here, the focus is explicitly on the question of God, or more precisely, on the idea of God that comes to mind.

According to Levinas, the history of philosophy in the West has been a history of philosophy asserting itself as master discourse: "The philosophical discourse of the West asserts the amplitude of an all-inclusiveness or an ultimate comprehension. It compels every other discourse to justify itself before philosophy" (DD 94/OG 55). This compulsion has been shaped by the belief that thought and reality coincide, that intelligibility is correlative with meaning, and phenomenality with intelligibility. Levinas writes:

---

3. This is a reference to the title of Levinas's 1982 volume, *De Dieu qui Vient à l'Idée* (1982), translated by Bettina Bergo as *Of God Who Comes to Mind* (1998). "God and Philosophy," first published in 1975, was later collected in this volume. This chapter works from these 1982/1998 editions of the essay.

> This dignity of an ultimate royal discourse comes to Western
> philosophy by virtue of the rigorous coincidence between the
> thought in which philosophy stands and the reality in which
> this thought thinks. For thought, this coincidence signifies the
> following: not to have to think beyond that which belongs to
> the "gesture or movement of being"; or at least not to have to
> think beyond that which modifies a previous adherence to the
> "gesture of being," such as ideal or formal notions. For the being
> of the real, this coincidence signifies: to illumine thought and
> what is thought by showing itself. To show itself, to be illu-
> mined, is precisely to have a meaning; it is precisely to have
> intelligibility par excellence, underlying any modification of
> meaning. [DD 94/OG 55]

Meaning always takes place within the context of being. For philosophy to give meaning to the idea of God, philosophy must understand
God within the context of being, and therefore as a being. This reading has posed a problem for the philosophical explication of the God
of the Bible, a God which on Levinas's reading signifies a something
beyond being, and therefore beyond philosophy:

> If the intellectualization of the biblical God—theology—does
> not reach the level of philosophical thought, it is not because
> theology thinks God as a being without making clear to begin
> with the "being of this being," but because in thematizing God,
> theology has brought him into the course of being, while the
> God of the Bible signifies in an unlikely manner the beyond of
> being, or transcendence. [DD 95/OG 56]

Conceiving of God as a being does not do justice to the biblical
God, the God who "signifies without analogy to an idea subject to
criteria, without analogy to an idea exposed to the summons
to show itself true or false" (DD 95/OG 56). We are thereby led
to the question of the primacy of philosophy in discourse concerning the God of the Bible: "Rational theology, fundamentally
ontological, endeavors to accommodate transcendence within the
domain of being by expressing it with adverbs of height applied
to the verb 'to be.' God is said to exist eminently or par excellence.

But does the height, or the height above height, which is thus expressed, still depend on ontology?" (DD 95/OG 56).

One strategy for dealing with the God of the Bible has been to remove the argument concerning that God from the register of philosophy and instead to construct it as a question of faith. Levinas is not willing to follow that move because it operates under the beliefs that (1) the God of the Bible is not intelligible as a meaningful concept, and that (2) philosophy's definitions of meaning and intelligibility are the only viable ones. Levinas is not willing to concede either of those points, and instead wants to argue that we can think of this God as meaningful precisely because there are other modes of thinking about meaning than those dictated by traditional philosophical discourse.

For Levinas, the question is: *How* can we speak of the meaning of God, indeed of meaning itself, without recourse to the language of being, without recourse to philosophy? This is the central question of the text. As he poses it:

> The problem that is posed, consequently, and which shall be our own, consists in asking ourselves whether meaning is equivalent to the *esse* of being; that is, whether the meaning which, in philosophy, is meaning is not already a restriction of meaning; whether it is not already a derivation or a drift from meaning; whether the meaning equivalent to essence— to the gesture of being, to being *qua* being—is not already approached in the presence which is the time of the Same. [DD 96/OG 57]

Is not the restriction of meaning to the meaning of being, the meaning of essence, a restriction of the idea of meaning itself? Is there not another register of meaning that sits not in the register of the Same, but of the Other? We are compelled to inquire into the possibility of a meaning that is prior to being—an other meaning that is otherwise than being:

> Our question is whether, beyond being, a meaning might not show itself whose priority, translated into ontological language,

will be called prior to being. It is not certain that, going beyond
the terms of being and beings, one necessarily falls back into
the discourse of opinion or faith. In fact, while remaining outside of reason, or while wanting to be there, faith and opinion
speak the language of being. Nothing is less opposed to ontology than the opinion of faith. To ask oneself, as we are attempting to do here, whether God cannot be uttered in a reasonable
discourse that would be neither ontology nor faith, is implicitly to doubt the formal opposition . . . between, on the one
hand, the God of Abraham, Isaac, and Jacob, invoked without
philosophy in faith, and on the other, the god of the philosophers. It is to doubt that this opposition constitutes an alternative. [DD 96–97/OG 57]

Levinas sees an alternative to the faith–reason opposition; he believes that there is another way of construing the transcendent. And
it is to this that the text addresses itself: the possibility of not just
the good beyond being, but the God beyond being as well.

Levinas begins by arguing that in the history of Western philosophy, meaning has always been couched within the manifestation of being, and vice versa. However, this is a philosophical
mistake, for if being is manifestation, then the manifestation of
being is nothing more than being's action of manifesting itself; it
is not the manifestation of some "reality." Truth, then, is not the
external reflection of an internal form, but merely an external reflection of an external reflection, whereas knowledge, or the consciousness of meaning, is only an inner reflection of an inner affect.
Levinas writes:

We have said that for Western philosophy meaning or intelligibility coincides with the manifestation of being, as if the very affair
of being led, in the form of intelligibility, toward clarity . . . But
if being is manifestation—if the exertion of action of being comes
back to this exhibition [of a being's phenomenal essence]—then
the manifestation of being is only the manifestation of "this exertion." That is, it is a manifestation of manifestation . . . But
knowledge—or thought, or experience—should not be understood as some sort of reflection of exteriority in an inner forum.

> The notion of reflection, an optical metaphor borrowed from
> thematized beings or events, is not the characteristic of knowl-
> edge. Knowledge only comprehends itself in its own essence,
> starting from consciousness, whose specificity eludes us when
> we define it with the aid of the concept of knowledge, which it-
> self supposes consciousness. [DD 97–98/OG 57–58]

The problem of consciousness is the problem of the self attempting to view all things as exterior from within the realm of the self
or the same. Consciousness reduces all things to objects of consciousness, and as objects they present themselves to consciousness as representations. But, according to Levinas, representation
is the reduction of all time to the present, and thus of all meaning
to presence. Presence is a reduction of other to same because it
understands beings only as objects at the service of the same, objects for the self to use for his pleasure. It is only in disrupting the
idea of "presence" that objects can stand as subjects, thereby retaining their status as other than the same. Consciousness, then, is
the reduction of all things to being and presence, and therefore to
the same.

The problem of consciousness is also a problem of temporality, for in consciousness all is remembered as an event, an occurrence, with a beginning—an origin. Here again everything can be
reduced to a phenomenon, and as such to presentation and re-
presentation. Levinas writes:

> Consciousness is a light that illuminates the world from one end
> to the other; all that sinks into the past is re-membered or is re-
> discovered by history. Reminiscence is the extreme conscious-
> ness that is also universal presence and ontology; all that which
> is able to fill the field of consciousness was, in its time, received,
> perceived, and had an origin. Through consciousness the past is
> but a modification of the present. Nothing can, or could, come
> to pass without presenting itself. [DD 100–101/OG 60]

In reducing the past to a modification of the present, we fail to account for the past as anything but synchronous with the present—

that is, in the register of the same. However, the ethical encounter with the other, as an an-archic past, is diachronous—not synchronous with the present: it has its own history, its own time, and its own register of meaning, a register of meaning that is not reducible to the same but, rather, exists within the realm of the other.[4] In reducing the past to the present, then, we constrict meaning to sameness, and in so doing constrict meaning to immanence: "Philosophy is representation, the reactualization of representation; that is, the emphasis of presence, the remaining the same of being in its simultaneity of presence, in its forever and in its immanence. Philosophy is not only knowledge of immanence, it is immanence itself" (DD 101/OG 61). Such a reduction, however, does not do justice to the actuality of that which "shakes" consciousness, that which "shakes" immanence: transcendence.

Levinas does not write of "experiencing" transcendence. Transcendence as such cannot be experienced, because calling it an experience posits that it can be explained and re-presented. But this contradicts the very idea of transcendence. Transcendence is not explainable using the categories of immanence and re-presentation: it exceeds them. Transcendence is not a phenomenon. The idea of narrating "religious experience," then, is problematic for Levinas. If an experience is "religious" (that is, of transcendence), then it is by definition outside the discourse of immanence, and therefore cannot be thought of as an "experience." To speak of religious experience, then, as if it is something that can be related, is to speak of the experience as if it can be re-presented, grasped within the categories of meaning and idea available to us only within being and immanence; to speak of religious experience is to reduce transcendence to immanence, and thus to erase it. Levinas writes:

> The "narrative" of religious experience does not shake philosophy and, consequently, could not break the presence and the immanence of which philosophy is the emphatic accomplishment. It is possible that the word "God" may have come to

---

4. We will further explore the idea of the an-archic past below.

philosophy from a religious discourse. But philosophy—even
if it refuses—understands this discourse as that of propositions
bearing on a theme; that is, as having a meaning that refers to
a disclosure, to a manifestation of presence. The messengers of
the religious experience do not conceive another signification
of meaning. The religious "revelation" is henceforth assimilated
to philosophical discourse . . . the religious being interprets
what he lived through as experience. In spite of himself, he
already interprets God, of whom he claims to have an experience, in terms of being, presence, and immanence. [DD 103/
OG 62]

Though the word "God" may have passed into philosophical usage,
it still signifies something beyond the philosophical discourse of
meaning as re-presentation. For Levinas, the word God and the idea
God signify something otherwise than presence and immanence.
God breaks up the "I think" and throws the self out of consciousness into insomnia.[5]

For Levinas, it was Descartes who most clearly presented the
concept of the transcendence of God breaking the unity and self-
presence of the I:

In his meditation on the idea of God, Descartes has sketched,
with unequaled rigor, the extraordinary course of a thought proceeding to the point of the breakup of the *I think*. While thinking of God as a being, Descartes thinks of him nevertheless as

---

5. Levinas on insomnia: "Always on the verge of awakening, sleep communicates with wakefulness . . . The category of insomnia cannot be reduced
to the tautological affirmation of the Same, or to the dialectical negation, or to
the "ecstasy" of thematizing intentionality . . . Insomnia as a category . . . does
not come to be inscribed in a table of categories [Kant] starting from a determining activity exerted upon the other as a given, by the unity of the Same (and
all activity is only identification and crystallization of the Same against the Other,
although affected by the Other) in order to assure the Other, consolidated in a
being, the gravity of being . . . [Insomnia] is cored out by the Other who tears
this rest, who tears it from the inner side of the state where equality tends to
settle. There precisely lies the irreducible, categorical character of insomnia:
the Other in the Same who does not alienate the Same, but precisely wakes him"
(DD 98–99/OG 58–59).

an eminent being, or he thinks of him as a being that *is* eminently. Before this *rapprochement* between the idea of God and the idea of being, we must certainly ask ourselves whether the adjective *eminent* and the adverb *eminently* do not refer to the height of the sky over our heads and thus overflow ontology. [DD 104/OG 62]

Descartes did not follow this through to what Levinas sees to be its logical consequence. By still thinking of God as a being, Descartes still thought of the transcendent within the register of the immanent. However, by thinking of God as "eminent," he did set the stage for our moving beyond this reduction. Levinas writes:

> Descartes maintains a substantialist language here, interpreting the immeasurableness of God as a superlative way of existing. But for us [Descartes'] unsurpassable contribution does not lie here. It is not the proofs of God's existence that matter to us here, but rather the breakup of consciousness, which is not a repression into the unconscious, but a sobering or a waking up that shakes the "dogmatic slumber" that sleeps at the bottom of all consciousness resting upon that object. As a *cogitatum* of a *cogitatio* that contains *at first sight* the *cogitatio*, is the idea of God (understood as signifying the uncontained *par excellence*) the very absolution of the absolute here? This idea of God surpasses every capacity, its "objective reality" as a *cogitatum* causes the "formal reality" of the *cogitatio* to break apart. Perhaps this overturns—in advance—the universal validity and the original character of intentionality. We shall say this: the idea of God causes the breakup of the thinking that—as investment, synopsis, and synthesis—merely encloses in a presence, re-presents, brings back to presence, or lets be. [DD 104–105/OG 62–63]

This idea of God, then, breaks the unity of the "I think" in precisely "what" is being thought. The "what" that is being thought exceeds the presence of being and the being of presence. The "I think" is broken apart by the thought it attempts to contain. What is this "what" being thought? What is this idea of God, this idea of the Infinite that comes to mind? And what follows from it? The idea of the Infinite is precisely the signification of something *non-finite within* the finite. As Levinas writes: "the in of the Infinite signified at once the *non-* and the *within*" (DD 106/OG 63). It is not a "what" filled with finite content. It is merely the fact of something non-finite, something that cannot be contained, something that exceeds my grasp. But it exists within me, as an idea "of" something more. It is this fact that breaks up and shatters the "I think," for I am, in fact, thinking of something that I cannot in fact "think," if by think we mean contain. I have the idea within me, but it is an idea of something not only larger than I am, but other than I am, and as such it disrupts my very understanding of what it is "to think."

As an idea that is beyond me, I find it as an idea that must have been put in me; I cannot claim responsibility for its presence because it is precisely what I am not. As such, it is an idea that I find in myself in my being in a state of ultimate passivity, more passive than any other passivity. It is beyond me, and yet within me; it is more than I am, and yet I "think" it. I cannot be responsible for its being there; it must have been put in me: "The breakup of the actuality of thought in the "idea of God" is a passivity more passive than any passivity, like the passivity of a trauma through which the idea of God would have been placed in us" (DD 106/OG 64).

The question remains, how am I to respond to this idea? I respond, Levinas tells us, with non-indifference. Non-indifference is a caring, an attitude, a comportment, a taking seriously. I cannot ignore it; I cannot turn away from it. I instead seek an understanding of this idea of God, this idea of the Infinite, as the trace of the Infinite within me that awakens me from my state of immanent consciousness into the vigilance of insomnia, a state of awareness of the beyond. I respond by refusing not to respond; I respond by answering the call it places on me.

It is this non-indifference that makes me a subject. Levinas writes:

> The difference between the Infinite and the finite is a non-indifference of the Infinite with regard to the finite, and is the

secret of subjectivity. The figure of the Infinite-placed-in-me, which if we believe Descartes is contemporary with my creation, would signify that the not-able-to-comprehend-the-Infinite-by-thought is, in some way, a positive relation with this thought. [DD 108/OG 65]

In other words, the fact of the idea of the Infinite within me provides the ground for a relation between the Infinite and the finite such that the beyond of the Infinite dumbfounds the cogito, and thereby wakes thought out of its self-sameness. In this, I stand in a positive relation to the Infinite by not turning away from it, by confronting the reality of the idea of it within me.

This relation is thinkable as a "relation" in that it wakes in the finite a response that occurs in passivity. It is not a relation to a personal God, to an other being. It is not a relation of reciprocal exchange and communication. It is a relation of asymmetrical call and response and ultimately of passive realization and assumption of responsibility. This response, which will become manifest as the assumption of responsibility, is at first to be understood as a recognition of a desire for the Infinite, a desire for the other that leaves itself as a trace in the same. The "in" of the Infinite

designates the depth of the affection by which subjectivity is affected through this "placing" of the Infinite within it, without prehension or comprehension . . . A passivity, or passion, in which Desire is recognized, in which the "more in the less" awakens with its most ardent, most notable, and most ancient flame, a thought that is destined to think more than it thinks. [DD 110–111/OG 66–67]

The positive meaning of the "in"—the "withinness" of the Infinite—awakens in me an appreciation and realization of the depth of affection of the other that has placed within me the thought that exceeds my capacity to think, the Idea that exceeds me. This coincides with the negative meaning of the Infinite, the "beyond" of the Infinite, which hollows out a desire that could not be filled, one nourished from its own increase, exalted as Desire—one that withdraws from its satisfaction as it draws near to the Desirable. This is a Desire for what is beyond satisfaction, and which does not identify, as need does, a term or an end. A desire without end, from beyond Being: dis-inter*estedness*, transcendence—desire for the Good. [DD 111/OG 67]

This negativity of the "in" of the Infinite, then, awakens within me the desire for this more, the desire for that which exceeds me, the desire for that which is greater than any thought I can think. This is the "good beyond being" Levinas attempted to articulate in *Otherwise than Being*. This "Good" is more than being, beyond being, and is the perfection of something more than I can grasp, the goodness of that which is more than I can think, the absoluteness of that which transcends the immanent. And my desire for it is my desire to be more than I am, my desire to continue to think more than I can think.

In this desire, the possibility of love awakens within me because "the 'more' . . . ravages and wakes up the 'less'" (DD 112/OG 67). In this, I am compelled to find more than I am alone, more than I am within the confines of the same. But love, recall, can degenerate into Eros. This runs counter to the Infinite as beyond me. So the question emerges: "Is the transcendence of the Desirable possible, beyond the interestedness and the eroticism in which the Beloved is found?" (DD 112/OG 68). According to Levinas:

For that the disinter*estedness* to be possible in the Desire for the Infinite—for the Desire beyond being, or transcendence, might not be an absorption into immanence, which would thus make its return—the Desirable, or God, must remain separated in the Desire; as desirable—near yet different—Holy. This can only be if the Desirable commands me to what is the nondesirable, to the undesirable *par excellence*; to another . . . We have shown elsewhere the substitution for another at the heart of this responsibility, which is thus an enucleation of the transcendental subject, thus also the transcendence of goodness, the nobility of pure *enduring*, an ipseity of pure election. Love without Eros. [DD 113/OG 68]

The desire for the Infinite can only remain disinterested, that is, can keep itself from being caught in the objectification of Eros, can keep itself from being reduced to the order of the immanent, if that desire remains separate from its object; that is, if the object of desire, the desired, the desirable, removes itself. And this can only be achieved if the desirable turns me away from itself toward another object. The Infinite must redirect desire away from itself and toward another—toward something undesirable. In this, its own otherness can be retained, and its transcendence protected. And so we are turned toward that something undesirable, that something other than the Good in and of itself, in order to protect our desire for the Good. We are commanded, for the sake of the preservation of a Love without Eros, to our responsibility for the other.[6]

Our desire for the Infinite turns us away from the Infinite as the object of our desire toward that which is undesirable—the other person. Levinas calls this movement "illeity" (roughly translatable as "himness.") Illeity is that movement by which God escapes our desire and turns us to our ethical responsibility to the other person. He writes:

> We have designated this matter for the Infinite, or for Good, to refer, from the heart of its very desirability, to the undesirable proximity of the others, by the term "illeity"; this is an extraordinary turning around of the desirability of the Desirable, of the supreme desirability calling to itself the rectilinear rectitude of Desire. A turning around by which the Desirable escapes the Desire. The goodness of the Good—of the Good that neither sleeps nor slumbers—inclines the movement it calls forth to turn it away from the Good and orient it toward the other, and only thus toward the Good. [DD 113–114/OG 69]

---

6. We will return to this discussion of desire in the conclusion.

This ethical turnabout, this orientation toward the other, is achieved by the Infinite within us. It is the trace of God within us, and the alterity of God orients us toward our responsibility, calls us into that responsibility. As such, it is "God's absolute remoteness, his transcendence [that] turns into my responsibility—the non-erotic *par excellence*—for the other" (DD 115/OG 69).

The ethical meaning of transcendence is now clear. The Infinite calls us out of our self-same identity of consciousness and into relation with the other person. This is only possible because of the proximity of the other person, because of her nearness to me. Without this, we would only have been operating on the level of an abstraction. It is the proximity of the neighbor that makes concrete this turning, this responsibility. It is because the neighbor is near that I can turn to her. As such, it is this proximity that allows me to turn my passive acceptance of the idea of God to an active giving over of self to other; proximity allows me to become ethical by assuming my responsibility as my own.

This responsibility to the other occurs before my own freedom, before my ability to choose. It is the absolute passivity of obligation awakened within me, the passivity of substitution. The consciousness of my "I think" is disrupted, and I am called to responsibility without the chance to reflect or consider. I am obligated before I can choose this obligation. In this I am held hostage by the other, guilty before even having acted. But it is only in my response that I assume the full extent of that responsibility. I am summoned, and I must answer: "I respond from the first to a summons" (DD 117/OG 71). This call and this response make the subject unique, for no other is called in this, and no other can take the place of the one summoned. Levinas calls this uniqueness and irreplaceability "election." I am elected, and no one else can answer the call made upon me:

> In appealing to me as to someone accused who can not challenge the accusation, responsibility binds me as irreplaceable and unique. It binds me as elected. To the very degree to which

> it appeals to my responsibility, it forbids me any replacement.
> As unreplaceable for this responsibility, I cannot slip away from
> the face of the neighbor without avoidance, or without fault,
> or without complexes; here I am pledged to the other without
> any possibility of abdication. [DD 118/OG 71]

As elect, I cannot avoid my obligation, cannot pass the responsibility on to another. I and only I am elected, no one else.

This idea of election in Levinas is the source of fraternity, of the idea of a brotherhood of responsible subjects. In my immediate responsibility for my neighbor, I am called to be his guardian, his protector. This is the source of brotherhood, for it is this responsibility that gives its name to fraternity, to responsibility for the brother. Fraternity does not ground responsibility; responsibility awakens me to fraternity. This an-archic responsibility—this trace of God within me that turns me toward the other person in preservation of its Infinity, this ethical moment—is what engenders fraternity. Transcendence is the root of the world of persons.

From this argument, Levinas comes to several conclusions. First, he posits that God is not simply the first other, but is rather something altogether different. He finds in God not simply the absolute other, but an otherwise than other, and hence beyond being. Levinas writes: "It is from the analysis just carried out that God is not simply the 'first other,' or the 'other par excellence,' or the 'absolutely other,' but other than the other, other otherwise, and other with an alterity prior to the alterity of the other, prior to the ethical obligation to the other and different from every neighbor, transcendent to the point of absence" (DD 115/OG 69). Levinas is pointing to God as not simply other than myself, but as otherwise than being, as that which disrupts being itself, which exceeds presence, and which escapes conceptualization. God is Infinite, otherwise, beyond.

Second, Levinas finds in this essay a new understanding of the religious as the ethical. No longer couched within terms of belief or reason, religion is now the answer to the call of election, the assuming of one's responsibility. He writes:

> A marvelous accusative: here I am under your gaze, obliged to
> you, your servant. In the name of God. Without thematization!
> The sentence in which God comes to be involved in words is
> not "I believe in God." The religious discourse prior to all reli-
> gious discourse is not dialogue. It is the "here I am," said to the
> neighbor to whom I am given over, and in which I announce
> peace, that is, my responsibility for the other. [DD 123/OG 75]

Religion is not belief, not a personal, singular call of a relation to a
thought, but a relation to the alterity of God, and thus a relation to
the other person. Religion is the assumption of one's responsibility toward the other in the answer to the call of election, in the "Here
I am."

Third, Levinas in this essay offers a new reading of prophetism
and a new reading of signification: what he calls "prophetic signification." He calls prophetism a "pure witnessing, pure because [it
is] prior to all disclosure" (DD 124/OG 76). The prophet is the one
who witnesses the call of God. And Levinas calls signification the
trope of "the-one-for-the-other" (DD 125/OG 76). Prophetic signification, then, is the pure witnessing of my being for-the-other—
that is, an answer to the call of the face of the other in my assuming
my responsibility for him. In my subjection to the other, I am a
sign not simply of responsibility, but of my responsibility before
God. In prophetic signification, then, Levinas offers an answer to
Derrida's challenge, claiming now that in fact "*Not to philosophize
would not be still to philosophize*," for the "intelligibility of transcendence is not ontological" and prophecy is not philosophy (DD 126
and 125/OG 76). My being for-the-other is not a subjection of
myself to the order of being, nor to the order of re-presentation
and synchronic meaning. Instead, my being for-the-other is a subjection to an other order beyond immanence, phenomenality, and
being. My being for-the-other is an other signification that is otherwise than philosophy.

We now begin to see what is perhaps the most important discovery Levinas makes in this essay: the re-presentation of his model
of the one-for-the-other as the structure of subjectivity grounded

in the idea of the Infinite within me. The subject is only subject
when he is subjected, called out of his hypostatic solitude of presence into the uncomfortable world of otherness, and he is only
called this way by God. On subjectivity, Levinas writes:

> Here is an exposition that does not resemble the self-conscious-
> ness or the recurrence of the subject to himself, confirming the
> ego by itself. This is rather the recurrence of awakening, which
> one can describe as the shiver of incarnation, through which
> giving takes on meaning, as the original dative of the for the
> other, in which the subject becomes heart and sensitiveness and
> the hands that give. Yet it is thus a position already de-posed
> from its kingdom of identity and substance, already in debt, "for
> the other" to the point of substitution for the other and alter-
> ing the immanence of the subject in his innermost identity. This
> is the subject, irreplaceable for the responsibility there assigned
> to him, and who therein discovers a new identity. [DD 119–
> 120/OG 73]

But this subjectivity cannot happen without the glory of the Infinite. He writes: "The glory of a long desire! The subject as hostage
has been neither the experience nor the proof of the Infinite, but
the witnessing of the Infinite, a modality of this glory" (DD 120/
OG 73). What is significant here is the way in which the grounding of the subject takes place explicitly through the idea of God,
through the Infinite within me. While this idea was hinted at in
both *Totality and Infinity* and *Otherwise than Being*, it is only now
that it receives its full exposition. Now the subject is truly the subject not only through the other person, but also through the trace
of God.

But in what way does this idea of the God, as the good beyond being, take root in me? The question I am asking here is not
a metaphysical one ("What puts it in me?"), but rather an ethical
one ("How does this idea manifest itself for me?"). The answer to
this question lies in the second theme that we need to elucidate in
order to arrive at a complete picture of Levinas's conception of the
ethical subject—the good as an-archic. In understanding the ethi-

cal encounter as "an-archical," we can see the true radicality of the Levinasian project, and it is only in working through that concept that we can come to make any sense of a project so outside of our normal mode of philosophizing. In turning our attention to subjectivity as an-archic subjectivity, then, we will come to full and proper reading of Levinas's views on ethical subjectivity.

From his earliest works, "time" has been an important theme in Levinas's thought. *Time and the Other* was a series of lectures delivered in 1946–47. Additionally, in interviews Levinas (1985) has offered Henri Bergson's (2001) *Time and Free Will* as one of the five greatest books in the history of Western philosophy, alongside Plato's *Phaedrus* (1956), Kant's (1965) *Critique of Pure Reason*, Hegel's (1977) *Phenomenology of Spirit*, and Heidegger's (1962) *Being and Time*.[7] It is not until late in his career that Levinas's views on time receive their fullest explication. Clearly, his understanding of time became extremely important in establishing his conceptions of substitution and an-archy in *Otherwise than Being*. But we find his clearest and most succinct treatment of the subject of time in a 1985 essay entitled "Diachrony and Representation."[8]

In "Diachrony and Representation," Levinas sets out to explain several key terms in his thought, the most important of which are an-archy, the immemorial past, and the pure future. Levinas begins the essay by noting that, in philosophy, the intelligible has always been correlated with vision. As the structure of seeing is the ability to represent one thing to another, it has the "thing being seen" as its object. Thus, vision is connected to intentionality. Intentionality—the aiming of thought at its object—is an aiming always done by the "I" of the "I think." This in turn opens up the question of consciousness. Consciousness, as the directedness of an I toward its object of thought, is a purely internal occurrence.

---

7. Levinas, *Ethics and Infinity* (1985, pp. 37–38).
8. The essay is the text of a lecture delivered in honor of Paul Ricoeur, and was first published in the Canadian journal *Revue de l'Université d'Ottawa*, and later in one of the last collections of Levinas's writings, *Entre Nous*, published in 1991.

In this, the object of thought remains object, being kept within the realm of the self and the same. The other is thereby reduced to the same, and its function becomes nothing more than its existing to satisfy the I, to fulfill the I's desire, its aim in the "I think," and to act as object of the I's drives.[9]

In vision as intentionality, the other is present to the I as presence, as "at-handedness" (main-tenance).[10] The other is reduced to an object of presence, a thing present for the I. Seeing, knowing, taking in hand, are all "linked to the structure of intentionality" and all intentionality is locked within the I, and thus within the egology of presence (EN 166/EN 160). In this, the temporality of thought as re-presentation is privileged, and the alterity of the other is seen as only an object for the I to grasp. Such a seeing of the other fails to give an account of the other in her otherness. Everything is reduced to the register of the same.

This privileging of presence is maintained in language as a means of representation between speakers. Dialogue, then, is seen as the entering into the thought of the other, and the taking of the other into the thought of the self; it is thereby part of a single consciousness in which the I think is the first and last cause. Everything is gathered into the presence of a single discourse, a work of re-presentation. Even the representation of the historian, the gathering of the past and present (and future) into a single narrative, is the reduction of the past into the present, into presence, as a thing— a book between two covers. The historical narrative makes tempo-

---

9. The question of "drives" here is fascinating, for it shows Levinas in implicit conversation with psychoanalysis. Neither Freud nor psychoanalysis is invoked by name, and yet each is implicated in this brief critique of the drives, by which the *I* uses the other to satisfy his desire. According to Levinas, as the drives are satisfied on the register of an "I," the unconscious, even as unconscious, still operates within the realm of the "I think," and is therefore caught within the realm of intentionality. It is because of this that Levinas will argue that unconsciousness is but a "deficient mode" of consciousness (EN 166/EN 160).

10. The reference is to Heidegger's terms *vorhanden* (presence-at-hand, occurrentness, objective presence), *zuhanden* (readiness-to-hand, availability, handiness), and *Dasein* (being-there, being-somewhere). See Heidegger 1962, especially paragraph 9, "The Theme of the Analytic of Dasein."

rality into a "thing, the gathering of the being of beings into a being" (EN 169/EN 163). All this occurs despite the alterity of the other, an alterity that announces itself in a disruption of our everyday understandings of time. Levinas tells us that such re-presentation has occurred

> despite the past that had *neither been present nor re-presented by anyone*—the immemorial past or an-archic past—and despite the inspired future, which *no one anticipates.* Such a past and future begin to signify time on the basis of the hermeneutic of the biblical "verses" of the text, without prior chronological reference to the metaphor of flux, nor to the still spatial images of the "hither" and of the "beyond." [EN 169/EN 163, italics added]

History is a synchrony of the now, excluding the reality of either an immemorial past, or what Levinas calls "an-archy"—a past that no one can represent because it exists outside of synchronous time—or an "inspired" or "pure" future—a future that no one can antici- pate because it exists outside of synchronous time. And, according to Levinas, these are the things for which we must be able to account. But in the process of writing a narrative history through the use of the "I think" (and the "I see," and the "I know," and the "I be- lieve" . . . .), alterity is "gather[ed] . . . into the unity of presence by the *I* of the intentional *I think*" (EN 168/EN 162). History as narra- tive therefore excludes that which we must take into account.

The immemorial past and the inspired future are modes of temporality not representable by historical narrative or rational discourse. The historical narrative and the intentionality it entails are not the only, nor even the primary, modes of the philosophi- cal; instead, there is an other rationality, one that takes account of the non-synchronous temporal moments of the immemorial past and the inspired (or pure) future, and it is to this diachronic read- ing of temporality that we must turn our attention. Levinas argues:

> The moment has come to ask whether this entry of each into the representation of the others, whether this agreement

between thoughts in the synchrony of the given, is the unique, original, and ultimate rationality of thought and discourse. One must ask whether this gathering of time into presence by intentionality—and thus whether the reduction of time to the essance of being, its reducibility to presence and representation—is the primordial intrigue of time. [EN 170/EN 164]

In place of time as presence, in place of temporality reduced to the register of the same, Levinas directs us otherwise.

A certain shift of focus from Levinas's earliest works is evident here, for the question is not simply about how to avoid "philosophy," as if it were some monolith in which being and the rationality of presence are the first and last words. The question is not how to move to an "otherwise" than rationality. Now the question is whether or not there might not be an *other* rationality awaiting our discovery:

We have tried to show in our essays that the judgments of true knowledge and thematic thought are summoned—or invented—on the basis of or apropos of certain exigencies that depend on the ethical significance of the other, inscribed in his or her face; imperatives in the face of the other who is incomparable to me and is unique . . . But I also think that the [ethical significance of the other] constitute[s] the rationality of an already derived order, that responsibility for the other signifies an original and concrete temporality, and that the universalization of presence presupposes it. [EN 171/EN 165]

Instead, time as diachronous—as an order in which the other is not reduced to the synchronous same—has its own rationality; time, therefore, can be examined beyond the confines of being and representation. In fact, Levinas argues, the reading of time as presence requires this other reading. It is to this other rationality, to this other reading of time, that Levinas directs us.

Levinas argues that the alterity of the other person is not a logical alterity, but rather a positive one. That is, it is not a purely formal otherness, in which the other would simply be another I,

and the I another other. Rather, the other person has an alterity
that stands apart from the sameness of the self and that cannot be
swallowed into the presence of being and representation. The other
person signifies a prior responsibility called forth in the I, a demand of my being "for-the-other." This for-the-otherness is, one
recalls, prior to consciousness, prior to all knowledge and seeing,
prior to intentionality. It is a signification prior to "the statements
of propositions communicating information and narrative" (EN
172/EN 166). Levinas reminds us: "The *for-the-other* arises in the
I as a commandment understood by the I in its very obedience, as
if obedience were its very accession to hearing the prescription, as
if the I obeyed before having heard, as if the intrigue of alterity were
woven prior to knowledge" (EN 172/EN 166). The I who obeys
before hearing, this is the one-for-the-other. In calling us to this
responsibility that is prior to my having heard it, the face of the
other is, for Levinas, an-archic.

The relation to the other person is my responsibility for his
mortality: a responsibility for his life, even to the point of my own
death. As such, I am held hostage to (but not by) the other person:
"The I as hostage to the other human being is precisely called to
answer for this death. Responsibility for the other in the I, independent of every engagement ever taken by this I and of all that
would have ever been accessible to its initiative and its freedom,
independent of everything that in the other could have 'regarded'
this I" (EN 173–174/EN 167).

My being hostage happens before I can question it, before I
can deliberate as to its origin or validity. I am commanded to answer for the death of my neighbor before I even realize what this
responsibility means. In this, I am called forth in the biblical commandment, "Thou shalt not kill (me)": "Responsibility for the
other—the face signifying to me 'Thou shalt not kill,' and consequently also 'you are responsible for the life of this absolutely
other other'—is responsibility for the one and only" (EN 174/EN
168). The one and only is both the uniqueness of the other person—she is the unique one for whom I am responsible—and the
uniqueness of my responsibility to her—I alone am called to this

responsibility. Levinas calls this uniqueness "*election*, the uniqueness of he who does not allow himself to be replaced" (EN 174/EN 168).

In being responsible for the other's life (and death), Levinas introduces the concept of (corporeally) occupying the other's place in the world; it is, in other words, because in existing I occupy space in the universe, because I take up matter and energy, space, food, air, and light, that I in actuality take life from another existent. As such, I truly am responsible for the other person, for in my continued existence I risk condemning him to death. This evokes in the I a shame for surviving, and brings in him the call and response "here I am," even if he cannot answer why:

> The risk of occupying—from the moment of the *Da* of my *Dasein*—the place of an other and thus, on the concrete level, of exiling him, of condemning him to a miserable condition in some "third" or "fourth" world, of bringing him death. Thus an unlimited responsibility emerges in this fear for the other, a responsibility with which one is never done, which does not cease with the neighbor's utmost extremity—despite the merciless and realistic expression of the doctor, "condemning" a patient—even if the responsibility comes to nothing more at that time—as we powerlessly face the death of the other—than saying "here I am," or—in the shame of surviving—than pondering the memory of one's wrongdoings. [EN 175–176/EN 169]

In my responsibility, I am compelled to respond to the other person, even if I do not know how. What am I to do, then? What is it that I offer? I own up to my existence, and thus to the fact of my responsibility for the other, her life and death. I answer the call of responsibility by simply acknowledging that I am here, in the face of the other, responsible for her. This is the biblical "Here I am."

My responsibility emerges as always having been, as prior to my response, as prior to even my ability to respond, for it is awakened in me as before my freedom, as before my cognition or intention. It has always already been: "A responsibility anterior to all the logical deliberation required by the reasoned decision. Deliberation, i.e., already the reduction of the face of the other to representation, to the objectivity of the visible, to its coercive power, which is of the world" (EN 176/EN 170). I do not deliberate; I do not consider the consequences. I do not even represent the face to myself as an object of my consciousness. My responsibility is anterior to this, prior to and beneath this. My responsibility is awakened in me as something already there, always already having been.

The awakening of this prior having-been by the other is decidedly not a remembering of a past event; it is not a past present. Levinas writes:

> The anteriority of responsibility is not that of an a priori idea interpreted on the basis of reminiscence—that is, referred to perception and the glimpsed intemporal presence based on the ideality of the idea or the eternity of a presence that does not pass, and whose duration or diachrony of time would be only a dissimulation, decline, deformation, or privation, in finite human consciousness.
>
> Here we have, in the ethical anteriority of responsibility (for-the-other, in its priority over deliberation), a past irreducible to a hypothetical present that it once was. A past without reference to an identity naively (or naturally) assured of its right to a presence, in which everything supposedly began. Here I am in this responsibility, thrown back toward something that was never my fault or of my own doing, something that was never within power or freedom, something that never was my presence and never came to me through memory. There is an ethical significance in that responsibility—without the remembered present of any past commitment—in that an-archic responsibility. [EN 176–177/EN 170]

This past is irreducible to a hypothetical present. It is not something that I can represent in my history or my narrative: it is not an event that can be reduced to an object or to being. It is an origin without origin, an original non-event that cannot be remembered, but that announces itself to me in the face of the other. This is an-archy: the anti-foundational foundation, the diachronic reality of an other past that grounds our subjectivity as ethical, as for-the-other; it gives meaning to the present, calls the I into *signi-fication* as the one-for-the-other. This past that was never a present takes hold of the I and makes him hostage; it calls him, elects him, and obsesses him. Levinas writes: "It is the significance of a past that concerns me, that regards 'me' and is 'my business,' beyond all reminiscence, re-tention, re-presentation, reference to a remembered present" (EN 177/EN 170–171). Levinas calls this my "*nonintentional* participation in the history of humanity, in the past of others" (EN 177/EN 171). This non-reducibility of the past to a past present, its non-synchronic history, is its diachronic reality.

In order to spell the concept out more clearly, Levinas proceeds to a negative description of what he calls responsibility for the other. He distinguishes it from a Kantian a priori, arguing that it is not a "simple modality of 'transcendental apperception'" (EN 177/EN 171). He distinguishes it from second-order ethical reflection, arguing that "it is not even a question here of receiving an order by first perceiving it and then subjecting oneself to it in a decision taken after having deliberated about it. In the proximity of the face, the subjection precedes the reasoned decision to assume the order that it bears" (EN 177/EN 171). Instead, again, it is a prior non-event to which the subject is subjected in absolute passivity. Passivity is not a simple receptivity, for again, such a definition posits an intentional consciousness. This inability to even be receptive is part of Levinas's understanding passivity: one cannot be both passive and receptive, for one *chooses* to be receptive. Instead, in this responsibility, one exists *before* one is receptive, passive in that one only comes "to be," that is, comes to see oneself as a being among others, in the assumption of this prior subjection. The past is an an-archical past that the subject is called to assume. Levinas writes:

> Here there is absolute foreignness of an unassumable alterity, refractory to its assimilation into presence, alien to the apperception of the "I think" that always assumes what strikes it by re-presenting it. Unequaled diachrony of the past. Subjection

preceding the understanding of the order—which attests to or measures an infinite authority. [EN 178/EN 171]

Levinas calls this a "past that is articulated—or 'thought'—without recourse to memory" (EN 178/EN 171).

Interestingly, Levinas does here invoke the language of Kant in a positive manner. He labels this prior obligation to the other a kind of categorical imperative, but in a very specific (and anachronistic) meaning of the term:

> an inveterate obligation, older than any commitment, taking on its full meaning in the imperative that, in the guise of the face of the other, commands the I. A categorical imperative: without regard—so to speak—for any freely taken decision that would "justify" the responsibility; without regard for any *alibi*. An immemorial past, signified without ever having been present, signified on the basis of responsibility "for the other," in which obedience is the mode proper for listening to the commandment. Harkening to a commandment that is therefore not the recall of some prior generous dispositions toward the other man, which, forgotten or secret, belong to the constitution of the *ego*, and are awakened as an a priori by the face of the other. This hearing of a commandment as already obedience is not a decision emerging from a deliberation—be it dialectical—disclosing itself in the face of the other, the prescription deriving its necessity from a theoretical conclusion. A commandment whose power no longer signifies a force greater than mine. The commandment here does not proceed from a force. It comes—in the guise of the face of the other—as the renunciation of all coercion, as the renunciation of its force and of all omnipotence. [EN 178/EN 172]

What Levinas means by categorical imperative requires our attention. It is an "imperative" in that it must be assumed by the I: the I is commanded. It is categorical in that it is unconditional, absolute: it cannot be taken freely, and so it cannot be avoided freely—it *is* before I myself *am*. But it is not Kant's categorical imperative, for in Kant there is reflection, second-order decision making, and an assumption of the imperative in the freedom of the I. Moreover, in Kant the categorical imperative takes the form of an a priori—it justifies itself not in experience but in its universal standing. Rather, the obligation of Levinas's "categorical imperative" exists prior to any consciousness, prior to any deliberation. This anterior responsibility of the diachrony of the immemorial past is Levinas's "categorical imperative."

My responsibility toward the other person is a responsibility awakened in me by "an authority signifying after and despite my death" (EN 179/EN 172). This points to what Levinas calls a "pure future" in which I am for-the-other (EN 179/EN 172). He writes:

> signifying to the finite I, to the I doomed to death, a meaning-ful order signifying beyond this death. Not, to be sure, any sort of promise of resurrection, but an obligation that death does not absolve and a future contrasting strongly with the synchronizable time of re-presentation, with a time offered to intentionality, in which the I think would keep the last word, investing what is imposed upon its powers of assuming. [EN 179/EN 172–173]

The obligation carries beyond and after my death, for the author-ity justifying it is beyond and after my death: the authority justify-ing my obligation is more than being. What I hear, then, in the imperative, is something that goes beyond the intentional, before and after my consciousness; what I hear is the "word of God" (EN 179/EN 172). The word of God signifies a future outside of syn-chronous time, not limited by its inclusion in the presence of the present. It is a pure future coming from an otherwise-than-being. Levinas explains:

> The futuration of the future does not reach me as a to-come, as the horizon of my anticipations of pro-tensions. Must one not, in this imperative meaning of the future that concerns me as non-in-difference to the other, as my responsibility for the stranger—must one not, in this rupture of the natural

order of being, understand what is improperly called super-
natural? Is it not to hear an order that would be the word of
God or, still more exactly, the very coming of God to mind and
its insertion into a vocabulary—whence the "recognizing" and
naming of God in every possible Revelation? The futuration of
the future—not as "proof of God's existence," but as "the fall
of God into meaning." [EN 179–180/EN 173]

This future is not a horizon, a future that I can see and can anticipate. It is not something representable in the single temporality of
history and the narrative of a future following from a present. Nor
is it the promise of the realization of a particular kind of progressive narrative: it is not the realization of a project in which we are
currently, in this time, engaged. Nor is it the "proof of God's existence" as some proof of an other order of time awaiting us in an
other future. It is clearly not a Messianic eschatology. Rather, in
the pure future of obligation, I am confronted with the word of God
and the fall of God into meaning. That is, I am confronted with the
fact of the "beyond" of the Infinite manifest "within" the finite. This
is the meaning of God's transcendence: the meaning of a future (and
a past) beyond (and before) me, before which I find myself elected.
He writes: "Does not responsibility for the other's death—the fear
for the other that no longer enters into the Heideggerian phenomenology of emotion, *Befindlichkeit*—consist in perceiving, in the
finite being of the moral I arrived at from the other's face, the
meaning of a future beyond what happens to me, beyond what, for
an I, is to come?" (EN 180/EN 174).[11]

---

11. One thing that is particularly striking here is a kind of transformation
of the Levinasian method. Recall that *Time and the Other* followed a rather strict
usage of phenomenological reduction: the analysis of the phenomenon of the
advent of the other as breaking up the synchrony of time. However, such an
analysis still operated under the assumption that the advent of the other happened *in* time to break up time; that is, there was still a narrative structure that
the argument followed in unpacking the event. But narrative no longer works
here. Now, the other is pure non-event, pure alterity. The other does not come
in time to disrupt time; rather, the other is disruption itself. In this, we note a
further shift away from the prior *of* consciousness (the *il y a*) to the prior *to*

The future is more than I am; it has meaning beyond me and my existence, beyond the realm of my self-same. In my subjection to the other, I submit myself to a transcendence, higher than, prior to, and beyond my own being. This is the subjection of myself to the word of God, the "A-Dieu" (EN 181/EN 174). It is a subjection of the "authority of excellence or of the Good" (EN 181/EN 174). It is transcendence itself. In this, Levinas has succeeded in showing us how time, in fact, belongs to an order other than pure synchrony. Time is not simply past, present, future, in the everyday, mundane sense of the terms. Instead, there is a "meaning of a past that has not been my present and does not concern my reminiscence, and of a future that command me in mortality or in the face of the other . . . [which] no longer articulate the representable time of immanence and its historical present" (EN 182/EN 175–176). Time has its own history; time is diachronous. And in that diachrony, I find responsibility as an-archy.

Now we come to a complete understanding of ethical subjectivity in Levinas: the ethical subject is the one signified as "for-the-other" in assuming the obligation of responsibility in which the subject finds himself elected, and this election and assumption are the discovery, in the face of the other, of the immemorial past, the an-archic foundation of my subjectivity. An-archy is the immemorial past of obligation I discover in the face of the other, and as such serves as the foundation of my being in the world, of my being a subject. An-archy is the diachronic assumption of the transcendent idea of the good beyond being as foundational for my subjectivity. This is Levinasian foundationalism: the assignation of responsibility and the taking on of the obligation to the other in the confrontation of the non-event of the immemorial past. The subject who takes up his responsibility, who assumes his obligation, is not divided, not empty, not conflicted. This subject is, however, motivated by factors it does not see or know. As such, it is driven by that which

---

consciousness (the immemorial past). Moving further away from traditional methods and argumentation, the radicality of Levinas's thought comes into full view, and clearer explication.

it does not contain or comprehend, by that which exceeds it. In this, it is subjected, constrained, obligated to an "other" order: the word of God. And the word of God is the absolute alterity, the other-than-other itself, that directs it toward the less desirable, toward that other who will hold it hostage and for whom it will be responsible—the other person.

The other person, through the word of God, becomes master of me, he to whom I subject myself. He is, as I am, whole. But he exceeds me in his commands, and I find myself submitted to him in my election. This is the meaning of Levinas's humanism of the other person: the subject as fully and wholly for-the-other-*person*. This subject is not split, not an other to itself; rather, it is for an other in itself. The other takes hold of it, and in this sense shatters the dominance of the "I think," but the subject is still whole when it assumes its prior obligation, when it takes on its responsibility. There is no conflict of conscious and unconscious desires and memories, no splitting of the subject, and no fiction of unity to which it falsely adheres. It is unified, as entirely for the other person. In this, a Levinasian humanism of the other person retains the unity associated with humanism, but none of the self-sufficient power of the humanist subject/self. Instead, this subject is decidedly created (in the strict sense of the term) by and for the other, and it is only in the order of the other that the self as such has any meaning. In the humanism of the other person, I am alienated from a self-sufficient freedom, a freedom that does not yet exist, for I am always already first obligated to an other, in my whole self, and it is that whole self I give to the other person who commands me from high, draws me near, and commands that I give him the bread out of my very mouth. This alienation does not "split" me; rather, it unifies me. It is this alienation that creates my sense of self, as *wholly* and *entirely* for-the-other. This is the portrait of a Levinasian ethical subject, and this is the meaning of a Levinasian humanism of the other person. In my an-archic responsibility as called forth in me by my facing alterity, my turning and seeing the trace of God in the face of the other, I take on my obligation and respond that I shall be responsible, taking on my signification as for-the-other;

confronted with the idea of God within me and turned toward the face of the other person, I stand as witness to the word of God, to the absolute Good, and I respond to the call of my neighbor, the commandment "Thou shalt not kill (me)," with the biblical phrase: I answer, "Here I am."

At last we have fully explicated Levinas's conception of the ethical subject. Now what of Lacan? We will find that Lacan takes us in a startlingly different direction. Though in the first three chapters of this book we have been able to read the two side by side, I mentioned at the end of Chapter 3 that we would not be able to do so in this chapter. And, indeed, we cannot. We cannot because where Levinas has a conception of the ethical subject, Lacan has a conception of the ethics of psychoanalysis. We cannot because where Levinas sees the good as (in an an-archic sense) foundational, Lacan will see it as pathogenic. We cannot because they simply go too far in different directions from each other. So, in isolation from Levinas, it is to Lacan that we now turn.

Now that we have set out the basic trajectory of the Lacanian subject (that is, the move from infancy through adolescence, and thereby the move from the Real to the Imaginary to the Symbolic— all from the perspective of the patient in analysis and from the perspective of the Symbolic itself), it is time to inquire more deeply into the meaning of subjectivity for Lacan, specifically in relation to the question of ethics. Recall that, for Lacan, the subject emerges in the confrontation with the other. The mirror stage provides the foundational moment for the creation of the fictive unity of the self, resulting in a primary alienation and aggression toward the other in the self; in the resolution of the Oedipus complex, the child moves from the Imaginary into the Symbolic and takes up a linguistic and sexed subject position in relation to the master signifier, the phallus. As such, the subject is always by and for the other. But what does this mean for the subject of psychoanalysis, for the patient, for the person? What are Lacan's understandings of time, human relation, love, and desire? What is the ethical subject according to psychoanalysis? And what is the relationship between

psychoanalysis and ethics? These are the questions to which we
will address ourselves here.

To arrive at a fully developed concept of the ethics of Lacanian
psychoanalysis, we must make sure we have a fuller understanding of Lacan's theory of the subject.[12] To do so, we will begin with
a final spelling out of Lacan's conception of subjectivity. We will
achieve this through an examination of Lacan's (1973/1981) seminar *The Four Fundamental Concepts of Psychoanalysis*. The *Four
Fundamental Concepts* was the first of Lacan's seminars to be translated into English, and it is one of the most widely read of Lacan's
works. In this seminar, Lacan identifies the four fundamental concepts of psychoanalysis as "the unconscious, repetition, the transference, and the drive" (S XI 21/S XI 12). In exploring these concepts,
psychoanalysis is seen as the search for the truth of the subject, and

---

12. When speaking of the Real as one of the three registers of existence
(alongside the Imaginary and the Symbolic), I will capitalize the term, and when
speaking of the real as the actual, lived experience of the subject, I will not. Additionally, when using it as an adjective, I will not capitalize it. For Lacan, discussion of the real (*le réel*) is nearly always discussion of the Real as an order of
existence. Rarely does he use "real" to simply mean "actual" or "historical" or
"concrete" or "material," all terms we might substitute for "real" in common
English usage. For Lacan, those terms all exist in the order of the Symbolic, and
are treated as such. Thus, in citing Lacan's texts you will note that "real" is not
capitalized, even though I do so in my own text. I follow the same rules with
capitalizing for the Symbolic, the Imaginary, and the Unconscious.

On the significance of the Real for our inquiry, Lacan writes:

It is at this point that I must refer to those guiding terms, those terms
of reference which I use, namely, the symbolic, the imaginary, and
the real.

More than once at the time when I was discussing the symbolic and
the imaginary and their reciprocal interaction, some of you wondered
what after all was "the real." Well, as odd as it may seem to that su-
perficial opinion which assumes any inquiry into ethics must concern the field of the ideal, if not of the unreal, I, on the contrary, will
proceed instead from the other direction by going more deeply into
the notion of the real. Insofar as Freud's position constitutes progress
here, the question of ethics is to be articulated from the point of view
of the location of man in relation to the real. [S VII 20–21/S VII 11]

in this search, Lacan sets out the goal of the seminar: an inquiry into the fact that "the truth of the subject, even when he is in the position of master, does not reside in himself, but, as analysis shows, in an object that is, of its nature, concealed" (S XI 13–14/S XI 5).

The first of the four fundamental concepts is the Unconscious. We will find that in an examination of the Unconscious we are led to an understanding of the ethical aims of psychoanalysis. Having learned that the Unconscious is structured like a language, that the Unconscious is that register of discourse that directs the subject but that is not transparent to him, and that the Unconscious is constituted in the Symbolic, we now focus on the Unconscious as the calling to our attention of a gap between the Symbolic and the Real, indeed as the very structure of lack itself. Lacan writes:

> I am trying to make you see by approximation that the Freud-
> ian unconscious is situated at that point, where, between cause
> and that which it affects, there is always something wrong. The
> important thing is not that the unconscious determines neuro-
> sis—of that one Freud can quite happily, like Pontius Pilate,
> wash his hands. Sooner or later, something would have been
> found, humoral determinates, for example—for Freud, it would
> be quite immaterial. For what the unconscious does is to show
> us the gap through which neurosis recreates a harmony with a
> real—a real that may well not be determined . . . Something of
> the order of the *non-realized*. [S XI 30/S XI 22]¹³

The Real is what is unavailable to the subject, that piece of his past that has been foreclosed. But the power of the Real does not subside with its foreclosure; the power of the Real is manifest as the unconscious desire for a return to the Real. As an unconscious desire, the desire for a return to the Real is an effect of the Symbolic foreclosure on the Real. But the foreclosure on the Real is also the retroactive construction of the Real, for the Real never existed until it was constructed as "that which the Symbolic is not." Our

_____

13. Notice that Lacan is here making a shift from the analytic to the philosophical.

ETHICAL SUBJECTIVITY **189**

unconscious desire to return to the Real is an effect of the signifying chain of the Symbolic. Understanding this from the perspective of the Symbolic and the patient in analysis, we shouldn't say
that the subject actually seeks a return to a prior unity; rather, we
should say that the subject acts *as if* he were seeking a return to a
prior unity—a unity that never even existed.

Lacan tells us that "the gap of the unconscious may be said to
be pre-ontological" (S XI 38/S XI 29). By this he means that "what
truly belongs to the unconscious . . . is neither being, nor non-being,
but the unrealized" (S XI 38/S XI 30). As such, it is precisely in the
gap between the Symbolic and the Real that the Unconscious is able
to exert its power—in the lack in the subject and its own unconscious feelings of incompleteness. The subject is the desiring subject—in search of a completeness that never existed. And although
the search for that unity enacts itself in the sexual arena, in the
search for the (m)other, and eventually, the partner as love object, the object of desire can never be realized precisely because
it is an unconscious fiction; in the Symbolic, desire is displaced
onto other objects, objects that can never satisfy the unsatisfiable.
And so, perhaps, to the extent that the Symbolic is the realm of
the lived, the gap is not only the gap between the Real and the
Symbolic, but also the gap between the Real and the real. As Lacan
argues, "what analytic experience enables us to declare is rather
the limited function of desire. Desire, more than any other point
in the range of human possibility, meets its limit somewhere"
(S XI 39/S XI 31).

What is the relationship of psychoanalysis to the desire that
meets its limit? It is not ego psychology's search for the normal-
ization of the subject to society. Instead, it is the search for knowledge, understanding, and, dare we say, truth. It is the search for
the Unconscious, not in order to destroy it, but in order to expose
it. This, for Lacan, is the ethical:

> The status of the unconscious, which, as I have shown, is so
> fragile on the ontic plane, is ethical. In his thirst for truth, Freud
> says, Whatever it is, I must go there, because, somewhere, this

unconscious reveals itself. And he says this on the basis of his experience of what was, up to that time, for the physician, the most rejected, the most concealed, the most contained, reality, that of the hysteric, in so far as it is—in a sense, from its origin—marked by the sign of deception. [S XI 41–42/S XI 33]

This is the ethical goal of psychoanalysis: the discovery of the truth of the Unconscious and its power over the subject. And this is the goal of the analysis of dreams. For Lacan, Freud does dream-work in order to show the patient that it is there that the Unconscious can be discovered, and it is there, in the Unconscious, that the subject is "home." Lacan writes: "I am saying that Freud addresses the subject in order to say to him [the subject] the following, which is new—*Here, in the field of the dream, you are at home. Wo es war, soll Ich werden*" (S XI 53/S XI 44).

The second of Lacan's four concepts is repetition. Repetition is, like the Unconscious, in large part concerned with the question of the Real. Lacan tells us:

No praxis is more oriented toward that which, at the heart of the experience, is the kernel of the real than psychoanalysis . . .

Where do we meet this for real? For what we have in the discovery of psychoanalysis is an encounter, an essential encounter—an appointment to which we are always called back with a real that eludes us. That is why I have put on the blackboard a few words that are for us, today, a reference-point of what we wish to propose.

First, the *tuché*, which we have borrowed, as I told you last time, from Aristotle, who uses it in his search for cause. We have translated it as *the encounter with the real*. The real is beyond the *automaton*, the return, the coming-back, the insistence of the signs by which we see ourselves governed by the pleasure principle. The real is that which always lies behind the automaton, and it is quite obvious, throughout Freud's research, that it is this that is the object of his concern. [S XI 63–64/S XI 53–54]

So, it is in the repetition that the Real is suggested, beyond the repetition that the Real lies. But what, precisely, is repetition, and what is being repeated? Lacan tells us that what is repeated is "always something that occurs . . . *as if by chance*" (S XI 65/S XI 54). For instance,

> we always point out that we must not be taken in when the subject tells us that something happened to him that day that prevented him from realizing his wish to come to the session. Things must not be taken at the level at which the subject puts them—in as much as what we are dealing with is precisely this obstacle, this hitch, that we find at every moment. [S XI 65/S XI 54]

Clearly every act, and every repetition, is meaningful: nothing happens without a *reason*. But what is this reason, and, again, what is it that is being repeated? To explain repetition, Lacan turns to Freud's (1961a) presentation of the *fort–da* game in *Beyond the Pleasure Principle*.

One of the most often cited in Freud's text, this moment is worth quoting at length here. The *fort–da* game is the story of a child playing with a string and reel, in which the child throws the reel out of sight and pulls it back into view with the string, all the while "oohing" and "aahing" at the wonder of disappearance and reappearance. Freud tells the story this way:

> This good little boy, however, had an occasional disturbing habit of taking any small objects he could get hold of and throwing them away from him into a corner, under the bed, and so on, so that hunting for his toys and picking them up was often quite a business. As he did this he gave vent to a loud, long-drawn out "o-o-o," accompanied by an expression of interest and satisfaction. His mother and the writer of the present account were agreed in thinking that this was not a mere interjection but represented the German word "fort" ["gone"]. I eventually realized that it was a game and that the only use he made of any of his toys was to play "gone" with them. One day

I made an observation which confirmed my view. The child had a wooden reel with a piece of string tied round it. It never occurred to him to pull it along the floor behind him, for instance, and play at its being a carriage. What he did was to hold the reel by the string and very skillfully throw it over the edge of his curtained cot, so that it disappeared into it, at the same time uttering his expressive "o-o-o-o." He then pulled the reel out of the cot again by the string and hailed its reappearance with a joyful "da" ["there"]. This, then, was the complete game— disappearance and return. As a rule one only witnessed its first act, which was repeated untiringly as a game in itself, though there is no doubt that the greater pleasure was attached to the second act. [pp. 13–14]

Freud interprets this game as the child's repetition of the act of his mother's comings and goings, but to what end? Why would the child reenact the clearly painful event of his mother leaving? Freud (1961a) continues:

The child cannot possibly have felt his mother's departure as something agreeable or even indifferent. How then does his repetition of this distressing experience as a game fit in with the pleasure principle? It may perhaps be said in reply that her departure had to be enacted as a necessary preliminary to her joyful return, and that it was in the latter that lay the true purpose of the game. But against this must be counted the observed fact that the first act, that of departure, was staged as a game in itself and far more frequently than the episode in its entirety, with its pleasurable ending.

No certain decision can be reached from the analysis of a single case like this. On an unprejudiced view one gets an impression that the child turned his experience into game from another motive. At the outset he was in a *passive* situation—he was over-powered by the experience; but by repeating it, unpleasurable though it was, as a game, he took an *active* part. These efforts might be put down to an instinct for mastery that was acting independently of whether the memory was in itself pleasurable or not. But still another interpretation must be attempted. Throwing away the object so that it was "gone" might satisfy an impulse of the child's, which was suppressed in his actual life, to revenge himself on his mother for going away from him. In that case, it would have a defiant meaning: "All right, then, go away! I don't need you. I'm sending you away myself." A year later, the same boy whom I had observed at his first game used to take a toy, if he was angry with it, and throw it on the floor, exclaiming: "Go to the fwont!" He had heard at that time that his absent father was "at the front," and was far from regretting his absence; on the contrary he made it quite clear that he had no desire to be disturbed in his sole possession of his mother. We know of other children who liked to express similar hostile impulses by throwing away objects instead of persons. We are therefore left in doubt as to whether the impulse to work over in the mind some overpowering experience so as to make oneself master of it can find expression as a primary event, and independently of the pleasure principle. For, in the case we have been discussing, the child may, after all, only have been able to repeat his unpleasant experience in play because the repetition carried along with it a yield of pleasure of another sort but nonetheless a direct one. [pp. 15–16]

For Freud, the repetition of the event serves two purposes. First, it makes the child an active participant in a situation in which he was only passively involved. Second, it allows the child to express his own desire for revenge on the object of his affection, the person who is leaving him (in the first game, the mother, in the second game, the father). In this, the child is protecting himself from pain by taking control of it. From all of this, Freud is able to posit the human subject's compulsion to repeat as in part a compulsion to control, in part a compulsion to protect oneself from the looming loss of pleasure by conquest, and in part a compulsion to enact revenge. But even more than these, the compulsion to repeat is just that—a compulsion, for it is as cathected in the Unconscious that the event gains the energy it needs to reassert itself in the repetition. The child repeats the event *because* it is painful, *because* the

Unconscious has latched on to it, *because* it has not been "worked through."

For our purposes, the questions are: How does Lacan interpret this scene and what does he then make of this repetition compulsion? The Lacanian intervention in psychoanalysis here is to link this central psychoanalytic concept to Freud's concept of the splitting of the subject. Lacan writes:

> This real is not the mother reduced to a little ball by some magical game worthy of the Jivaros—it is a small part of the subject that detaches itself from him while still remaining his, still retained . . . If it is true that the signifier is the first mark of the subject, how can we fail to recognize here—from the very fact that this game is accompanied by one of the first oppositions to appear—that it is in the object to which the opposition is applied in act, the real, that we must designate the subject . . . The activity as a whole symbolizes repetition, but not at all that of some need that might demand the return of the mother, and which would be expressed quite simply in a cry. It is the repetition of the mother's departure as cause of a *Spaltung* in the subject—overcome by the alternating game, *fort–da*, which is a *here* or *there*, and whose aim, in its alteration, is simply that of being the *fort* of a *da*, and the *da* of a *fort*. It is aimed at what, essentially, is not there, qua represented—for it is the game itself that is the *Repräsentanz* of the *Vorstellung*. What will become of the *Vorstellung* when, once again, this *Repräsentanz* of the mother—in her outline made up of the brush-strokes and gouaches of desire—will be lacking? [S XI 72–73/S XI 62–63]

The repetition here represents the splitting of the subject—the gap between consciousness and the Unconscious, the gap between demand and desire, the gap between the Imaginary and Symbolic, the gap between the Symbolic and Real, not to mention the conflicts within the Unconscious itself. The repetition shows desire's inability to be achieved and the displacement of desire from one object to another—that is, the disjunction in desire between object and aim. The repetition is the expression of this splitting, this lack, in an attempt to gain what never in fact was, and what in turn never can actually be.

From this Lacan argues that in the case of the Unconscious and repetition

> the cause of the unconscious . . . this cause must be conceived as, fundamentally, a lost cause. And it is the only chance one has of winning it.

> That is why, in the misunderstood concept of repetition, I stress the importance of the ever-avoided encounter, of the missed opportunity. The function of the missing lies at the center of analytic repetition. The appointment is always missed—this is what constitutes . . . the vanity of repetition. [S XI 144/S XI 128]

For Lacan, the Unconscious is "a function of the impossible on which a certainty is based" (S XI 145/S XI 129). In the repetition, "the subject is looking for his certainty" (S XI 145/S XI 129). But we know that certainty is a fiction, as is unity, and that the subject can never find what was never there. What is an analyst to do, then? How is the repetition to be stopped, and how can the realization be made? The answer lies in the third of our four concepts: the transference.

Laplanche and Pontalis (1973) define transference as "a process of actualization of unconscious wishes" (p. 455). A more technical definition might be: a mechanism by which the "cure" of psychoanalytic treatment comes about in which there is in analysis the repetition of the trauma whereby the analyst becomes the object of the patient's aggression and love. It is in the transferential relationship that the trauma is worked through, the repression lifted, and the symptoms purged. Of course, throughout Seminar XI Lacan goes to great length to distinguish between repetition and transference. Still, their relationship is not in doubt.

As Evans (1996) shows, Lacan distinguishes between two components of transference, the Imaginary and the Symbolic:

> [Lacan] continues to elaborate on the symbolic nature of transference, which he identifies with the compulsion to repeat, the

> insistence of the symbolic determinants of the subject. This is to be distinguished from the imaginary aspect of transference, namely, the affective reactions of love and aggressivity. In this distinction between the symbolic and imaginary aspects of transference, Lacan provides a useful way of understanding the paradoxical function of the transference in psychoanalytic treatment; in its symbolic aspect (repetition) it helps the treatment process by revealing the signifiers of the subject's history, while in its imaginary aspect (love and hate) it acts as a resistance. [p. 212]

Acknowledging its symbolic and imaginary components (representation and affect, repetition and resistance), Lacan offers a nuanced treatment of the term.[14] Transference is connected to the Symbolic and the Imaginary in these ways precisely because, as Lacan argues, *"the transference is the enactment of the reality of the unconscious"* (S XI 167/S XI 149).

As the enactment of the reality of the Unconscious, transference is inextricably tied up with Lacan's fourth fundamental concept of psychoanalysis: the drive. Drive is a translation of Freud's term *Trieb*. Strachey translated the term as "instinct," but this is seriously flawed, for it inscribes the *Trieb* in the order of the biological, when clearly for Freud the *Trieb* is a psychical phenomenon (we have previously referred to it as a psychical ordering of bodily instincts). Lacan *also* argues convincingly that the drive is not natural, not biological, but rather psychical.[15] Recall that the

---

14. The reason the Symbolic is the site of repetition is because the Symbolic is the site of desire. We will deal with this in more detail below.

15. He gives as an example the satisfaction of an aim and the idea of sublimation as "successful" substitution. In one of his more notorious comments, he writes:

> Sublimation is also satisfaction of the drive, whereas it is *zielgehemmt*, inhibited as to its aim—it does not attain it. Sublimation is nonetheless satisfaction of the drive, without repression.

> In other words—for the moment, I am not fucking. I am talking to you. Well! I can have exactly the same satisfaction as if I were fucking.

psychical drive is the imaginary ordering of the "instinct" in which the "instinct" is directed to an object. In the drive, then, we

> That's what it means. Indeed, it raises the question of whether in fact I am not fucking at this moment. Between these two terms—drive and satisfaction—there is set up an extreme antinomy that reminds us that the use of the function of the drive has for me no other purpose than to put to question what is meant by satisfaction. [S XI 186/ S XI 165–166]

Of course, the "success" of sublimation is illusory, for the drive, though satisfied, is never fully satisfied. Consider for example, that the oral drive is not about hunger; rather, the oral drive is about satisfying the desire for pleasure that became associated with the desire for nourishment for the infant. That is, the oral drive is about the satisfying pleasure of the breast. Lacan continues:

> Even when you stuff the mouth—the mouth that opens in the register of the drive—it is not the food that satisfies it, it is, as one says, the pleasure of the mouth. That is why, in analytic experience, the oral drive is encountered at the final term, in a situation in which it does no more than order the menu. This is done, no doubt, with the mouth, which is fundamental to the satisfaction—what goes from the mouth comes back to the mouth, and is exhausted in that pleasure that I have just called, by reference to the usual term, the pleasure of the mouth.

> This is what Freud tells us. Let us look at what he says—As far as the object in the drive is concerned, let it be clear that it is, strictly speaking, of no importance. It is a matter of total indifference. One must never read Freud without one's ears cocked. When one reads such things, one really ought to prick up one's ears.

> How should one conceive of the object of the drive, so that one can say that, in the drive, whatever it may be, it is indifferent? As far as the oral drive is concerned, for example, it is obvious that it is not a question of food, nor of the memory of food, nor the echo of food, nor the mother's care, but of something that is called the breast, and which seems to go of its own accord because it belongs to the same series. [S XI 188–189/S XI 167–168]

We will return to the concept of sublimation as illusory or incomplete satisfaction below.

encounter the gap between the Imaginary and the Real.[16] As such, every drive is partial, for it never coincides entirely with the "instinct" it is supposed to satisfy.[17] Lacan writes:

> Every drive being, by its essence as a drive, a partial drive, no drive represents—a notion that Freud raises for a moment when he asks himself whether it is love that realizes it—the totality of the *Sexualstrebung*, of the sexual tendency, as it might be conceived as making present in the psyche the function of *Fortpflanzung*, or reproduction, if this function entered the psyche at all. [S XI 228/S XI 203–204]

From this Lacan concludes that the drive most closely resembles a montage: the drive is a plural-collective of possible objects around which an aim is ordered. As a partial drive, the drive can never retrieve the prior state of unity (the Real) it thinks it originally once was; the drive may lead the subject toward a prior unity, but it can never reach that goal.[18]

---

16. The gap between the Imaginary and the Real also turns our attention to the gap between the Symbolic and the Imaginary and the gap between the Symbolic and the Real. In turn, we are led to an investigation of "desire." We return to this in detail below.

17. Here we must remember that these constructions are not "real" and that all such constructions are retroactive. We only have access to these retroactive constructions through the Symbolic.

18. Alenka Zupancic (2000) draws an important and eloquent distinction between desire and the drive. As she tells us:

> There is also a fundamental difference between desire and the drive. Desire sustains itself by remaining unsatisfied. As for the drive, the fact that it 'understands that this is not the way it will be satisfied' does not stop it from finding satisfaction 'elsewhere'. Thus, in contrast to desire, the drive sustains itself on the very fact that it is satisfied. [p. 242].

This is a sophisticated and nuanced reading, for of course the drive does find some satisfaction. Still, reading Lacan within the context of the three registers, it seems to me that the drive's satisfaction is never *fully* achieved, and in this sense is destined to fail in much the same way as does desire. For more on this, see also footnote 14 above.

As transference is the scene on which the Unconscious is manifest in the analytic relationship, it is the drive that is played out in the transference. As such, the frustration of the Unconscious is the frustration of the impossibility of satisfying the drive. The fantasy of retrieval remains, but it is only ever fantasy, because the gap exists. Moreover, the fantasy of retrieval is all the more a fantasy because the object of retrieval, that which we seek to restore, is itself a fantasy. Still, we continue in the search, hopeful that it is somewhere out there for us. But it is a search at which we are destined to fail.

Transference also rests on the idea of the subject who is supposed to know. A patient enters analysis because he thinks the analyst knows something that she does not, something that he can learn from her. He assumes that the analyst is in possession of an essential knowledge that will cure him. In this, he places on the analyst a capacity that she herself does not have, and he goes to her hoping that she will impart that knowledge. This is the search for certainty. In Descartes, this search was a search for God. In modern atheistic times, God, as Lacan will ironically tell us, lies in the Unconscious, and so the search for certainty is displaced from God onto the master of the Unconscious: the analyst. Now all the pieces of the puzzle come together—the Unconscious, repetition, transference, and the drive—here, in the analyst as the subject who is supposed to know. In transference, the search for unity is repeated, and the frustration of that search is manifest. The search for unity coincides with the search for certainty, and this search culminates in the positing of the analyst as "the subject who is supposed to know" (S XI 256/S XI 230). It is at this point that the analyst must do away with all authority as the one who knows, and instead must impart to the patient the reality of her not knowing. The patient must be made aware not only of his own impotence, but hers as well. The analyst must be "liquidated." In this, the power of the Unconscious is asserted, the operation of the drive is exposed, the transference is acknowledged, and the repetition completed. This is the knowledge the analyst imparts to the patient, then— the knowledge of castration. Lacan writes:

It would be odd all the same if this subject who is supposed to know, supposed to know something about you, and who, in fact, knows nothing, should be regarded as liquidated, at the very moment when, at the end of the analysis, he begins at last, about you at least, to know something. It is therefore at the moment when he takes on most substance that the subject who is supposed to know ought to be supposed to have been vaporized. [S XI 297–298/S XI 267]

The argument comes full circle. In the liquidation of the deception of the subject supposed to know, the patient comes to understand his subjectivity as defined in relation to the Other, and in this comes to recognize the illusion of selfhood. Aggression and love collide, and the symbolic representations as manifest in language repeat themselves; in these things, the power of the Unconscious is uncovered, the fiction of the self is revealed, and the identification of patient with analyst allows a repudiation of the analyst as the subject supposed to know. The antihumanism of the argument now comes in full view. The liberation of psychoanalysis is not a stronger ego exercising control over the id at the direction of the superego. The liberation of psychoanalysis is the understanding of the workings of one's unconscious repetitions, thereby allowing the subject to put aside the specific effects of this aspect of the quest for mastery, the effects of which are causing the specific illness, the specific neurosis at hand, and in turn allowing the subject to accept at least in part some of the consequences of his split subjectivity—split within the Unconscious, split between conscious and unconscious impulses, split between Symbolic and Imaginary, split between Symbolic and Real, and dictated by the field of the Other. So here, in all its glory, is Lacan's vision of the antihumanist subject.

We now have the liquidation of "the subject supposed to know," with the realization by the subject in analysis of the illusory nature of the analyst's knowledge, and in turn of his own. But the question still remains, from the recognition of Lacan's vision of the antihumanist subject: How do we get to ethics? We have already argued that the ethical *goal* of psychoanalysis is the discovery of the truth of the Unconscious and its power over the subject. But what does this mean? In what way is that ethical? How is this picture of ethics different from others? Similar to others? What, in reality, is the ethics of Lacanian psychoanalysis? Lacan addresses these questions in the seminar of 1959–60, *The Ethics of Psychoanalysis* (1986/1992).[19] It is to this seminar that we now turn.

The basic trajectory of the seminar is a description of what an ethics of psychoanalysis is through a detailed reading of what an ethics of psychoanalysis is not. An ethics of psychoanalysis is not an ethics of "the good." It is aimed at neither uncovering the good as universal moral principle (Kant), nor the pursuit of the pleasure of good (Aristotle), nor working for the greatest good for the greatest number (Bentham).[20] These approaches all represent, for Lacan, examples of the pathogenic nature of civilized morality.

Lacan, as always, is writing with Freudian thought as his foundation. Freud presents his account of morality as pathogenic in several of his works, the most prominent treatment occurring in *Civilization and Its Discontents*. There Freud argues that it is

---

19. The seminar on ethics took place four years before the seminar on the four fundamental concepts; from a historical perspective, then, we can read the seminar on ethics as prefiguring the later discussion.

20. Lacan's treatment of these three thinkers is highly sophisticated and highly nuanced. By summarizing them here, I do not wish to do violence to the comprehensiveness of Lacan's reading. For a comprehensive and instructive study of Lacan's interpretations, see John Rajchman's *Truth and Eros: Foucault, Lacan, and the Question of Ethics* (1991), especially pages 44–71. Rajchman does an excellent job of unpacking Lacan's treatment of Aristotle, Kant, and Bentham. Rajchman's constructive point is ultimately that both Lacan and Foucault succeed in calling into question our conventional understandings of ethics, thereby opening up the possibility of our thinking about ethics in a different way, and he directs us to Lacan and Foucault as the jumping off points for our future thought. Thus the penultimate question of the book is the Lacanian question, "What is the place of eros—of jouissance, of our suffering and pleasure—in the truths by which we live?" (p. 147). However, Rajchman does not tell us much more of what ethics becomes when we ask those questions, or what answers we might find. Here I hope to give a little more in the way of concrete answers, both in the sense of what Lacan tells us about ethics and "ethics" (see footnote 28 below), and I hope to offer some preliminary answers to these new types of questions that Rajchman thinks need to be asked.

precisely the conflicts between the individual's superego, the introjected demands of civilization and its code of morality, and the individual's desire (what Freud here identifies as the "id") that lead to psychic conflict.[21] Where a subject's desires conflict with the superego and its prescribed moral dictates, one is forced either to transgress accepted social norms, which can lead to negative psychical consequences, or to repress one's desires and conform to those norms, which causes psychic illness and ultimately leads to neurosis. Civilization and its psychic counterpart, the superego, then, are inherently in conflict with an individual's desire.[22] Building on Freud, Lacan locates the *ethical* project of psychoanalysis, then, within the realm of desire. He writes: "It nevertheless remains true that analysis is the experience that has restored to favor in the strongest possible way the productive function of desire as such. This is so evidently the case that one can, in short, say that the genesis of the moral dimension in Freud's theoretical elaboration is located nowhere else than in desire itself" (S VII 11/S VII 3).

In his analysis of traditional ethical systems Lacan shows how the search for the good and the expression of desire stand in each other's way. He writes: "The dimension of the good erects a strong wall across the path of our desire. It is, in fact, at every moment and always, the first barrier that we have to deal with" (S VII 270/ S VII 230). The very idea of the good, then, is that which stands in the way of the subject realizing his desire. In analysis, the conflict between the good and desire is revealed to the patient and the illness is cured; that is, the patient comes to understand the symptoms and the defenses at work and the repression lifts. One of the revelations of analysis, then, is the revelation of the conflict between desire and the pursuit of the good that stands in desire's way. Lacan writes: "Our daily experience proves to us that beneath what

---

21. As Zupancic (2000) puts it, "The 'Freudian blow' to philosophical ethics can be summarized as follows: what philosophy calls the moral law—and, more precisely, what Kant calls the categorical imperative—is in fact nothing other than the superego" (p. 1).

22. This conflict, remember, all happens on the level of the Unconscious.

we call the subject's defenses, the paths leading to the pursuit of the good . . . reveal themselves to us constantly . . . the whole analytical experience [then] is no more than an invitation to the revelation of his desire [as that which stands in the way of the good—and vice versa]" (S VII 261/S VII 221).

From this Lacan argues that what analysis demands is a renunciation of the pursuit of the good as the ideal toward which the subject must strive: "a radical repudiation of a certain ideal of the good is necessary" (S VII 270/S VII 230). An ethics of psychoanalysis aims the patient away from a pursuit of the good and toward her desire, which points the patient toward her Unconscious. It is only in examining the workings of the Unconscious that we can discover this conflict that exists, for this conflict is an unconscious one.

In relation to the ethical, this process directs our attention to the Real: in our examination of the Real we come to see more clearly the conflicts of our Unconscious as ethical because it is onto the Real that we graft our sense of the moral as a basic driving force. As Lacan writes: "Moral action is, in effect, grafted on to the real" (S VII 30/S VII 21). We unconsciously attach ourselves to a pursuit of the good because we mistakenly place the good within the register of the Real. Lacan calls that which we place in the register of the Real "*das Ding*" (the thing). We have mistakenly located that search for the ideal as the search for *das Ding*—the lost object of our desire—that is, as existing in the Real; this is the mistake of traditional ethics. It is in *attention* to the Real, then, that we can come to see the pathogenic nature of civilized morality: "Insofar as Freud's position on ethics constitutes progress here, the question of ethics is to be articulated from the point of view of the location of man in relation to the real" (S VII 21/S VII 11). For psychoanalysis, the good is *not* the Real; rather, the Real is a register that exerts itself in the psyche as the retroactive construction of that place that existed before the Imaginary, before the ego. The Real is *the all*, the unity of everything, not a place of moral codes and universal ethical beliefs. And the Real can never be achieved, for it is an unconscious fantasy. The Real is not the ideal, but rather is the *impossible*.[23] The unity of the Real (which never truly existed) can, of course, never again come to be. It is in attention to the Real that we can come to see what psychoanalysis *does* have to teach us positively about ethics. For if the experience of psychoanalysis is not about a search for the "ideal" so much as it is about the uncovering of the unconscious desire, and if it is in the Symbolic order that desire manifests itself, then it is in the Real that the *roots* of desire seemingly (and retroactively) manifest themselves.

Concretely, this has several implications for the proper reading of an ethics of psychoanalysis. In opposition to the prescriptions of ego psychology, Lacan argues that an ethics of psychoanalysis is not one that simply places the superego at the forefront of moral decision-making, or one that submits all claims of desire to the dictates of the introjected social law. For Lacan, ego psychology stresses ethics as the search for and imposition of an ideal on the subject. Lacan is adamant that such a reading of psychoanalytic ethics will not suffice: "Moral experience is not simply linked to that slow recognition of the function of that which was defined and made autonomous by Freud under the term of superego" (S VII 15/S VII 7). He regards the submission of desire to the superego and the process of building a stronger ego around which such "choices" can be made as fundamentally misdirected. Such attempts fail to take into account the fictivity of the unified self, and fail to account for the fact of the split nature of the subject.

This does not mean that psychoanalysis directs us in the opposite direction, either. An ethics of psychoanalysis is not one of liberation of libidinal drives over and against the dictates of a prescribed morality. Lacan argues convincingly that "Freud was in no way a progressive" (S VII 216/S VII 183). An ethics of psychoanalysis cannot direct us toward a liberation of our pleasure.[24]

---

23. Of course, this takes place on the level of the unconscious. We don't actually have an idea of the Real as either the unity or the ideal; rather, we act as if we have an idea of this earlier unity we call the Real, and we act as if we have come to graft our sense of the moral onto it.

24. Freud (1977) is clear about this in many places. Consider the following statement from his *Introductory Lectures*:

As Evans (1996) argues: "Psychoanalysis . . . is not simply a libertine ethos" (p. 56). Here, Lacan is clearly siding with Freud's (1961b) argument in *Civilization and Its Discontents*, where pessimism wins out over any system of prescribed morality.[25]

For Lacan, factors other than pessimism are also at work here—most prominently an argument against the *possibility* of fully realizing pleasure.[26] Lacan tells us that some argue that what is demanded of the analyst in analysis, as the end of analysis, is "happiness." A reading of psychoanalysis centered on the Unconscious, however, does not bring the patient happiness at all, for the uncovering of the workings of the Unconscious and the recogni-

---

But, Ladies and Gentlemen, who has so seriously misinformed you? A recommendation to the patient to "live a full life" sexually could not possibly play a part in analytic therapy—if only because we ourselves have declared that an obstinate conflict is taking place in him between a libidinal impulse and sexual repression, between a sensual and an ascetic trend. This could not possibly be solved by our helping one of these trends to victory over its opponent. [p. 538]

On the "goal" of psychoanalysis, Freud continues: "A true decision can only be reached when they [the component parts of the conflict] both meet on the same ground. To make this possible is, I think, the sole task of our therapy" (ibid., p. 539). Of course, Lacan's goal of the dissolution of the subject supposed to know is slightly different, a clearly antihumanist take on Freud's originally quite humanist goal. Still, it is one that is thoroughly in line with one highly intelligible reading of Freud.

25. This is not to say that Lacan does not direct us toward our eros, for he does. Fink (1995) makes this point well, particularly in juxtaposition with ego pscyhology, when he says, "While therapists in our society are expected to interact with their patients in ways that are considered by dominant contemporary social, political, and psychological discourses to be for their own *good*, analysts act instead so as to further their analysands' *Eros*" (p. 146). Still, directing a patient toward her eros is different than directing society at large to the liberation of pleasure. Such a move wouldn't work, for liberation at large is, for Freud and Lacan, a social (and symbolic) impossibility. Fink agrees in telling us that psychoanalysis is "a praxis of jouissance, and jouissance is anything but practical" (ibid., p. 146).

26. This is not to suggest that Freud's argument is simply built on his pessimism. It is simply to (1) point out that in *Civilization and Its Discontents* Freud clearly rejects a libertine ethos, and (2) that Lacan, in his treatment of the subject, takes the argument in directions Freud did not follow in that work.

tion of the impossibility of unity and coherence are not happy events, but rather are ones in which the subject is forced to confront his fictions as fictions. Lacan writes:

> [The] aspiration to happiness will always imply a place where miracles happen, a promise, a mirage of original genius or an opening up of freedom, or if we caricature it, the possession of all women for a man and of an ideal man for a woman. To make oneself the guarantor of the possibility that a subject will in some way be able to find happiness even in analysis is a form of fraud.
>
> There is absolutely no reason why we should make ourselves the guarantors of the bourgeois dream. [S VII 350/S VII 303]

The goal of analysis, then, is not the lifting of unconscious desires and the conformity of one's Unconscious to the social in order that *happiness* is achieved. Instead, for Lacan, "the true termination of an analysis . . . [should] confront the one who undergoes it with the reality of the human condition" (S VII 351/S VII 303). The goal is understanding the reality of the fictions of identity and happiness, realizing the impossibility of a return to a unity that never was by realizing the impossibility of mastery, by realizing one's own fantasmatic castration.

An ethics of psychoanalysis articulates the prevalence of the Unconscious in our decision making. In this, psychoanalytic theory directs our attention to the gap between the Symbolic and the Real, making us take account of this gap and forcing us to come to terms with it. In analysis, this is realized by our seeing that we have been acting as if we have a notion of an earlier unity to which we seek to return. That is, we act as if we desire to return to the Real. In recognizing the fiction of the Real, we recognize the impossibility of realizing it. Symbolic desire can never fulfill the need articulated as a desire to return to the Real. As patients, then, we are forced to confront the fact of our fictions and the force they play in structuring our desire. Lacan writes:

[I]t is within this opposition between fiction and reality that is to be found the rocking motion of Freudian experience.

Once the separation between the fictitious and the real has been effected, things are no longer situated where one might expect. In Freud the characteristic of pleasure, as that dimension which binds man, is to be found on the side of the fictitious. The fictitious is not, in effect, in its essence that which deceives, but is precisely what I call the symbolic.

That the unconscious is structured as a function of the symbolic, that it is the return of a sign that the pleasure principle makes man seek out, that the pleasurable element which directs man in his behavior without his knowledge (namely, that which gives him pleasure, because it is a form of euphony), that that which one seeks and finds again is the trace rather than the trail—one has to appreciate the great importance of all of this in Freud's thought, if one is to understand the function of reality. [S VII 22/S VII 12–13]

By separating the fictitious from the real, Lacan is, in effect, showing how our unconscious fantasies are fictions, but fictions that act as if they are truths. For Lacan, the fictions of the Symbolic may not be "true" in the sense of being "real," but this does not mean they are illusory, for they operate in our Unconscious as if they were true. Thus, Lacan argues that "every truth has the structure of fiction" (S VII 22/S VII 12).

Seeing the Unconscious as a function of the Symbolic directs our attention to the gap between the Symbolic and the Real. In realizing this, we can assume our own, as well as the analyst's, castration. This does not do away with desire: desire remains the first and last cause; but it does allow us to relinquish the specific symptoms and defenses at work when we desire too much a return to this fictional place we call the Real. This attention to the gap between the Symbolic and the Real takes us back to our earlier discussion of the difference between demand and desire.[27] Lacan writes:

---

27. See my treatment of this theme in Chapter 2.

In daring to formulate a satisfaction that isn't rewarded with a repression, the theme that is central or preeminent is, What is desire? And in this connection, I can only remind you of what I have articulated in the past: realizing one's desire is necessarily always raised from the point of view of an absolute condition. It is precisely to the extent that the demand always under- or overshoots itself that, because it articulates itself through the signifier, it always demands something else; that in every satisfaction of a need, it insists on something else; that the satisfaction formulated spreads out and conforms to this gap; that the desire is formed as something supporting this metonymy, namely, as something the demand means beyond whatever it is able to formulate. [S VII 340/S VII 294]

On the surface, the call of demand is the call to satisfy the instinctual need of the Real. However, demand always demands more—it demands love of the (m)other, which comes in the Imaginary. Thus, desire emerges in the gap between demand and need as the failure of demand to meet itself. Desire can never be satisfied because it demands the impossible. Desire, then, is the failure of demand to *articulate* itself in the Symbolic. The signifier fails to articulate the signified. This gap between demand and desire, then, is a function of the gap between the Symbolic and the Imaginary, which is in turn a function of the gap between the Imaginary and the Real. These gaps remain and always will; desire can never be fulfilled in its entirety because the Imaginary phallus and the Real phallus are not one and the same. The Symbolic exists by separating itself out from the Real, and does so because of the gap between the Imaginary and the Real. Illness results from our failures to deal with the impossibility of satisfaction due to these unbridgeable gaps.[28]

---

28. Jonathan Lee (1990) has an instructive discussion of the impossibility of the real as what makes the subject of psychoanalysis "ethical." He argues that the "ethical subject carries out his actions in an asymptomatic relation to the always elusive real" (p. 168). I like this formulation. However, I disagree with Lee when he finishes this sentence, "forever attempting and yet failing to achieve the purity of the Kantian good will" (ibid.). Clearly, it is the knowledge of the impossibility of achievement of the Real that keeps the subject asymptomatic (that

None of this is to say that *satisfaction* is not *a* goal of the psychoanalytic situation, for the lifting of repression *is* a satisfaction. This, for instance, is the goal of sublimation. Sublimation is an important but underdeveloped category in Freud's writings. Laplanche and Pontalis (1973) define it as a

> process postulated by Freud to account for human activities which have no apparent connection with sexuality but which are assumed to be motivated by the force of the sexual instinct. The main types of activity described by Freud as sublimated are artistic creation and intellectual inquiry.
>
> The instinct is said to be sublimated in so far as it is diverted towards a new non-sexual aim and in so far as its objects are socially valued ones. [p. 431]

In sublimation, the sexual drive is redirected; that is, the drive is directed toward a different object, and, in fact, a different aim. Through sublimation, the economic forces of the drives are satisfied without there being a need for the repression of the socially unacceptable object and aim, specifically the sexually perverse. Lacan focuses on the possibility of object-change as the defining factor in how sublimation works. As Evans (1996) argues, Lacan's focus is not *simply* on the possibility of a change to a new object presenting itself to the desire, but the position of that object "in the structure of fantasy" (p. 198). Lacan defines sublimation as the possibility of "satisfaction without repression" (S VII 340/S VII 293). What allows this is "not [the change to] a new object or a previous object, but the change of object in itself" (S VII 340/S VII 293). In being able to lift repression by making known the contents and impulses of the Unconscious, desire is revealed as "noth-

---

is, healthy). But this does not mean Lacan endorses an endless pursuit of that impossibility. While I do not argue that Lacan thinks that we give up our desire for the impossible Real by erasing this desire from our lives altogether, neither do I argue that Lacan thinks that we continue in the pursuit in the same way we did prior to the realization of the Real's impossibility. He does not. Lee's language of the "forever attempting" seems to me to push this a bit too far.

ing more than the metonymy of the discourse of demand," that is, as the ordering of the Imaginary by the Symbolic (S VII 340/S VII 293). Thus, we are reminded of the fact that the object of desire has no value in and of itself as object, but has value only in the role it plays in fantasy as satisfying imaginary demand. In discovering this, the object of that desire *is* changed: we sublimate.[29] However, though sublimation may direct us to the possibility of a satisfaction without repression, it will never be a full and complete satisfaction. It is never enough; it will never succeed fully.[30]

One thing the patient achieves in analysis is the realization of the conflicts of his Unconscious (in this case, that conflict is the enactment of the gap between his desire and his demand) and the impossibility of achieving that unity toward which he is seemingly striving. In uncovering the fact of unconscious motivation, the patient lets go of this part of the fantasy of unity; that is, he lets go of the particular symptoms and defenses enacted in this manifestation of that fantasy, but the fantasy itself never disappears. In this, part of what psychoanalysis offers is knowledge of the nature of our desire, and the extent to which we can never achieve this fantasmatic ideal of unity. Happiness, conformity, ideality, these things are our unconscious fantasies of being able to achieve an original sexual fulfillment in the Real. Psychoanalysis exposes these things as fictions: the Real is the impossible. So, while one can sublimate and in turn substitute one desire for another, or at least substitute one object of desire for another, this will never fully succeed. Neither demand nor desire can ever satisfy need, their counterpart in the Real, for unity is a retroactively established fantasy manifested as a desire to return to the Real, but the Real never existed. In un-

---

29. Sublimation often, and in fact more often, occurs at the unconscious level, in which the preconscious censor redirects the drive before it can transgress and cause the symptoms of illness associated with the repression of that desire to transgress.

30. Jean-Michel Rabaté (2000a) shows us how critical of the concept of sublimation Lacan is. I agree, and would further point out that while for both Freud and Lacan sublimation can never offer full satisfaction, Lacan is ultimately more critical of sublimation than Freud is. Freud seems to think of sublimation as a viable option to repression; Lacan does not.

covering the workings of one's unconscious desire, then, one is able to realize that the fulfillment of that desire is an impossibility.

An ethics of psychoanalysis allows us to see the importance of our desire in structuring our actions, thereby allowing us to see the Unconscious as the primary motivating factor in our lives. How is this an ethics? What makes this ethical? For Lacan, then, the question of a psychoanalytic ethics explicitly is: "Have you acted in conformity with the desire that is in you?" (S VII 362/S VII 314). Lacan writes:

> What needs to be unmasked . . . is the point on which [traditional] morality turns. And that is nothing less than the impossibility in which we recognize the topology of our desire. The breakthrough is achieved by Kant when he posits that the moral imperative is not concerned with what may or may not be done. To the extent that it imposes the necessity of a practical reason, obligation affirms an unconditional "Thou shalt" . . .
>
> Now we analysts are able to recognize that place as the place occupied by desire. Our experience gives rise to a reversal that locates in the center an incommensurable measure, an infinite measure, that is called desire. [S VII 364/S VII 315–316]

If ethics is about the world of the "ought," then for Lacan the ought is the movement of our desire, for our desire is manifest as an ought. Desire is that which compels us, and desire *as* an ought is Lacan's play on the categorical imperative, Lacan's play on the very question of ethics. What we assess in determining whether or not we have acted "ethically" is not whether or not we have acted in accord with an internal(ized) moral law, but whether or not we have acted on our desire. "Ethics," for Lacan then, is not what we traditionally think of as ethics at all. Lacan turns the term, and the very idea of ethics, on its head.[31] Thus, Lacan states: "the only thing one

---

31. Notice that at this point I begin to place "ethics" in quotation marks when referring to Lacan's positive reading of an "ethics of psychoanalysis." I do this in order to signal to the reader Lacan's continuous ironizing and appropriation of the term.

can be culpable of is giving ground relative to one's desire" (S VII 370/S VII 321). For it is giving ground relative to one's desire, that is, placing something else before our desire by denying our desire, that is the source of (ethical) culpability in a psychoanalytic framework; and it is allowing our desire to drive us that is the source of the judgment of culpability from a traditional ethical position. (Lacan is clearly playing on the idea of culpability here.) In this Lacan means both that (1) *traditional* ethical systems hold us responsible when we give way to desire, and (2) the only thing we can be truly culpable for from a *psychoanalytic* perspective is *not* acting in accord with our desire.[32]

One must be careful, however, with Lacan's language here, for it is all too easy to slip into a humanist reading of his account. According to psychoanalysis, one can *never* act without *regard* to one's desire: desire is always that which motivates us. Whether we act in accord with our desire or go against it, it is the desire that drives us, for we only go against our desire to the extent that we *actively* (but unconsciously) put something in its way. Again, desire, in psychoanalysis, is primary. Moreover, desire is never something we can ever know. That is, we don't know what our desire is or what it is for, we only "know" that we desire, and that somehow this desire is connected to a fantasmatic search for an original unity. The things we consciously learn are (1) the fact of our desire; (2) the fact of a conflict in our Unconscious; and (3) the specific sources and defenses of the symptoms we are, at this moment, attempting to lift. Beyond that, desire remains in the Unconscious, and continues to do its work there. Acting "in accord" with our desire, then, really means acting without repression. So, the question for the patient and analyst becomes, what was the source of this repression and how do we lift it?

In a psychoanalytically informed "ethics," no conception of the good can or should hold sway over our desire. This does not mean that Lacan is arguing for some Nietzschean dismissal of the

---

32. It seems to me that this *is* a moral judgment on Lacan's part. That is, he is placing value on "acting in accord with one's desire."

ETHICAL SUBJECTIVITY   **213**

ethical as such.[33] Rather, Lacan is arguing for an informed position concerning the reality of the Unconscious. As such, the ethical question of psychoanalytic inquiry is not whether or not an action was in conformity with an idea of the good, whether it was right or wrong. The ethics of psychoanalysis is not concerned with moral judgments about past events. The ethics of psychoanalysis is an uncovering of the reality of the Unconscious and the fact of our desire. The ethical question of psychoanalysis is an inquiring into our understanding of the extent to which an action was "in accord" with our desire. That is, it is a local exploration of a local event—the inquiring into the question, "How are your symptoms and defenses connected to a particular unconscious conflict between your desire and your idea of the good?" Lacan posits the question of ethics, then, not as a matter of "How do we judge what just happened?" but rather as a question of "What now?" He writes: "The important thing is not knowing whether man is good or bad in the beginning; the important thing is what will transpire once [one has acted]" (S VII 375/S VII 325). We should not interpret this as an attempt to use the "past" to determine the "future"; Lacan is far too antihumanist to lead us down the liberal path of progressive narrativity. The only way to interpret this statement is as an analytic statement, not as a philosophical one.[34] Lacan's "What now?" is a question as to the direction of the patient's cure. The cure only happens by the lifting of the repression, thereby alleviating the suffering repression causes. In coming to terms with the Unconscious, with desire, the patient lifts the repression and thereby lifts the symptoms, and allows the battle between a certain movement of desire and its defenses to cease. If we ultimately *did* want to posit some ultimate "moral" goal of psychoanalysis, from a traditional perspective, this would be it: seeing ourselves as desiring subjects can help to alleviate the suffering

33. This certainly might be one direction in which we could take Lacan. However, he himself does not develop any such "system." What I propose to do with Lacan's insight will be addressed in the conclusion.

34. "Analytic" meaning "concerning the patient in analysis."

of repression. This does not lead to happiness, as we have already seen. It does not lead to a better-developed ego, or to a stronger means of mastery. It only leads to the acknowledgment of the workings of the Unconscious, and, in turn, to better psychic health. But even to posit that as a moral goal of analysis is to push Lacan in places he would not want to venture.

Where does this leave us? Where are we to go now? It seems as if, after all our attempts at reading Levinas and Lacan side by side, we are, in the end, left with two theories so incompatible as to have rendered this entire project moot. And, indeed, on the surface this certainly seems to be the case. But perhaps there is a way to bring the two back together, if not in conversation then at least in some sort of a mutual truce. Perhaps there are underlying points of contact, even agreement, even on this point on which they most strongly disagree—the nature of the ethical—through which we can move forward with both. Or perhaps, refusing to reduce one to the other, refusing to obscure disagreement with forced agreement, we can find a way to bring these two thinkers together in spite of—or perhaps even because of—their disagreements! It is to this project, the project of how to bring Levinas and Lacan together, that we must turn our attention in the conclusion. I will do so by looking at the ways others have attempted to do this, and then proceed to examine my own attempt to achieve this project, by means other than assimilation.

Conclusion: Post-Humanist Ethical Subjectivity

What is it to be an ethical subject? What in subjectivity can be called ethical? In the philosophical landscape of today, one dominated by critiques of Enlightenment humanism, traditional answers to these questions, answers that have attempted to define the ethics of the self with reference to universal powers or capacities such as reason, the passions, the virtues, or even a narrative life, no longer apply. Today, in our post-humanist landscape, what answers can we provide to these questions?

In this book I have approached these questions from the perspective of two of the most provocative thinkers of the twentieth century, two thinkers who dealt extensively with the questions of subjectivity, ethics, and their origins—Emmanuel Levinas and Jacques Lacan. Choosing to read Levinas and Lacan together may have seemed an odd project to many. On the surface, their projects may seem completely irreconcilable. Having now read them together, I hope to have shown that this is not entirely the case. The points of agreement and contact are far greater than previously recognized. For both, the subject is formed in response to an intervention of the other, in which the other disrupts the solitude and hypostasis of self-same existence, calling the subject to an order outside itself, beyond itself, to which it must accede. For both, the subject's sexed position is indicative of an order outside of the sameness of the self, and calls the subject into relation with an other. For both, the subject's ability to speak is predicated on a preexisting system of meaning, though only for one is this indicative of an ethical order prior to signification. However, although the intervention of the other stands as the foundational metaphor for understanding subjectivity in both Levinas and Lacan, in the end, in discussing more directly the questions of origins, ethics, God, and the Unconscious, we found that the two thinkers radically diverged.

Having asked how Levinas and Lacan answer our questions, I have added to a collection of literature that has read these two thinkers together, looked beyond the surface disagreements, and found hidden areas of agreement, or at least productive conversation. This collection of literature is small, but, I am happy to say, growing, and has had the benefit of several important works published in the last several years, including Reinhard's (1995) "Kant with Sade, Levinas with Lacan," the edited volume *Levinas and Lacan: The Missed Encounter* (Harasym 1998), and Critchley's *Ethics—Politics—Subjectivity* (1999). It is in light of these contributions that I have offered this reading.

Among these works, one stands out as deserving special mention, for it is, in part, from this reading that I wish to distinguish my own. That reading is Critchley's. His reading is significant, for it is the one that, I believe, pushes the connection between Levinas and Lacan the furthest. Critchley (1999) offers his innovative reading of Levinas and Lacan in two chapters: "The Original Traumatism: Levinas and Psychoanalysis," and "*Das Ding*: Levinas and Lacan," and his argument is twofold. First, he wishes to show that the discussions of subjectivity that we find in Levinas and psychoanalysis share a similar structure—what Critchley calls "original traumatism." Second, he wishes to argue that the originary phenomena (and I use this word with obvious reservation) that found the subject as ethical in Levinas and in Lacan—

the face of the other person and the encounter with the Real—
can be read as equivalent.

The first point is simple enough. For Levinas, the subject is
founded in a confrontation with the other in which the self is emp-
tied out by a "non-intentional affectivity" that "tears into my subjectivity like an explosion, like a bomb that detonates without
warning, like a bullet that hits me in the dark, fired from an un-
seen gun and by an unknown assailant" (Critchley 1999, p. 190).
As he shows, this description easily translates into psychoanalytic
terminology: "*subjectivity would seem to be constituted for Levinas
in a transferential relation to an original trauma*" (p. 190). On this
point, it is hard to disagree with Critchley.

The second point is a little trickier. Critchley goes on to say
that Levinas's description of the face of the other is correlative to
Lacan's description of the encounter with the Real. In "*Das Ding*:
Levinas and Lacan," Critchley relates the following:

> I remember a friend saying to me several years ago, "What pre-
> vents the face of the other in Levinas from being *das Ding*?" I
> didn't know quite what he meant at the time, but the ques-
> tion was clearly meant critically. I would like to answer the
> question directly now by saying that nothing prevents the face
> of the other being *das Ding* and, furthermore, that there is a
> common formal structure to ethical experience in Levinas and
> Lacan. [p. 199]

Das Ding is the term Lacan uses in the seminar on ethics to describe that lost object of desire that we place in the register of the
Real, and that sense of realness that we ascribe to the moral.
Critchley goes on to present a sophisticated and, for the most part,
highly accurate and instructive reading of the shared insights and
obvious divergences between Levinas and Lacan. Critchley's starting point, however, is flawed. As the an-archic stands outside of
the realm of discursive signification, it also stands outside of the
Lacanian Symbolic (the order of signification). It is tempting,
therefore, to locate the ethical structure of subjectivity within the
Lacanian Real (the register of prediscursive unity). However, to do

so would be to make a fundamental mistake. It is certainly not the case that nothing prevents the face of the other from being *das Ding*. Rather, much prevents the face of the other from being *das Ding*— precisely because *das Ding* in Lacan can best be understood as primarily a function of *exclusion*.

Recall that for Lacan the Real is that register of meaning on which psychic reality claims to rest, to which the symbol claims to refer, and in which the object that love tries to recover is supposed to lie. It is the original, impossible all that is supposed by the subject to have existed prior to differentiation. However, the Real only *is* in relation to the Symbolic, only comes into being as having been created as that which has been foreclosed upon by the Symbolic. The Real is composed of that which is excluded *into* the Real. The Real in Lacan is a fantasmatic retroactive construction—one that, from our place in the Symbolic, we determine had, prior to the Imaginary (hence the fantasmatic component), resisted symbolization and signification. The Symbolic is always privileged, always primary, always *first*. In Levinas, by contrast, the immemorial past may be outside of signification and symbolization, but it is neither a posited retroactive *construction* nor an excluded *result* of the order of language and being. Although outside of synchronous time and re-presentational being, the an-archical foundation of the ethical encounter is absolutely primary, and in this, is *a* real, not "Real." Thus it is precisely at the point at which Levinas and Lacan may seem to be closest together that they are actually farthest apart. To read too much Levinas into Lacan or too much Lacan into Levinas is to run the risk of serious reduction.[1]

---

1. In his essay "The Real of Sexual Difference," Slavoj Žižek (2002) offers an extremely sophisiticated critique of Critchley's conflation of Levinas and Lacan. While Žižek mistakenly links the Real with excrement (a Kristevan reading that misses the point—the Real, however, is not the abject) and while his argument skillfully unfolds through a reading of the post-secular critique of onto-theology, Žižek does note the disparity between the Real and *das Ding* when he notes that "the Real is there as the empty place, as a structure, a construction that is never actual or experienced as such but can only be retroactively constructed and has to be presupposed as such—the Real as symbolic construction" (p. 64). Although

Perhaps we can better understand the operative difference here if we look more closely at what Levinas and Lacan mean when they talk of the "origins" of ethics. To do this, let us first ask the question, What do these two thinkers mean by the term "origin"? We begin with Levinas.

For Levinas, an origin is an-archic—a proto-foundation, a non-event from the immemorial past that grounds my subjectivity as ethical. But let us be more concrete. We already know that my subjectivity is "ethical" because my responsibility to the other person emerges as always already having been, prior to my response, prior even to my ability to respond. In this, it is awakened in me as *before* my freedom, before my cognition or intention. In the face of the other, I cannot deliberate, I cannot consider the consequences; I cannot even re-present the other's face to myself as an object of reflection for my consciousness. My responsibility is *anterior* to this, prior to and beneath these possibilities, already there, always already having been. The awakening of this prior having-been by the other is decidedly not a remembering of a past event, for it cannot be understood as object, thought, or being. It is an *originless origin*, a *foundationless foundation*—the recalling of an *originary* non-event that cannot be remembered because it never properly *happened*. But in announcing itself to me in the face of the other, the immemorial past tells me it is a piece of my past in that it is at the very heart and soul of *who* and *how* I am in the world of others. It is in this sense that Levinas calls it an "an-archy": a *without-foundation* that, nevertheless, *founds* and *grounds* my subjectivity. It undergirds what it is for me to exist among others in the world. It gives meaning to the present, calls me into *signification* as the one-for-the-other. With every step I take, with every assertion of my power, I am preceded by it. I cannot escape it. I can ignore it, but it will not go away. I am guilty before ever having acted, for every act will be an act of violence to the other. This fact follows me wherever I go.

I formulated my critique of Critchley several years before I encountered the Žižek essay, I am extremely grateful to this paper for offering a similar critique, one that also strengthens my reading.

When I turn myself toward it, it takes me hostage, obsesses me, reminds me of my originary election, and, if I choose, I can accept that it is my pure, inspired future, in the response, "Here I am."

The immemorial past itself isn't an event (rather Levinas calls it an "enigma"). It is a non-phenomenon that never "happened" in an ordinary, synchronous sense of the word. It structures my subjectivity in the world, though, because it has already predetermined what it is for me to act, to think, to do, to exist. I have access to it, to that past, when I confront the other person in the present. This confrontation reminds me, recalls in me this founding "moment," this underlying structure of who and how (and why) we are. So, even though this immemorial past did not "happen" in the ordinary sense of the word, it is very real. It exists as prior to this world, as lying beneath and before it. As an an-archy, it is an *arché* nonetheless. And as an anti-origin, it is originary. The *origins* of ethics are found, then, in these moments in which I am awakened to my immemorial past—that is, in which I am awakened to the ethical structure of my subjectivity.

For Lacan, on the other hand, the answer to the question of origins is a little less straightforward. It rests in one of Lacan's most interesting and difficult contributions to psychoanalytic theory— the idea of the three registers, the Real, the Imaginary, and the Symbolic. If we were to need to describe these to a non-Lacanian, one way would be to define them as "stages." This would be a convenient way to begin to understand them, but, as we shall see, it would be very misleading if we were to stop there. It may seem as if the three registers unfold temporally and developmentally in the child's existence, but they do not. From a developmental perspective, we might speak of what occurs as follows: The Real represents the life of the infant, both in the womb and (roughly) in the first six months of its existence. In this stage, the child does not differentiate between itself and others; its world is one of original unity, with the mother, with its environment, with the all. The Imaginary is initiated in the mirror stage, which emerges starting around the child's sixth month, and lasts, in waning degrees, through the resolution of the Oedipus complex. In the mirror stage, the infant is confronted with a specular image, one that is whole, unified, and in control. The infant comes to recognize that this image is both itself and its other, and attempts to assume the unity that this image has, but that it itself lacks. Lacan calls this image the "ideal I." In recognizing the image of the other (hence the term "Imaginary"), the infant begins the process of differentiation between self and other and organizes itself around the dyadic relationship it experiences with its respective others (the specular image and the (m)other) and the "ideal I" it sees in them. The Symbolic stage emerges in increments, and exerts itself in full force in the resolution of the Oedipus complex. To resolve the Oedipus complex, the child is forced to give up its incestuous love for the parental objects, and instead take up its sex-appropriate love object. In assuming its appropriate *object*, the child assumes its appropriate (or inappropriate) *subject position* (its ego-ideal) in relation to the master signifier, the phallus. That is, it sexes itself by assuming either a male or a female subject-position. As these positions exist in relation to the symbol "phallus," and as this symbol is the organizing principle of language, Lacan calls this the Symbolic order.

Clearly the procedure as we have just described it is straightforward, and makes Lacan's theory of the registers accessible. However, the problem that arises in defining these registers as stages, as temporal and developmental periods through which the child moves, is that such a definition misses the radicality of Lacan's insights. It is not the case that the Real precedes the Imaginary, which precedes the Symbolic. According to Lacan, the child is always already located in the Symbolic order. Lacan goes to great lengths to make this point. We live in the Symbolic. While the Imaginary and the Real may be part of our history, we only ever have access to them through the Symbolic. This is true for the patient in analysis who looks back on the events of his childhood—the subject who experiences illness as a conflict in the Unconscious wherein some portion of it desires to return to something pre-Symbolic (the Imaginary or the Real), or in which conflict arises because traces of the Imaginary or the Real are exerting pressure on the Unconscious against the demands of the Symbolic. It is also true for any subject who confronts his past, for in confronting his past the subject experiences it, as Lacan writes in the Rome Discourse, "already as facts of history" (E 261/E 52). The events of the past only exert power on us insofar as they are *interpreted*— experienced as in *conflict* or in *congruence* with events in our present. They do not exist as simple pasts, but rather as pasts that structure the here and now. Even better, they exist as events that the present retroactively establishes as congruent or conflictual, and therefore as significant.

Not only is it true of the analysand, and of the subject confronting her past, that the past has meaning because of the present, but it is *also* true—and here is one of the more radical claims that Lacan makes that most readers miss—of the child *having* the experiences that it later *comes* to understand as *having been* part of the Imaginary or the Real. Not even the preadolescent child exists outside the Symbolic. Not even the infant is wholly outside the Symbolic. All so-called prior events happen in a world that is always already structured by the Symbolic. Thus, Lacan warns us not to view a past event that now holds significance as "a mere stage in some instinctual maturation" (E 262/E 53). Instead, he insists that a past event or stage is "no less purely historical when it is actually experienced than when it is reconstituted in thought" (E 262/E 53).

Given the fact that the Symbolic is always at work, that even the infant is already situated in it, we need to stop conceptualizing the Real as that which "precedes" the Imaginary, and so on, and instead reconceptualize both the Imaginary and the Real as retroactively constructed from within and from the Symbolic. The Imaginary is no longer the time of the mirror stage. Instead, the mirror stage is the remembrance of what I term a "past that is experienced in a present," by which I mean "from the standpoint of the Symbolic." It is only *in the present*, as *symbols* of a *supposed* past to which the patient's unconscious *now* wishes to return, that these events *exist* in any real and meaningful way for us. It is only as events already in the history of the Symbolic that the events ever really "happened" for us in the first place.

Thus Lacan is able to claim that "The Symbolic function presents itself as a double movement within the subject: man makes an object of his action, but only in order to restore to this action in due time its place as a grounding" (E 285/E 73). This is a wonderful quote, for when we look into it carefully we see a hidden meaning. It is in the Imaginary that the infant comes to be able to differentiate subject and object. It is the Real that the subject believes is his original grounding. What Lacan is talking about here is how the Imaginary and the Real are made—constructed by and out of the Symbolic. Thus, with a few substitutions and a little tweaking, the quote I find underneath the quote reads: "The Symbolic function presents itself as a double movement within the subject: man makes the Imaginary, but only in order to give to his actions their status as having originated in the Real."

In light of this insight into Lacan's conception of the Imaginary and the Real, much of his discussion takes on a different light. For instance, take Lacan's (1973/1981) reading of Freud's "*Wo es war, soll Ich werden.*" In the *Seminar XI, The Four Fundamental Concepts*, he correlates the *Ich* not with the ego, but with the I, the subject, and thus with the Symbolic. Similarly, the *es* is no longer the id, but "the it"—what preceded the subject, in other words the Real. Thus, he tells us that when "the subject is there to rediscover where it was," the I "anticipates the Real." That is, the I anticipates what is yet to come as the past that only exists for us now, and that only exists for us now as the place we claim we once were but are not. We can also understand what Lacan (1988) means when, in *Seminar I*, he talks of the "juncture of the Symbolic and of the Imaginary in the constitution of the Real" (p. 174). It is always from the later that the Real comes to be—when it comes to be as that to which the later desires to return.

So, in the end, what is an origin, for Lacan? It is an event from the past that, insofar as it exists for us now, in the present, in the Unconscious, conflicts with the demands of the Symbolic, holds power over us as that supposedly originary event, that supposedly originary realm to which we wish to return. But in this, it is a fiction. It is a fiction that holds power over us as if it *were* real, and in this, it is part of our reality. However, it is *not* "real" in the sense that it "once *was* as we *remember it* to have been," for it was *not* so, if it ever really was at all. We were never unified; we were never in control; we were never in "the all." We have always been in the Symbolic, subjected, separated, differentiated, though this subjection may grow stronger and more concrete as the years go on. The Real as the original origin, as the primal space of undifferentiation, does not exist, has never existed, outside the realm of phantasy— as the desire that it was once there, the desire to return to it. Its reality is undeniable, but we easily misunderstand it. The Real exists for us, as real, here and now; that does not mean it existed "then." In a very real sense, then, for Lacan, *the past only "happens" because the present retroactively establishes it as having happened.*

I believe we can spell this out even more clearly with reference to another of Lacan's key concepts—the *objet petit a.* Critchley (1999) makes the claim that the *objet petit a* is substituted for *das Ding* in Lacan's later work, or at least that both signifiers share the same signified. (*Das Ding* is used in Seminar VII of 1959–60 [1986/ 1992], whereas the *objet petit a* plays a central role in Seminar XI of 1964 [1973/1981]). The *objet petit a* is Lacanian algebra for the original object that desire believes it is after, but cannot have. Desire is the Symbolic counterpart to Imaginary demand and Real need. Need is best exemplified by the infant's hunger. Demand is best exemplified by the child's cry. Desire, however, emerges in the realization that what the child needs and what it demands are not the same thing, for in addition to demanding that its hunger be satiated, it demands that all its energies be discharged, that all its pleasure be satiated. That is, it demands the impossible. In the Symbolic, the child comes to associate this demand for complete cessation of all unpleasures with the unconditional love it desires of the parent. But that unconditional love is no more possible than is the complete cessation of all unpleasure possible, for unconditional love comes to be represented by complete unity—that is, by a return to the Real. The *objet petit a* is *this* object of desire—unconditional love, cessation of all unpleasure, the return to the pure, complete, undifferentiated all. But as we saw with Lacan's discussion of the Real, the *objet petit a* is no less retroactive in origin than is *das Ding*. Thus, in *Seminar XI* (1973/1981) Lacan writes: "The *objet petit a* is not the origin of the oral drive. It is not introduced as the original food, it is introduced from the fact that no food will ever satisfy the oral drive, except by circumventing the eternally lacking object" (S XI 201–202/S XI 180). The past object that desire seeks, the *objet petit a*, *das Ding*, is introduced by the impossibility of satisfaction. Introduced to the subject, made into an object, created as a past. The subject's establishing of the origin is achieved, according to Lacan, in a retroactive positing.[2]

It should now be clear how far apart Levinas and Lacan stand on the question of origins. And, if Levinas and Lacan mean different things in speaking of origin, they clearly mean different things when discussing the origin of the ethical. It is now quite easy to see why Critchley (1999) is mistaken in his claim that the face can be *das Ding*. As the Lacanian Real is a retroactive construction of, from, and by the Symbolic, the an-archic stands outside (and before) the Real, as well. The Real in Lacan is only ever a fantasmatic retroactive construction, toward which, from our place in the Symbolic, we desire to return. The Symbolic is both *more important* and *first*. In Levinas, by contrast, the immemorial past may be outside of signification and symbolization, but it is not posited as a *retroactive construction*.[3] Although outside of synchronous time and re-presentational being, the an-archical foundation of the ethical

---

2. We could as well make this point by examining Lacan's treatment of *tuché* and the automaton in *Seminar XI*. As Paul Verhaeghe (2001) explains it, "the Symbolic determines the emergence of *tuché*, of the Real as a negative product of the Symbolic" (p. 77).

3. Nor is it posited as an excluded *result* of the order of language and being. Another way to get at this difference is to see that the Real is only "the all" in light of the differentiation of the Symbolic, that is, in light of the fact that language operates through the binary of absence and presence. In this, the Real is a result of language. The immemorial past structures the possibility of communication in Levinas. It is outside of and before language. The saying precedes the said, though on this point Critchley (1999) and I disagree again.

encounter is absolutely primary, and in this, is a very *real* "Real." Moreover, the immemorial past, as an-archic, may not be an event that happened within synchronous history, but as an enigma from a diachronic history. It still stands as a metaphysical foundation of our subjectivity as ethical (thus the term "ethical subjectivity") even when Levinas thinks he has moved beyond metaphysics.

Levinas and Lacan mean very different things in describing subjectivity as ethical. On the one hand, Levinas calls the positing of the ethical structure of human subjectivity "an-archy." By so doing, Levinas is directing us to (1) the foundational status of the ethical, and (2) the ethical as otherwise than being and beyond essence. Levinas is making an argument about the very nature of subjectivity itself. The argument is not about ethical action or moral codes; an-archy is not a foundation for a positive ethics. Rather, an-archy is nothing more or less than the foundation of subjectivity. When constructing a moral code or a system of law and justice, as Levinas himself suggests we do, my being for-the-other can serve as a negative guideline. It stands as a corrective to systems that reduce the human subject to an object; it stands as a warning against totality and a reminder of the infinite. It cannot, however, act as a positive guideline. Ethical responsibility can never tell others how I *should* act in a situation, nor can it tell society what a code of ethics or justice should look like. It cannot even stand as a foundation to which I myself appeal when making decisions—that is, as a regulative ideal. Ethical responsibility is neither ideal nor idea, and therefore cannot be appealed to. It is not something that I can reflect upon when trying to act ethically, for as soon as I reflect I have reduced it to the realm of representation; were I to do that, then I would no longer be speaking about ethical responsibility as an an-archical foundation at all, and instead would have done a fundamental violence to the ethical by turning it into being. As an an-archical foundation, then, the ethical stands forever out of my cognitive reach: I cannot reflect upon it in my moral decision-making, for it is beyond and before any power of reflection. Ethical responsibility as an an-archical foundation of subjectivity, then, serves as a universal without content. It is the very structure of the subject, and in it I am faced with the fact of my subjectivity as ethical. This I can neither escape nor ignore. Moreover, as the structure of my subjectivity it says nothing to me about human activity or the world of interpersonal relations. It simply tells me how I am structured at the deepest an-archic level. It alerts me to the immemorial past in which my very subjectivity was given structure and form, but without content. I discover my subjectivity as a signification of my being for-the-other, and I assume the structure of my subjectivity as ethical in the biblical response, "Here I am." But foundational an-archy ends there; there is nothing more it can tell me. Ethical subjectivity is an empty formalism, in the very *best* sense of the term. In this, Levinas's idea of the ethical as an-archic foundation does stand outside signification as representation, and therefore is otherwise than being.

On the other hand, Lacan tells us that traditional conceptions of morality are pathogenic. They thrust our Unconscious into conflict, and our desire remains always unrealizable. This conflict in our Unconscious directs our attention to the Real, because it is onto the Real that we graft our sense of the moral as basic driving force. For psychoanalysis, however, the good is not the Real. The Real is the register of meaning that exerts itself in the psyche as the place that existed before the Imaginary, before the ego; however, the Real can never be achieved because, as a retroactive construction, it is an unconscious fantasy. The Real is, in realty, not the ideal, but rather *the impossible*. Instead of following the path of the ideal by asking the question of traditional ethics, "What is the good?" psychoanalysis directs us to ask the question, "Have we acted in conformity with the desire that is in us?" Desire is the inescapable ought; it refuses to go away, and no matter how well we repress it, it does disappear. Desire is, moreover, from the perspective of traditional ethics, the "ought" that we ought to repress. What we assess in determining whether or not we have acted "ethically," says Lacan, should *not* be whether or not we have acted in accord with "the good," but whether or not we have acted in conformity with our desire. "Ethics," for Lacan, is not, then, what we traditionally think of as ethics at all. Lacan turns ethics on its head. Now, from the perspective of Lacanian psychoanalysis, to be ethical we must instead attempt to act "in accord with our desire." But, we ask, "Which desire?" for desire is a web of unconscious forces, unconscious wishes that we want to achieve, and to satisfy, and they include the internalized moral law no less than the sexual drive. The superego, remember, is a transformation of part of the id, and both exert pressure in the Unconscious—as *desiring agencies*. This means that an ethics of psychoanalysis can direct us neither toward a traditional moralistic position nor toward a libertine ethos, for either position causes us to act against part of our desire. Instead, an ethics of psychoanalysis directs our attention to the gap between the Symbolic and the Real and forces us to come to terms with it: first by making us realize that we have been acting on our unconscious desire to return to the Real, second by making us see that we have unconsciously come to see the Real not only as original unity but also as the ideal, and third by making us consciously realize that any return to the Real, whatever it is, is impossible. This does not mean we end up overcoming *either* our libidinal desires (love) *or* our moral desires (the good). Rather, we simply come to recognize them both *as* unconscious desires, as driving oughts. And then we attempt to act in accord with them, to "act in conformity with desire that is in us." But how can we act in accord with a desire that is in conflict with itself? That is the situation that psychoanalysis leaves us with—the knowledge that our *Unconscious*, which is the driving force in our lives, is always a site of conflict. Acting "in accord" with our desire, then, really means nothing other than acting *without repression*.[4]

---

4. In this, it is far less about what we do than about how we do it. Which is not to say that this prescription has no normative force—I'm not trying to liken it to Heideggerian authenticity. Instead, it is to focus on the present and the future more than on the past. Lacan posits the question of "ethics," then, not as a question of "How do we judge what just happened?" but rather as a question of "What now?" As he tells us: "The important thing is not knowing whether man is good or bad in the beginning; the important thing is what will transpire once [one has acted]" (S VII 375/S VII 325). So, our desire for the good stands in the way of our desire for libidinal satisfaction. Because any "idea of the good" we have is grafted onto the Real, it claims a status as the foundation of our subjec-

Critchley's (1999) claim is simply mistaken. The face of the other is not *das Ding*. The Lacan whose views I have just outlined seems far less reconcilable with Levinas than the Lacan that Critchley has proposed. But can we still bring Levinas and Lacan together? I believe so. Before I suggest how, let me remind you that in this sketch I am proposing something that neither Levinas nor Lacan would have found palatable. I am consciously doing a fundamental violence to both of their positions. Moreover, I am proposing something which, as a philosophical position, does not entirely cohere. That is, it is not entirely coherent. Rather, it is conflicted; it is in disagreement with itself. It proposes that ethics are both good and bad. It proposes that they will hurt us while they help us. It proposes that they are pathogenic, but that we cannot do without them. In short, it is in one sense a very psychoanalytic position, and not a very Levinasian one, and in another sense, vice versa. But I believe it is a constructive position that moves us out of the rather static place philosophical ethics has been in for many years now. Moreover, I think that it does so not in spite of, but rather because of its inconsistencies and conflicts.

Let me begin by reminding the reader that I believe that the project of bringing Levinas and Lacan together must be done without attempting to efface their differences or disagreements in any way. As such, it must be done in the spirit of true dialogue, in which difference and opposition are not only not ignored, but rather are celebrated, precisely because it is in their opposition that they have the most to offer.

Although I believe that Levinas is fundamentally right when he posits the structure of our subjectivity as ethical, as for-the-other, I also believe that Lacan would be quite right in seeing our adherence to that structure as pathogenic, and it is at this juncture that I wish to bring the two together. More concretely, I believe that

---

tivity. However, as we already know, the Real is only ever a retroactive construction. Any attempts to give foundational status to our idea of the good will conflict with our unconscious, and will thus result in psychic illness. Instead of appealing to the reality of the ideal, then, Lacan locates the ethical in the unconscious, and therefore in the Symbolic.

Levinas's conception of the original signification of the subject (my being the one-for-the-other) is a fundamental structure of subjectivity. In my judgment, it is in fact also, from a Lacanian perspective, the grafting of a certain conception of the subject onto the Real, and any such grafting, I believe, would indeed be pathogenic. Though it seems that the positions of Levinas and Lacan cannot both be true, it is precisely the truth of both positions that I am arguing. It is impossible to know as an epistemic certainty the truth of either of these statements. Clearly Lacan's argument is based on certain truths uncovered in the analytic situation, the importance of which cannot be underestimated. That such a beyond, or that the positing of such a beyond, functions pathogenically is a truth of analysis. Lacan, however, is working on the level of signification and discourse and psychic formation, whereas Levinas is positing something philosophically beyond.[5]

So, Levinas's reading of the structure of subjectivity as foundationally ethical is, I believe, fundamentally correct. Yet if we simply see the immemorial past as actually occupying a real (anarchical) space, we fail to see the extent to which it does *function* as if it were grafted onto the Lacanian Real. That is, if we uncritically accept the an-archic reality of ethical subjectivity, we will undoubtedly be led into psychic conflict, for, as Lacan would argue, we will construct this notion of ethical subjectivity into an idea of the good, and this idea of the good, the subject as the one-for-the-other, will be given a certain status in the unconscious as part of the Real. It will thereby be put in conflict with the desire of the unconscious, a desire that also wishes a return to the Real, but to the original sense of the Real—the Real as undifferentiation. Any simple positing of the reality of the ethical subject will lead to a positing of it as Real, then, and, in turn, to pathology. This is the psychoanalytic insight that Levinas fails to see. Lacan's critique of

---

5. This is not to say that the beyond is not real on some level *as* that anarchic foundation, as that immemorial past (real, of course, without "existing"—that is, *not* on the level of being).

the positing of the ethical onto the Real is also, I believe, fundamentally correct.[6]

We can already see the dilemma that a co-reading puts us in. As soon as one thinker offers us something, the other thinker seems to demand the opposite. How may we best proceed? Perhaps we should return to the method of Chapter 4, and proceed diachronically. Maybe then we can better see the insights of each thinker.

Let us begin with the importance of the Lacanian position. Lacan clearly offers, so far as I can see, three things that Levinas fails to give us. First, Lacan offers a subtler picture of the *human subject*—as ruled by conflicting unconscious forces—and thereby leads us out of Levinas's overly humanist presentation of the subject as fully conscious and transparent. Even in his vision of the

---

6. Following Lacan, we do not want to argue that a simple understanding of these issues will allow the subject to avoid psychic conflict. Conflict is the very structure of the psyche, both in the battle between the conscious and unconscious and in the battles within the unconscious itself. And on some level conflict will always lead to the neuroses of everyday life. Still, a certain vigilance to the idea that we have grafted our conception of the subject as ethical *onto* the Real will better prepare us for the conflicts that do arise, and allow us better access to a knowledge of the specific symptoms and defenses that might emerge in these conflicts. Recall that analysis does not ally itself with one side or another of the conflict—it simply brings the conflict into the conscious, where it can be dealt with by the patient without illness (that is, without repression and the resulting symptoms). As such, it is not necessary to mediate an "agreement" between Levinas and Lacan. It is simply necessary to remain conscious of the fact of their disagreement, and to hold this as conscious knowledge. In fact, such attention to the conflicts of the unconscious are part and parcel of psychoanalytic theory. Attention to the subject as the split subject is *essential* to the health of the patient. Without an understanding of the fact of desire and the unconscious, we are easily susceptible to losing what little control we do have in a world in which we are not masters. We are easily susceptible to tying ourselves to a search for mastery and unity that is not only destined to fail, but that can cause us great psychic distress and harm. Knowledge of the fictions of the Real and knowledge of the power of the unconscious allow us to come to terms better with the conflicts of daily life. Psychoanalytic insights lead to a far healthier life in synchronous time. In the synchronic time of the subject, the unconscious is an undeniable fact. For me, as for Lacan, it is un-"ethical" to deny that.

subject as subjected, even in his view of the subject as split, and as determined in a relation to a transcendence and an otherness that founds the possibility of the self's subjectivity, Levinas still leaves intact too much Cartesian power, at least in the realm of knowledge, though not in the realms of freedom and action. This position ignores the insights not only of Freud and Lacan, but also those brought forward by Foucault, Lévi-Strauss, or even Peter Berger. By positing the subject as subject to forces not only beyond the self, but also beyond consciousness, Lacan offers insights that are, it seems to me, simply indispensable in the wake of antihumanism.

Second, Lacan offers an *erotic* element sadly lost in Levinas's later work.[7] Whereas *Time and the Other* and *Totality and Infinity* had powerful discussions of the erotic body, they were discussions marred by a serious masculinism, and could not be rescued by simply reinterpreting his discussion as "gendered" instead of "sexed."[8] When Levinas gave up the metaphysical language of his early work for the "ethical language" of his later work, a serious discussion of the erotic body disappeared.[9] There remained in *Otherwise than Being* a strong presentation of the body as hungry, as suffering, as helpless—in short, as embodied. But it was a body devoid of sexuality. Lacan forces us to reintroduce sexuality as a driving force in our encounter with the other. Moreover, he does so without reducing sexuality to the sexed body, a move that is simply indefensible after the work of Judith Butler (1999), and, more importantly, Kate Bornstein (1995), Riki Anne Wilchins (1997), Alice Domurat Dreger (1998), and Anne Fausto-Sterling (2000). By reintroduc-

---

7. The best work published to date on the erotic in Levinas's work, in particular as it pertains to the ethical, is the recent article by Lisa Walsh, entitled "Between Maternity and Paternity: Figuring Ethical Subjectivity" (2001).

8. This is a move that not only the otherwise profound interpreter Richard Cohen (1994) makes, but also one that Levinas himself suggests in the interviews in *Ethics and Infinity*.

9. Some have argued that Levinas's discussion of the maternal has within it an erotic sensibility, but again I disagree. See my discussion on this matter in Chapter 2. Also, as noted above, the best reading of the maternal in Levinas is in Walsh's article.

ing the eroticism of our desire for the other, the desire to touch and be touched, the desire to draw near and even consume, Lacan (and even more so Freud) gives us a deeper and more profound reading of the actual lived encounter of persons in contact with each other as sexually charged.

Third, Lacan, as always through Freud, offers the indispensable idea of "the good" as pathogenic. On this point, I am simply in total agreement. It is an insight, I believe, that we can confirm through history as much as through psychoanalysis, and one about which volumes have been and will continue to be written.

But Lacan on his own will not do. For one thing, there is more going on in us than simply the Unconscious he describes. That there seems to be an an-archic structure at work in structuring our subjectivity is hard to deny. Still, one might deny it. Thus it becomes even more important that Levinas not only describes something that I might think is true, for this is easy enough to disagree with, but also prescribes something that I think we *need*, and it is this that is harder to dismiss. If Kantian reason can no longer be claimed as a cross-cultural ideal, if Utilitarianism can be so clearly abused, if virtues are too context-specific to be viable—if, in short, Fackenheim (1994) is right in his belief that "thought" is no longer possible after the Holocaust—we seem to be afloat with no grounding whatsoever. Some postmoderns might celebrate this; yet when we look carefully at their work we discover a profound hypocrisy. Mark Taylor (1987) clearly has an "idea of the good" at work in his texts. But where does it come from? Even Derrida has moved closer and closer to justice as a universal category, however unformed and empty a concept he seems to want it to be.

Without some ideal guiding is, we seem to lack any ground on which to stand. But Lacan and Freud are right that ideals tend to do more harm than good. Derrida is right that any adherence to ideals needs to be constantly called into question. John Caputo (1993) is right that the road ahead is always under construction. Is there some sort of "ideal," then, that will *not* succumb to the conflicts of the Unconscious? That will not lead to pathology?

That will not be reified into a god? That we will remember isn't unquestionable?

I do *not* think there is.

And this is where Levinas comes back in the picture.

Levinas's position is not about ethical action or moral codes; it does not offer a foundation for a positive ethics. It does not have an "ideal." At least not always. Rather, through a phenomenological analysis of something that resists phenomenology (the face, the approach), it directs us to a re-collection of the subject's immemorial past (the structure of her self as subjected to an an-archic responsibility). Through the claim that the subject is ethical, the origins of ethics are located in the constitution of subjectivity-in-the-world.[10] The subject discovers his subjectivity as always already the signification of being-for-the-other, and he assumes that ethical structure in the biblical response, "Here I am." The face, as that which calls us into intersubjective relation, is itself an originary signification. The face, then, is the pseudo-ground of intersubjective discourse. It not only allows human beings to interact, but it also requires that they do so. It does not dictate how they will act or offer an ideal in relation to which we can evaluate actions. It does, however, give us a structural point of reference. We can now look at ourselves and ask if we act based on an assumption of our originary structural responsibility or as a turning away from it.

Some may find this idea of an originary structural responsibility an empty concept, but it is here a matter of the emptier the better. It is precisely this that will keep us further from the notions of substance essentialism and conceptual universalism. We can have original responsibility without an "idea of the good." In fact, so far as it remains non-ontological (that is, so long as it claims a status that cannot be assimilated into the Real), the face resists being reified into an "idea of the good" that will conflict with our unconscious. Resistance, however, is sometimes futile. Levinas himself does not stop where I think he should. He takes his theory too far, and although his discussions of God place God outside the

_____

10. Here the echoes of Husserl are stronger than ever.

register of Being, God still becomes, for him, an "idea of the good," and that is problematic. So long as Levinas holds on to this, he cannot escape the pathology that will necessarily ensue, ontology or not.

Even if he were successful in resisting the idea God, an attenuated Levinas such as the one I am putting forward would nonetheless fall prey to the temptations of conceptual universalism, substance essentialism, and their inevitable counterpart, colonialism. Yet by trying as hard as possible to keep this program one of structure and not of content, one of responsibility without responsibilities, one of law without laws, we may avoid some of the more serious dangers. And so long as we remain vigilant, questioning, deconstructive, and psychoanalytic, we will usually catch ourselves when we slip—eventually, at least.

Beyond what Lacan and Levinas offer each other in regard to what is lacking, there is one final point to be made, and it is in terms of what each offers the other in terms of what needs augmenting. The central issue here involves what is perhaps one of the most important subjects that must be addressed in a theory of ethical subjectivity—that is, desire. Here each thinker gives us something essential, and by bringing the two together, we can again move the issue forward. Levinas give us an account of our structural desire for the other; Lacan gives us a psychical reading of desire for the other. Levinas demonstrates our originary structural ethicality, and shows us through eloquent and adept phenomenological description the desire we have for transcendence. In "God and Philosophy" in particular, Levinas advances a sophisticated theory of desire. But the fact remains, even if Levinas's description is apt, which I believe it is, that we most often do not move toward the other in and out of this originary desire. Why do we assume instead of flee? Why do we sometimes lash out instead of caress? Why do we choose love that is ethical instead of love that consumes? Levinas tells us that alongside our more originary desire for transcendence there is also a wish to consume the other into our own being, for the transcendence of the other is a weight too heavy to bear. And all this works on one level. But the psychological component is

missing in Levinas's argument. In limiting himself to a phenomenological analysis of the *structure* of our subjectivity, Levinas can
offer little insight into the nature of the *commitment* one takes on
in assuming one's responsibility. More is going on here than what
we find in the structural issues that Levinas addresses himself to.
Lacan's psychical reading of desire, then, makes a move that
Levinas's reading cannot. On the psychical level, are love and
aggressivity really opposites? Is all desire doomed to be a desire
for consumption? Can we perhaps psychically *desire* the good of
the other? Although Lacan does not offer positive answers to these
questions any more than Levinas does, at least he opens up the realm
of psychical desire as one worthy of exploring. Here we can use Lacan
with Levinas to offer a fuller reading of desire—to complement
Levinas's structural reading with Lacan's psychical reading—and
in this perhaps we can also discover some of the aspects missing in
Levinas's account. Of course, Lacan's account of the desire we have
in the face of the other is fundamentally limited to an aggressive
wish to consume based on an originary alienation. Here Lacan is
limited and limiting. Perhaps here Levinas can offer us some clues
as to how to move forward. Such a turn back to Levinas is instructive, for in his structural analysis perhaps he has uncovered some
psychical structures as well, which, though uninterrogated on the
realm of the psyche, can nevertheless be read on the level of the
psyche. Clearly neither thinker will be sufficient on his own here,
but both together allow us positive movement forward. This will
have to be more than a simple equation of Levinas + Lacan = Desire, of course. We will have to use each thinker not only to aug-
ment but also to correct the other, and we will have to think beyond
both of them. Still, looking at the two together here is clearly a
valuable move, and opens up new directions for our inquiry.

By augmenting Lacan with Levinas, we can posit a (generally)
nonpathogenic picture of the ethical that goes beyond our unconscious desire and opens up the possibility of a more deeply committed ethical subjectivity. We are not hereby positing any kind of
equivalence between a Levinasian concept and a Lacanian concept;
rather, we are attempting a mélange of the two that deliberately

does violence to the integrity of each as unique projects, yet offers us innovative and profound possibilities. Though I've only given glimpses here of what it will look like, I believe that a marriage of Levinas's vision of the ethical and Lacan's of psychoanalysis may help us arrive at a new picture of the ethical subject: the subject-desiring-the-good-of-the-other.

Have I succeeded in my task? I imagine I may have convinced a few readers of the usefulness of these thinkers. Yet I also anticipate heavy skepticism. My moving from one to the other may have been conveyed well enough, but how, the reader may ask, might this picture look as a marriage? How might this vision of ethical subjectivity look when discussing Levinas and Lacan together? To satisfy the reader looking for a more unified picture, allow me to offer some brief concluding remarks that may provide another way to approach the question than the ones outlined in the preceding paragraphs (though always with the caveat that unity is not what this project is about).

Levinas posits the very structure of our subjectivity as ethical. Lacan posits the very structure of our subjectivity as desiring. In a theory of ethical subjectivity, these two contradictory ideas need not exclude each other. Attention to one without the other can lead to unresolvable psychic conflict. Attention to either without the other can lead to a fundamentally unethical position of ir-responsibility. However, to hold both of these positions as true offers a paradigm that neither one on its own can provide. Without the positing of an ethical subjectivity, it is all too easy to deny the responsibility of the one-for-the-other and to spiral into certain nihilism; without the positing of the an-archy of that subjectivity, is it all too easy to deny the priority of otherness and to spiral into the totality that denies the infinite; and without the positing of the other as beyond the self, it is all too easy to continue in an absorption of all into being, of the other into the same. At the same time, without the positing of desire as the foundation of subjectivity, we fail to recognize ourselves as subjects driven by our own demands and desires, as subjects in fact driven by drives, and we thereby fail to account for the fact of our selves as subjects in the

Symbolic order. Additionally, unless we posit subjectivity as split, we fail to recognize the reality of the Unconscious and thereby risk being unable to escape psychical illness. As I have said before, and while recognizing that Levinas's and Lacan's readings are in conflict with one another, it seems to me that we cannot dispense with either one—we must have both the idea of subjectivity as structurally ethical, and the idea of subjectivity as structurally split. A subject who fails to pay attention to what structures it as ethical would fail to see itself as bound to the other, and in this would fail to see a basic fact of its existence, ultimately, then, being unable to take upon itself the call of election—of my being called as the unique bearer of the responsibility for the life and death of the unique other. In a related way, an ethical subject who fails to see itself as split, and who fails to see the ways in which its adherence to the ethical are in some sense pathogenic, would leave itself open to serious psychic conflict; as such, it would be unable to take upon itself its signification as for-the-other, remaining instead entirely bound by an unconscious battle between its desire and the idea of the good. That subject would be "unethical" in both the Levinasian and the Lacanian sense of the word; it would know only symptom and defense and would realize neither its potential to be an ethical agent accepting itself as for-the-other nor its potential as an "ethical" agent able to function healthily for and out of itself. A subject who sees belief in the ethical as only pathogenic, however, would doom itself to a life in which desire is the *only* cause; it would never know the glory of the infinite, and would contribute to the order of totality in which the other would be consumed by the same. Finally, a proper vision of ethical subjectivity must account for *both* ethical signification and an "ethics" of desire, for *both* the an-archy of the immemorial past and the power of the Unconscious. A theory of ethical subjectivity thus requires both Levinas and Lacan, not in spite of the fact, but precisely *because* of the fact that they disagree. The subject desiring-the-good-of-the-other is the only ethical subject.

References

Althusser, L. (1971). *Lenin and Philosophy*. New York: Monthly Review Press.

Balibar, E. (1994). Subjection and subjectivation. In *Supposing the Subject*, ed. J. Copjec, pp. 1–15. New York: Verso.

Barnard, S. (2002). Diachrony, *tuché*, and the ethical subject in Levinas and Lacan. In *Psychology for the Other: Levinas, Ethics, and the Practice of Psychology*, ed. E. Gantt and R. Williams. Pittsburgh, PA: Duquesne University Press.

Barnard, S., and Fink, B., eds. (2002). *Reading Seminar XX*. New York: SUNY Press.

Barzilai, S. (1999). *Lacan and the Matter of Origins*. Stanford, CA: Stanford University Press.

Beauvoir, S. (1948). *Ethics of Ambiguity*. New York: Citadel.

Berger, P., and Luckmann, T. (1967). *The Social Construction of Reality*. New York: Anchor.

Bergo, B. (2004). Levinasian responsibility and Freudian analysis: Is the unthinkable an Un-conscious? In *Addressing Levinas*, ed. E. Nelson. Evanston, IL: Northwestern University Press.

Bergson, H. (2001). *Time and Free Will*. Mineola, NY: Dover.

Bernasconi, R., and Critchley, S. (1991). *Re-reading Levinas*. Bloomington, IN: Indiana University Press.

Bornstein, K. (1995). *Gender Outlaw*. New York: Vintage.

Bowie, M. (1991). *Lacan*. Cambridge, MA: Harvard University Press.

Butler, J. (1999). *Gender Trouble*. New York: Routledge.

Butler, J., and Scott, J., eds. (1992). *Feminists Theorize the Political*. New York: Routledge.

Caputo, J. (1993). *Against Ethics*. Bloomington: Indiana University Press.

Chalier, C. (1991). Ethics and the feminine. In *Re-reading Levinas*, ed. R. Bernasconi and S. Critchley. Bloomington: Indiana University Press.

—————— (2002). *What Ought I to Do?* Ithaca, NY: Cornell University Press.

Chanter, T. (1995). *Ethics of Eros: Irigaray's Rewriting of the Philosophers*. New York: Routledge.

Cohen, R. (1994). *Elevations: The Height of the Good in Rosenzweig and Levinas*. Chicago: University of Chicago Press.

Copjec, J., ed. (1994). *Supposing the Subject*. New York: Verso.

Critchley, S. (1992). *The Ethics of Deconstruction*. Cambridge, UK: Basil Blackwell.

—————— (1996). Prolegomena to any post-deconstructive subjectivity. In *Deconstructive Subjectivities*, ed. S. Critchley and P. Dews, pp. 13–45. Albany, NY: SUNY Press.

—————— (1999). *Ethics—Politics—Subjectivity*. New York: Verso.

Critchley, S. and Dews, P., eds. (1996). *Deconstructive Subjectivities*. Albany, NY: SUNY Press.

Davis, C. (1996). *Levinas: An Introduction*. Notre Dame, IN: University of Notre Dame Press.

Derrida, J. (1972). *Margins of Philosophy*. Chicago: University of Chicago Press.

—————— (1978). *Writing and Difference*. Chicago: University of Chicago Press.

—————— (1987). *Of Spirit: Heidegger and the Question*. Chicago: University of Chicago Press.

—————— (1988. *Limited Inc*. Evanston, IL: Northwestern University Press.

Dor, J. (1998). *An Introduction to the Reading of Lacan*. New York: Other Press.

Drabinski, J. (2001). *Sensibility and Singularity: The Problem of Phenomenology in Levinas*. Albany, NY: SUNY Press.

Dreger, A. (1998). *Hermaphrodites and the Medical Invention of Sex*. Cambridge, MA: Harvard University Press.

Elliot, P., and Roen, K. (1998). Transgenderism and the question of embodiment. *GLQ: A Journal of Lesbian and Gay Studies* 4(2):231–261.

Evans, D. (1996). *An Introductory Dictionary of Lacanian Psychoanalysis*. New York: Routledge.

Fackenheim, E. (1994). *To Mend the World*. Bloomington: Indiana University Press.

Fausto-Sterling, A. (2000). *Sexing the Body*. New York: Basic Books.

Fink, B. (1995). *The Lacanian Subject: Between Language and Jouissance*. Princeton, NJ: Princeton University Press.

——— (2002). Knowledge and jouissance. In *Reading Seminar XX*, ed. S. Barnard and B. Fink. New York: SUNY Press.

Foucault, M. (1970). *The Order of Things*. New York: Random House.

——— (1977). *Discipline and Punish*. New York: Random House.

——— (2000). The subject and power. In *Power: Essential Works of Foucault*, volume 3, pp. 326–348. New York: The New Press.

Freud, S. (1960). *The Ego and the Id*. New York: Norton.

——— (1961a). *Beyond the Pleasure Principle*. New York: Norton.

——— (1961b). *Civilization and Its Discontents*. New York: Norton.

——— (1962). *Three Essay on the Theory of Sexuality*. New York: Basic Books.

——— (1963). *Sexuality and the Psychology of Love*. New York: Macmillan.

——— (1965). *The Interpretation of Dreams*. New York: Avon.

——— (1977). *Introductory Lectures on Psychoanalysis*. New York: Norton.

——— (1991). *General Psychological Theory*. New York: Simon and Schuster.

Fryer, D. (1996). Of spirit: Heidegger and Derrida on metaphysics, ethics, and National Socialism. *Inquiry: An Interdisciplinary Journal of Philosophy* 39(1):21–44.

——— (2003a). Introduction: symbols of the human: phenomenology, poststructuralism, and culture. *Listening: Journal of Religion and Culture* 37(2) (Spring): 78–83.

——— (2003b). Toward a phenomenology of gender: on Butler, positivism, and the question of experience. *Listening: Journal of Religion and Culture* 37(2) (Spring): 136–162.

Fuss, D. (1996). *Human, All Too Human*. New York: Routledge.

Gallop, J. (1985). *Reading Lacan*. Ithaca, NY: Cornell University Press.

Gantt, E., and Williams, R., eds. (2002). *Psychology for the Other: Levinas*,

Ethics, and the Practice of Psychology. Pittsburgh, PA: Duquesne University Press.

Gibbs, R. (1992). *Correlations in Rosenzweig and Levinas*. Princeton, NJ: Princeton University Press.

———— (2000). *Why Ethics?* Princeton, NJ: Princeton University Press.

Gordon, L. (1995a). *Bad Faith and Anti-Black Racism*. Atlantic Highlands, NJ: Humanities Press.

———— (1995b). *Fanon and the Crisis of European Man*. New York: Routledge.

Grosz, E. (1990). *Jacques Lacan: A Feminist Introduction*. New York: Routledge.

———— (1994). *Volatile Bodies*. Bloomington: Indiana University Press.

Habermas, J. (1995). *The Philosophical Discourse of Modernity*. Cambridge, MA: MIT Press.

Harasym, S., ed. (1998). *Levinas and Lacan: The Missed Encounter*. Albany, NY: SUNY Press.

Haraway, D. (1992). Ecce Homo, ain't (Ar'n't) I a woman, and inappropriate/d others: the human in a post-humanist landscape. In *Feminists Theorize the Political*, ed. J. Butler and J. Scott. New York: Routledge.

Hegel, G. (1977). *Phenomenology of Spirit*. New York: Oxford University Press.

Heidegger, M. (1962). *Being and Time*. London: Basil Blackwell.

Hume, D. (1978). *A Treatise on Human Nature*. Oxford, UK: Oxford University Press.

Husserl, E. (1962). *Ideas: General Introduction to Pure Phenomenology*. New York: Macmillan.

———— (1999). *Cartesian Meditations*. Boston: Kluwer Academic Publishers.

Irigary, L. (1985a). *Speculum, of the Other Woman*. Ithaca, NY: Cornell University Press.

———— (1985b). *This Sex Which Is Not One*. Ithaca, NY: Cornell University Press.

Kant, I. (1960). *Religion Within the Limits of Reason Alone*. New York: Harper & Row.

———— (1965). *Critique of Pure Reason*. New York: St. Martin's.

———— (1997). *Critique of Practical Reason*. New York: Cambridge University Press.

Kearney, R., and Dooley, M. (1999). *Questioning Ethics*. New York: Routledge.

Lacan, J. (1966). *Écrits*. Paris. Éditions de Seuil. Partial trans. A. Sheridan as *Écrits: A Selection*. New York: Norton, 1997.

────── (1973). *Le Seminaire de Jacques Lacan XI: Les quatre concepts fondamentaux de la psychanalyse*. Paris: Éditions de Seuil. Trans. A. Sheridan as *The Four Fundamental Concepts of Psychoanalysis*. New York: Norton, 1981.

────── (1974). Les complexes familaux dans la formation de l'individu: essai d'analyse d'une fonction en psychologie. Paris: Navarin.

────── (1975). *Le Seminaire de Jacques Lacan XX: Encore*. Paris: Éditions de Seuil. Trans. B. Fink as *The Seminar: Book XX: Feminine Sexuality*. New York, Norton, 1988.

────── (1986). *Le Seminaire de Jacques Lacan VII: L'éthique de la psychanalyse*. Paris: Éditions de Seuil. Trans. D. Porter as *The Seminar: Book VII. The Ethics of Psychoanalysis*. New York: Norton, 1992.

Lacoue-Labarthe, P. (1990). *Heidegger, Art and Politics: The Fiction of the Political*. New York: Basil Blackwell.

Laplanche, J. and Pontalis, J.-B. (1973). *The Language of Psychoanalysis*. New York: Norton.

Lee, J. S. (1990). *Jacques Lacan*. Amherst: University of Massachusetts Press.

Levinas, E. (1961). *Totalité et Infini*. Dordrecht, Netherlands: M. Nijhoff. Trans. A. Lingis as *Totality and Infinity*. Pittsburgh, PA: Duquesne University Press, 1969.

────── (1963). *De L'Existence à l'existant*. Paris: J. VRIN. Trans. A. Lingis as *Existence and Existents*. Boston: Kluwer Academic Publishers, 1995.

────── (1967). *En Decouvrant l'existence avec Husserl et Heidegger*. Paris: J. VRIN.

────── (1974). *Autrement qu'être ou au-delà de l'Essence*. Dordrecht, Netherlands: M. Nijhoff. Trans. A. Lingis as *Otherwise than Being or Beyond Essence*. Boston: Kluwer Academic Publishers, 1991.

────── (1979). *Le Temps et l'autre*. Paris: Fata Morgana. Trans. R. Cohen as *Time and the Other*. Pittsburgh, PA: Duquesne University Press, 1987.

────── (1982). *Humanisme de l'autre homme*. Paris: Fata Morgana.

────── (1982). *Ethique et infini*. Paris: Librairie Arthème Fayard et Radio. Trans. R. Cohen as *Ethics and Infinity*. Pittsburgh, PA: Duquesne University Press, 1985.

────── (1982). *De Dieu qui Vient à l'Idée*. Paris: J. VRIN. Trans. B. Bergo as *Of God Who Comes to Mind*. Stanford, CA: Stanford University Press, 1998.

────── (1982b). L'Au-Delà du Verset. Paris: Les Éditions Minuit. Trans.

G. Mole as *Beyond the Verse*. Bloomington: Indiana University Press, 1994.

———— (1991). *Entre Nous: Essais sur le penser à-l'autre*. Paris: Éditions Grasset & Fasquelle. Trans. M. Smith and B. Harshav as *Entre Nous: Thinking-of-the-Other*. New York: Columbia University Press, 1998.

———— (1993). *Collected Philosophical Papers*. Trans. A. Lingis. Boston: Kluwer Academic Publishers.

———— (1995). *The Theory of Intuition in Husserl's Phenomenology*. Evanston, IL: Northwestern University Press.

MacIntyre, A. (1981). *After Virtue*. Notre Dame, IN: University of Notre Dame Press.

Madison, G., and Fairbairn, M. (1999). *The Ethics of Postmodernity*. Evanston, IL: Northwestern University Press.

Manning, R. (1993). *Interpreting Otherwise than Heidegger*. Pittsburgh, PA: Duquesne University Press.

Moran, D. (2000). *An Introduction to Phenomenology*. New York: Routledge.

Nobus, D. (1999a). Life and death in the glass: a new look at the mirror stage. In *Key Concepts of Lacanian Psychoanalysis*, ed. D. Nobus, pp. 101–138. New York: Other Press.

———— (1999b). *Key Concepts of Lacanian Psychoanalysis*. New York: Other Press.

Outka G., and Reeder, J., eds. (1993). *Prospects for a Common Morality*. Princeton, NJ: Princeton University Press.

Peperzak, A. (1993). *To the Other*. West Lafayette, IN: Purdue University Press.

———— (1995). *Ethics as First Philosophy*. New York: Routledge.

———— (1997). *Beyond: The Philosophy of Emmanuel Levinas*. Evanston, IL: Northwestern University Press.

Plato (1956). *Phaedrus*. New York: Macmillan.

———— (1987). *The Republic*. New York: Penguin Books.

Rabaté, J.-M. (2000a). Construing Lacan. In *Lacan in America*, pp. xvii–xlii. New York: Other Press.

———— (2000b). *Lacan in America*. New York: Other Press.

———— (2001). *Jacques Lacan*. New York: Palgrave.

Rajchman, J. (1991). *Truth and Eros: Foucault, Lacan, and the Question of Ethics*. New York: Routledge.

Rawls, J. (1971). *Theory of Justice*. Cambridge, MA: Harvard University Press.

———— (2001). *Justice as Fairness*. Cambridge, MA: Harvard University Press.

Reinhard, K. (1995). Kant with Sade, Levinas with Lacan. *Modern Language Notes*, 110:785–808.

Rosenzweig, F. (1985). *The Star of Redemption*. Notre Dame, IN: University of Notre Dame Press.

Roudinesco, E. (1997). *Jacques Lacan*. New York: Columbia University Press.

Santer, E. (2001). *On the Psychotheology of Everyday Life: Reflections on Freud and Rosenzweig*. Chicago: University of Chicago Press.

Sartre, J.-P. (1960). *The Transcendence of the Ego*. New York: Hill and Wang.

———— (1991). *Being and Nothingness*. London: Routledge.

———— (1992). *Notebook for an Ethics*. Chicago: University of Chicago Press.

Shepherdson, C. (1994). The role of gender and the imperative of sex. In *Supposing the Subject*, ed. J. Copjec. New York: Verso.

Stout, J. (1988). *Ethics After Babel*. New York: Beacon Press.

Taylor, M. (1987). *Altarity*. Chicago: University of Chicago Press.

Tucker, R. C., ed. (1978). *The Marx-Engels Reader*. New York: Norton.

Van Haute, P. (2002). *Against Adaptation: Lacan's "Subversion" of the Subject: A Close Reading*. New York: Other Press.

Vanier, A. (2000). *Lacan*. New York: Other Press.

Van Pelt, T. (2000). *The Other Side of Desire: Lacan's Theory of the Registers*. Albany, NY: SUNY Press.

Verhaeghe, P. (2001). *Beyond Gender: From Subject to Drive*. New York: Other Press.

Walsh, L. (2001). Between maternity and paternity: figuring ethical subjectivity. *differences* 12 (Spring):79–111.

Wilchins, R. A. (1997). *Read My Lips*. Ithaca, NY: Firebrand Books.

Wyschogrod, E. (1974). *Emmanuel Levinas*. The Hague, Netherlands: M. Nijhoff.

Žižek, S. (2002). The real of sexual difference. In *Reading Seminar XX*, ed. S. Barnard and B. Fink, pp. 57–75. New York: SUNY Press.

Zupancic, A. (2000). *Ethics of the Real*. New York: Verso.

Index

Althusser, L., 16n33
Anti-humanism, 2, 8, 11–14, 17,
    21, 43, 116, 200, 213
Aristotle, 22, 201

Balibar, E., 16n33, 17
Barnard, S., 3n2, 6n6, 105n20
Barzilai, S., 50n19
Beauvoir, S.
Bentham, J., 22, 201
Berger, P., 232
Bergo, B., 2n2, 157n3
Bergson, H., 173
Bernasconi, R., 4n4
Bornstein, K., 232
Bowie, M., 4n4, 43, 55n24
Buber, M., 18
Butler, J., 232

Caputo, J., 15n32, 233
Chalier, C., 100n17

Cohen, R., 2n1, 32
Colonialism, 235
Continental philosophy,
    endorsement of anti-humanism,
        13
    ethics of, 18
    fundamental questions in, 5,
        14–15, 19–20
Critchley, S., 2n2, 4n4, 5n6,
    15n32, 18n34, 216–218, 224,
    229

Davis, C., 2n1, 4n4, 118n1
Derrida, J., 2, 15, 15, 23, 40n13,
    60n26, 83n6, 157, 171, 233
Descartes, R., 9, 19, 20, 163–164,
    199, 232
    Cartesian ego, 101
    Cartesian cogito, 149
Deutsch, H., 91
Dor, J., 4n4

Drabinski, J., 2n1, 38n9, 121n2
Dreger, A., 232

Eliot, P., 109n22
Eribon, D., 8
Evans, D., 92n14, 95, 97n16, 150, 195, 205, 209
Essentialism,
  substance, 234, 235
Ethical subject, the, 8, 30, 104, 144–145, 150, 185, 215, 234, 237
  as desiring-the-good-of-the-other, 30, 237
Ethical subjectivity, 5, 8, 18, 19, 21–23, 28–30, 69, 147, 153, 184, 226–227, 229–230, 235–236, 237
Ethics, 114, 155–156, 186, 200–201, 226, 236–237
  as pathogenic, 229–230, 238
  Continental vs. analytic conceptions, 15

Fackenheim, E., 233
Fausto-Sterling, A., 232
Fink, B., 4n4, 6n6, 105n20, 106, 107n21, 108, 108n22, 110n24, 111n25, 111n26, 205n25
Foucault, M., 8, 9n10, 15, 16n33, 19, 21, 232
Freud, S., 1, 18, 21, 23, 25, 26, 46–47, 91–93, 95–97, 132, 148, 157, 188, 204–205, 207, 209, 232, 233
  castration complex, 86, 88
  consciousness, 1, 65–66
  dreams, 132–133, 136–137, 190
  drive (*Trieb*), 196–197, 209

ego, 65–66, 201–202
  as bodily 65–66
  ethics as pathogenic, 1, 18, 201–202, 233
  fort-da game, 191–194
  id, 65, 201–202
  importance of language, 132–133
  libido, 66, 97
  name of the father, the, 93
  normal, 87, 88
  Oedipus complex, 86, 87–88, 89, 97
  pre-conscious, 65
  primary narcissism, 65, 94
  psychological consequences of the, 72
  anatomical difference between the sexes, 72, 86–88, 97
  sexual life of children, 64
  sublimation, 209
  super-ego, 65–66, 88, 201–202, 204
  talking cure, 132
  transference, 64
  Unconscious, the, 64, 65, 148–149, 190, 193–194
Fuss, D., 6n6

Gallop, J., 4n4, 27n42, 45–46, 55n24, 57–58
Gibbs, R., 2n1, 4n5, 11n21, 15n32, 29n45, 60
Gordon, L., 9n10, 15n32, 66n30
Grosz, E., 26–27

Habermans, J., 9
Haraway, D., 6n6

Hegel, G.W.F., 1, 19, 20, 121, 173
Heidegger, M., 1, 19, 23, 33, 36–37, 118–120, 121–122, 124, 128, 173, 174n10, 183
Horney, K., 91
Humanism, 5, 8–14, 32, 43, 185, 215, 231
  revised view of, 13–14
  tenets of, 10–11
Husserl, E., 2, 9, 15, 16, 19, 20n36, 23, 26, 37, 38n10, 124–125, 128

Intervention of the other, the, 36, 37, 38, 40, 42, 68
Irigaray, L., 2, 15n32, 16n33, 23n38, 66n30, 104

Jones, E., 91

Kant, I., 1, 9, 19, 20, 22, 121, 173, 181–182, 201, 233
  categorical imperative, 181–182, 201
  Kantian a priori, 180
Klein, M., 91
Kris, E., 44n14

Lacan, J.
  aggressivity, 59, 63–67, 111, 142, 200
  alienation, 51, 98, 110, 134, 152, 186
  analyst, the, 108, 133–136, 142, 143, 195, 199–201, 212
    as the subject-supposed-to-know, 199–201
  analyst, as, 1, 7, 47

anti-humanist, as, 8–9, 21, 48, 59, 72, 91, 98, 114, 116, 149, 200, 213
biology and sex, 108–109
body-in-pieces, 46–51, 56, *see also* fragmented body
castration, 47, 86, 110
castration complex, 88–89, 98
charge of conservatism against, 96–97, 98
consciousness, 22
das Ding, 203, 217–218, 224–225
demand, 92–94, 194, 207–208, 209–210, 224–225
desire, 66, 93–94, 106, 107, 109, 142, 186, 189, 194, 202, 207–208, 209–214, 224–225, 227–228, 235–236
  the ought of, 211
  object and aim of, 194
drive, the, 187, 196–199
  as montage, 198
École Freudienne de Paris (EFP), 44
ego, the, 54, 56, 64–66, 97, 223
  the impotence of, 98
ego-ideal, 221
entry into psychoanalytic movement, 42–47
Eros, 111
ethical subject, 150–151
ethical subjectivity, 23
father, the, 93, 95
feminine, the, 114
fort-da game, interpretation of, 191, 194–195
fragmented body, 47–48, 56–59, 63, *see also* body-in-pieces

Lacan, J. (*continued*)
  I, the, 46, 50, 54–56, 95, 223
  ideal-I, the, 50–51, 54–56, 63
  Imaginary, the, 52–54, 92, 94,
      95, 131, 134, 139–141,
      150, 186, 193, 194, 195–
      196, 198, 200, 203, 208,
      210, 221–225, 227
  jouissance, 108, 110–111
  Lacanian geometry, 105
  language, 112, 113, 117, 131,
      132–133, 136–144, 148,
      150
    as formative of sexual
      difference, 113
    as foundation of analysis, 133
  Law of the Father, the, 89, 93
  libido, 97
  love, 109, 111, 186, 195, 200
  masculinism, 114
  Mirror stage, the, 43–59, 64,
      66, 85, 94–95, 97, 186, 222
  (mis)representation, 51
  morality
    as pathogenic, 1, 186, 201–
      204, 227, 233
  (m)other, the, 92–94, 106, 189,
      208, 221
  objet petit a, 111n26, 224–225
  Oedipus complex, 85–86, 88–
      89, 93, 97–98, 138–139,
      186
  ontology, 59, 112, 113
  Other, the, 92, 94, 105, 107,
      111, 143, 151–152, 200
  patient in analysis, the, 47–49,
      54, 89, 133–136, 143,
      186, 189, 199, 202,
      210, 212

phallus, the, 66, 85, 89–91, 95–
    98, 106–107, 108, 109,
    111, 113, 131, 186, 221
  as signifier, 91, 107
  difference from penis, 90–91
psychoanalysis (analysis), 133–
    136, 141, 143–144, 148,
    186, 189, 195, 200, 202,
    203–204, 210
  as ethical, 22, 23, 131, 144,
    186, 189–190, 200–214
  as a theory of the speaking
    subject, 131
  ethical aims of, 188, 190, 200
  four fundamental concepts
    of, 187–200
  goal of, 205
  introduction of linguistic
    theory to, 91
Real, the, 7, 52–54, 92, 94, 111,
    131, 134, 150, 186, 188–
    189, 193, 194, 198, 200,
    203–204, 206–208, 210,
    217–218, 219–226, 227–
    228, 230–231
repetition, 187, 190–195, 199,
    200
repression, 209, 213–214
retroactivity, 53–54, 94n15,
    150, 203, 210–211, 218,
    221–224, 225
return to Freud, 64
satisfaction, impossibility of,
    205–210
self, the, 46–49, 105
seminar, the, 104–105
sexual difference, 97
sexed subjectivity, 72, 85–99,
    104–113

sexuation, 109–112

signified, the, 98, 113, 148–149, 208

signifier, the, 98, 112, 113, 148–149, 208

Société Française de Psychanalyse (SFP), 44

Société Psychanalytique de Paris (SPP), 44

speech, 132–136, 138, 143–144

subject, the, 22, 50, 59, 85–86, 89, 140–141, 144, 187

  as desiring, 189

  as linguistic, 85, 131

  as sexed, 114, 131, 186

  the splitting of, 194–199

  who is supposed to know, 199–201

subjectivity, 85–86, 99, 139, 143, 187, 200

  as split, 200

sublimation, 209–210

Symbolic, the, 53–54, 71, 85, 86, 89, 94–95, 96, 98, 110, 111, 131, 134, 137–143, 144, 148, 151, 152, 186, 188, 189, 193, 194, 195–196, 200, 203–204, 206–208, 210, 217–218, 219–225, 228

transference, 47, 187, 195–196, 199–200, 217

Unconscious, the, 1, 21, 22, 47, 69, 131, 135, 139, 142, 143, 144, 148–150, 187, 188–190, 193–200, 203, 205–206, 209, 210–214, 223, 233

  structured like a language, 138, 152, 188

woman, the, 109–110

Lacoue-Labarthe, P., 12n28

Laplance, J. and J.-B. Pontalis, 137–138, 195, 209

Lee, J., 4n4, 208n28

Levinas, E.

  a-Dieu, 184

  alienation, 75, 185

  alterity, 38, 40, 74–75, 176–177

  an-archy, 60–61, 68, 79, 160–161, 173, 175–177, 179, 184, 219–220, 236–237

  caress, the, 75–76, 79, 100

  categorical imperative, 181–182

  consciousness, 160–162, 165, 169, 173–174

    as a problem of temporality, 160–162

  death, 36–38, 40, 73–74, 182

  desire, 167–169, 235–236

  diachrony, 162, 176, 184

  election, 69, 169–170, 177–178, 185, 238

  Eros, 78–85, 167–168

  ethical, the, 22, 42, 69, 80, 117, 144, 145, 147, 155, 156

  ethical language, 61, 68, 117

  ethical metaphysics, 67

  ethical subjectivity, 179, 184

  existing, 33–35

  existent, the, 33–38, 40–42

  exteriority, 39

  face, the 39–43, 103, 117, 148, 177, 178, 184, 185, 186, 217–218, 229, 234

  fecundity, 77–81

  feminine, the, 38, 74–80, 83–85, 100, 103

Levinas, E. (*continued*)
  feminist critiques of, 84–85
  foundationalism, 79, 184–186,
    219
  fraternity, 78, 170
  God, 157–172, 182–186, 234–
    235
    as otherwise than other, 170
  here I am, 62, 178, 186, 227,
    234
  hostage, the, 117, 148, 177–
    178, 185
  humanism of the other person,
    21, 59
  hypostasis, 34–35
  I, the, 34–35, 41, 62, 68, 69, 82,
    163, 174
  il y a, 34
  illeity, 168–169
  immemorial past, 79, 173, 175,
    184, 219–220
  incarnation, 100–102
  infinite, 41, 164–172
    within me, 172
  insomnia, 163, 165
  inspired future, 74, 78, 83, 175,
    220, *see also* pure future
  language, 40–41, 117–131,
    144–148
    as sign, 126
    as temporalization, 125–126
  love, 75–77, 79, 167, 168
  masculine, the, 75
  masculinism, 72, 113–114
  maternity, 100–103, 114
  metaphysics, 32, 72, 74, 100,
    103, 117
  multiplicity, 38

obsession, 180
obsession with Holocaust, 26
ontology, 61, 72, 83, 99, 102,
  103, 114, 117–120, 127–
  128, 144
other, the, 36–37, 60, 75, 101,
  103, 117, 129, 130, 156,
  159, 162, 174
  structure of, the, 72–74
other person, the, 40–43, 61–
  63, 72–73, 169, 176, 185
passivity, 100, 129–130, 165–
  166, 180
paternity, 77
phenomenologist, as, 1, 6–7,
  20, 26, 60, 67–68, 114, 234
post-humanist, as, 21, 43, 72,
  103, 114, 116
prophetism, 171
proximity, 60, 123, 146–148, 169
pure future, 76, 173, 175, 182–
  184, *see also* inspired
  future
relation to psychoanalysis, 1
religion, 170–171
responsibility, 42, 43, 59, 61,
  62, 67, 69, 81, 102–103,
  115, 117, 122, 123, 130,
  166, 168–170, 177–186,
  219, 234, 238
said, the, 117, 122–123, 126–
  130, 147–148
saying, the, 117, 122–123, 126–
  131, 146–148
  as constitutive of ethical
    subjectivity, 130–131
sexual difference, 74
singularity, 145–147

solitude, 33–35, 43
stranger, the, 103
subject, the, 38, 59, 62, 82, 121,
    127, 147, 157, 172
    as ethical, 22, 42, 117, 128–
        129, 130–131, 157, 172,
        173, 184–186, 236
    as for-the-other, 42, 43, 63,
        101, 102, 121, 128–129,
        147, 148, 171, 177, 184,
        185, 229
    as linguistic, 123, 131
    as sexually hierarchized, 72
subjectivity, 6, 22, 67–68, 82–
    84, 103, 120, 121, 145,
    171–172, 184
    as the other in the same,
        121–122
substitution, 60–63, 84–85,
    100–101, 117, 122, 129–
    131, 148
Thou shalt not kill (me), 42,
    117, 177, 186
time, 33, 123–126, 173–176, 184
    as diachronous, 176, 184
    as verb, 124–126
trace, the, 103, 165, 166
    of God, 169, 170, 172, 185
transcendence, 40, 77, 78, 81–
    84, 156–157, 162–163,
    167–170, 184
vision, 40, 174
vulnerability, 101–103
Levi-Strauss, C., 232
Lingis, A., 104

Manning, R., 2n1
Marcuse, H., 15

Marx, K., 10n12, 15
Metaphysics, 20
Miller, J.-A., 104
Moran, D., 2n1

Nobus, D., 4n4, 52

Ontology, 112, 116, 120

Peperzak, 4n4, 7n7
Phenomenology, 2, 6, 16, 20, 23,
    26, 61, 234, 235–236
Plato, 121, 173
Post-humanism, 5, 8, 14, 17–19,
    21, 29, 32, 43, 116, 215
Psychoanalysis, 1, 2, 20, 21, 23,
    25, 47, 64, 91, 97, 132–133,
    204, 216
    as historical enterprise, 2, 22,
        26

Rabaté, J.-M., 4n4, 4n5, 210n30
Rajchman, J., 3n3, 6n6, 15n32,
    201n20
Rawls, J., 9
Reinhard, K., 3n2, 156n1, 216
Richardson, W., 28
Roen, K., 109n22
Rosenzweig, F., 36n6
Roudinesco, E., 8, 104n19

Santer, E., 3n3, 15n32
Sartre, J.-P., 1, 8–9, 19
    as humanist, 8
Sex as ambiguous term, 107
Sexual difference, 71–72, 115
Shepherdson, C., 89n13, 109n22
Sheridan, A., 45

254   INDEX

Subjectivity, 8, 15, 16, 18, 69, 71,
    86, 115–116, 117, 121–122,
    148, 155–156, 215, 216,
    226–227, 229–230, 234
  as subjection and subjugation,
    16–17
  Continental ethics, and, 15–17

Taylor, M., 233

Universalism,
  conceptual, 234, 235
Utilitarianism, 233

Van Pelt, T., 6n6, 7n9
Verhaeghe, P., 225n2

Wahl, J., 23, 32, 38n8
Walsh, L., 6n6, 102n18, 232n7,
    232n9
Weed, E., 138n8
Wilchins, R. 232
Wyschogrod, E., 4n4

Žižek, S., 218n1
Zupancic, A., 3n3, 7n9, 15n32,
    198n18, 202n21